ABOUT ISLAND PRESS

Island Press is the only nonprofit organization in the United States whose principal purpose is the publication of books on environmental issues and natural resource management. We provide solutions-oriented information to professionals, public officials, business and community leaders, and concerned citizens who are shaping responses to environmental problems.

In 1994, Island Press celebrated its tenth anniversary as the leading provider of timely and practical books that take a multidisciplinary approach to critical environmental concerns. Our growing list of titles reflects our commitment to bringing the best of an expanding body of literature to the environmental community throughout North America and the world.

Support for Island Press is provided by Apple Computer, Inc., The Bullitt Foundation, The Geraldine R. Dodge Foundation, The Energy Foundation, The Ford Foundation, The W. Alton Jones Foundation, The Lyndhurst Foundation, The John D. and Catherine T. MacArthur Foundation, The Andrew W. Mellon Foundation, The Joyce Mertz-Gilmore Foundation, The National Fish and Wildlife Foundation, The Pew Charitable Trusts, The Pew Global Stewardship Initiative, The Rockefeller Philanthropic Collaborative, Inc., and individual donors.

ABOUT GALLATIN INSTITUTE

Founded in 1991, the Gallatin Institute is dedicated to advancing the work of writers of the contemporary American West, in part by orchestrating the publication of new works and in part by helping to educate western writers. Through focused seminars and symposia, Gallatin Institute exposes writers and others to the best available thinking of ecologists, historians, economists, anthropologists, and sociologists, as well as grassroots community leaders from throughout the region.

The activities of the Institute are premised on two observations. First, the American West, which thrived for a century on the basis of a coherent set of cultural, economic, and political institutions all related to the exploitation of natural resources, is undergoing a massive shift—a transition that is painful to a citizenry reliant upon those institutions. Second, in U.S. history, writers have been among the most important catalysts for cultural shifts and evolution in public policy. Gallatin believes that it will be writers, more than any other professionals, who will both explain and nurture the slow transformation of the public lands in the West from a cultural mindset of exploitation to one of responsible stewardship.

THE NEXT WEST

Edited by
John A. Baden and Donald Snow

THE NEXT WEST

Public Lands, Community, and
Economy in the American West

Gallatin Institute

Island Press

WASHINGTON, D.C. / COVELO, CALIFORNIA

Grateful acknowledgment is expressed for permission to publish the following material:
Stephen Bodio, "Struck with Consequence." This essay first appeared in *Northern Lights*, Volume 10, Number 2, Fall 1994. Reprinted by permission of the author.
Tom Wolf, "Blood and Cotton." This essay first appeared under the title "The Northern San Luis Valley" in *Colorado's Sangre de Cristo Mountains* by Tom Wolf (Boulder: University Press of Colorado, 1995). Reprinted by permission of the author.
Karl Hess, Jr., "John Wesley Powell and the Unmaking of the West." A shorter version of this essay appeared in *Environmental History*, Volume 2, Number 1, January 1997. Reprinted by permission of the author.
Thomas Michael Power, "Ideology, Wishful Thinking, and Pragmatic Reform." A different version of this essay appeared as "The Price of Everything," by Thomas Michael Power and Paul Rauber in *Sierra*, November–December 1993. Reprinted by permission from the Sierra Club.

Library of Congress Cataloging-in-Publication Data
The next West / edited by John A. Baden and Donald Snow.
     p.   cm.
    Includes bibliographical references and index.
    ISBN 1-55963-459-6 (cloth). — ISBN 1-55963-460-X (paper)
    1. West (U.S.)—Economic conditions. 2. West (U.S.)–
–Environmental conditions. 3. Land use—West (U.S.) 4. Forest policy—West (U.S.) I. Baden, John. II. Snow, Donald.
HC107.A17N49   1997
333.7′0978—dc21   96-52664
                                       CIP

Printed on recycled, acid-free paper ∞ ⊛
Manufactured in the United States of America
10 9 8 7 6 5 4 3 2 1

CONTENTS

PREFACE

Unlikely partnerships may be the hallmark of the West in the closing years of the twentieth century. Had any of our readers known the editors of this book a dozen years ago, they could affirm that our collaboration in this project was unlikely indeed.

We two first met in 1980 at a legislative gathering under the copper dome of Montana's capitol. We're both a little foggy about the purpose of the meeting we attended, but it had something to do with the Montana Cattlemen's Association and the Sagebrush Rebellion. John A. Baden, who describes himself as "a libertarian at the corpuscular level," was at that moment leaning toward involvement with the Cattlemen in their attempts to steer Old Montana into the Rebellion (an involvement that did not occur). Donald Snow, the son of a union coal miner and a Democrat to the bone, couldn't believe that anyone in Montana was even *having* that conversation, least of all inside the venerable halls of the state capitol.

But worms and events both turn, and nearly a decade later we had embarked together on a project, sponsored by the Foundation for Research on Economics and the Environment (FREE), to bring together a group of young environmental writers and a group of environmental economists for the purpose of discussing a better future for the American West.

Dubbed simply the Writers-Economists Series, these seminars operated on the simple premise of cross-fertilization. It was Baden's idea that writers and economists needed each other—writers needed economists for their deeper insights into why things like incentives and markets matter; economists needed writers because so many, he believed, lacked both felicity of expression and a willingness to engage in nonnumerical discussions of concepts as fuzzy as "a sense of place." The Writers-Economists Series was an odd idea, and a gamble, but it paid off. Over the next few years, FREE sponsored six of those seminars. As the roster of writers grew and the list of economists diversified into sociologists, ecologists, political scientists, and philosophers, the seminars became all the more interesting.

Indeed, by 1991 the seminars had knitted themselves into a new nonprofit organization, the Gallatin Institute. Gallatin is dedicated to advancing the work of emerging writers in the West—not all writers, to be sure, but those who take a special interest in the natural environment and the human community. The work of the Institute is premised on two observations.

First, the American West, which thrived for about one hundred years on the basis of a coherent set of cultural, economic, and political institutions, is undergoing a massive cultural shift—a transition that is often painful to a citizenry dependent on those institutions.

Second, throughout U.S. history, writers have been major catalysts for important cultural shifts and evolution in public policy. Gallatin believes it will be writers, more than any other professionals, who will both explain and nurture the transformation of public lands in the West. Their collective works, if carefully and thoughtfully orchestrated, will contribute greatly to a new cultural, economic, and political coherence that will better serve the region and nation in the coming century.

The East has long told the West what it is and what it shall become, and nowhere is that tendency more apparent than in the world of publishing. Gallatin also exists simply to bring new works of truly western character to the attention of readers everywhere.

The essays in this volume were collected from seminars held between 1993 and 1994. No one seminar or set of ideas served as the instigator for this collection, yet by the close of our September 1994 seminar, held near the headwaters of Montana's Gallatin River, it was clear that diverse ideas pointing to the concept of a Next West were beginning to emerge and take shape. We had all heard, read, and in some cases written much on the New West, which by then was mostly a litany of what is; we decided to set our sights on what could be.

But these essays are not attempts at crystal-ball gazing or efforts in any sense to predict or even nominate the future of the public lands of the West. Rather, they are suggestive of a future—actually, several futures—rooted firmly in the present and the past. As much as anything, they reflect recitations of mistakes and a willingness to be bold enough to make some new ones. We hope you enjoy them, learn and benefit somehow from them, and see on their pages at least a smattering of the wisdom that seems to grow from any number of unlikely partnerships in the modern West.

John A. Baden
GALLATIN GATEWAY, MONTANA

Donald Snow
MISSOULA, MONTANA

ACKNOWLEDGMENTS

The Gallatin Institute is an odd creature. Not strictly literary in its approach, not strictly policy and economics in its focus, it is an organization composed of writers, scientists, social scientists, and activists who possess a passion for the American West and a concern for its future. The Gallatin group shares a commitment to discourse, debate, and the open exchange of ideas among honest people of goodwill. But its nonprescriptive, ecumenical approach makes the Institute difficult to pigeonhole, so it falls between many cracks in the world of philanthropy.

Still, a few people have recognized the value of Gallatin's unorthodox nature and made investments in this highly speculative enterprise. They include Jeff Olson and Walt Coward of the Ford Foundation, Bill Dennis of Liberty Fund, Inc., Dr. Michael Harbordt of the Temple Inland Corporation, and Dick Larry, an annual visitor to Montana who has long encouraged and supported our efforts. We thank and salute these men and the generous organizations they represent. In addition, we are very grateful to the staff and board of directors of the Liz Claiborne and Art Ortenberg Foundation, who have offered both financial and moral support.

The staff of the Gallatin Institute have been hardworking, patient, and enthusiastic. They have organized each of the Institute's seminars, gathered and distributed the readings, taken care of creature comforts at our assemblies, run a million airport shuttles, and helped get us past every obstacle. We are grateful for the good work performed by Peter Baldwin, Christy Fullen, Pete Geddes, Molly Holz, Karla Mills, Doug Noonan, and Donna Rae Robbins. In the months and years preceding creation of the Gallatin Institute, the staff of the Foundation for Research on Economics and the Environment ably steered the Writers-Economists Series. They included Jill Bowman, Kim DeBruycker, Tracy Fenne, Julie Forner, Christy Lindsey, Wendy Millet, and Tim O'Brien.

Our special thanks go to Suzanne Rowen, who brought focus, enthusiasm, professional business skills, and a sharp and lovely pen to the original planning efforts of the Gallatin Institute.

Finally, we acknowledge and thank the host of Gallatin Senior Fellows and the writers, scholars, and activists who have attended Institute seminars, offered their best work, and stayed aboard through some difficult times. Whereas scholars are often well supported by universities and other endowed institutions, independent, emerging writers of *belles lettres* are among the most underpaid, underappreciated professionals in North America. We hope a few more can find shelter and support through our nascent Institute.

INTRODUCTION

DONALD SNOW

It has often been said that the American West, more than any other portion of the country, is a work in progress—a region that seems always to be becoming but is never finished, a place in perpetual motion, always traveling, never arriving. I believe that the West's condition of permanently becoming is due primarily to the continued existence of the massive base of public lands in the western states; about half of the West's magnificent acreage is federal and is therefore, in many important respects, open and uncommitted in ways private lands seldom are. The ultimate destiny of the federal lands—if they have an ultimate destiny—has always been in question, and the people who live in proximity to those lands, or who live elsewhere but take a strong interest in them, will always ask questions about them, will always challenge and attempt to correct the prevailing regime, whatever it is.

It is also true that the West is a region of overworked adjectives and that over the many years in which interest in the region has grown, we have spawned a lexicon of descriptors that hang on the West like so many cheap suits. We were (and are) an *Old* West, lately being challenged by a *New* West,

1

which no one seems to be able to define but nearly everyone talks about. We have been a *Wild* West, it is true (isn't it?), and tourists today still go into watering holes as disparate as the Silver Dollar Bar in Jackson Hole and Trixie's Antler Saloon in the Blackfoot River valley above Missoula (or into the Bob Marshall Wilderness, for that matter) with the expectation that they will somehow get to participate in Old West wildness. The word *yee-haw* seems to pop up a lot in these parts; other places do not seem to be burdened with it. Indian people have often looked askance at the moniker *wild*, applied to both society and habitat; perhaps we should have paid some attention to their skepticism long ago.

And, of course, there is the tiredest adjective of all: the *Real* West. It's a descriptor worn smooth as cliché by now, so we seldom ask ourselves why the West needs to make claims to the real. Other regions don't seem to share such insecurity. We never hear anyone claim to know the Real South or the Real New England. Does the film *Fargo* somehow capture the Real Midwest? Lately, what with housing costs skyrocketing in every mountain state, I'm thinking that in the case of the West, Real must simply be shorthand for Real Estate, but I'm sure I'm wrong again.

We who have worked on this book thus realize that we risk adding to this silliness by contributing yet another adjective to the overmodified West— the *Next* West—but at the same time, we see value in the region's long-standing unfinishedness. There will indeed be a "next West," whether anyone calls it that or not, because it's in the nature of the region to shift and shift again.

This book offers some speculation on the next great shift in the American West, and it does so in part by dwelling on what has gone on before. A bit of revisionism takes place on these pages—in Karl Hess's essay on Major John Wesley Powell, especially—and revisionism, too, has become a hallmark of much intellectual activity applied to the West. Historians keep telling and retelling the region's story, reflecting shifts in social and political values as much as increases in our fund of factual knowledge. But in our collection, there is a revisionism of a different kind as well. Call it eco-revisionism, and let the prefix *eco* stand at once for both economy and ecology.

In a nutshell, the Next West under discussion on these pages is a West in which sound economics and sound ecology finally merge and, perhaps, do so under the banner of a new kind of environmentalism suggested by several of the essayists here. Without trying to predict the future or to nominate any definite policy alternatives that could lead to a different future for the West, these writers, environmentalists all, challenge one another and several prevailing paradigms at once.

Some of these writers challenge a set of ideas that economist Thomas Michael Power often refers to as folk economics. The hallmark of folk economics (which, by the way, is still espoused as gospel in many of the West's university business schools) seems to be that there is a basic economy in the West, tied to the extraction of raw natural resources, and that most other significant economic activity is anchored to that base. At the root of folk economics is the ancient belief that "all wealth comes from the ground." In the West, that idea has terrible political and environmental consequences, for it means that if you can't mine it, cut it, or grow crops or livestock on it, "it" is economically insignificant or, at least, less significant. But as Power and a host of other economists have shown, the basic-economy model is both fatally flawed and, in a region so full of public lands, environmentally pernicious. A Next West, then, must be a region that makes a clear accounting of its *entire* economy, not merely the portions of the economy that are favored and held in place by a host of commodity interests with settled expectations and even more deeply settled lobbyists.

In addition, more than one of the writers are moved to challenge the idea, commonly held by some environmentalists, that economics and ecology live miles apart and can never be reconciled. Indeed, even during the Writers-Economists Series of seminars that led to the creation of this book, described in the preface, we ran across several environmental writers who virtually hissed at the word *economist* and admitted as much—and actually, it's no wonder. They remember the days not long ago when every identified economist in sight seemed always to work on behalf of the exploiters and when the American people were confidently assured by economists that clear-cut logging on every mountainside and strip mining of every available seam of coal or pod of uranium were the only ways to secure the nation's future against OPEC-like embargoes or shortages or job famines. But as several of the authors herein counsel, it is important to distinguish between commerce and economics. A great deal of very successful commerce is based on perfectly rotten economics.

All this leads to the issue of subsidies. Although there is much disagreement among the writers represented in this book, most of them would probably concur with the statement that a great deal of the West's environmental dilemma at the end of the twentieth century grows from the fact that far too much of the region's economy and far too many of its communities have existed on the hollow promise of subsidies. To be sure, when most of the West's subsidies were levered into place—usually through some combination of administrative and legislative action—no one set out explicitly to create a new subsidy or perhaps even thought much about it. But the effects were almost

always the same and almost always unfortunate. The greatest subsidy of all—
measured by both economic and environmental impact—is probably the institutionalized giveaway of the public's water to irrigators and other users,
who have spent the past century emptying the region's rivers and streams
and converting as many as possible into reservoirs. That this unconditional
good of "water conservation" would be challenged by anyone seems to many
lifelong westerners a perfectly lunatic proposition, but again, many of those
good-hearted folks are wedded to Power's folk economics, which blinds
them to the full implications of the subsidies they and their region have long
enjoyed. The writers in this volume are not saying that all subsidies must
stop, but they do tend to agree that until the most egregious subsidies are
ended, neither wise economics nor sound environmental management will
really stand a chance in the West.

These are all key issues amplified in this book, but perhaps the heart of
the matter ultimately resides in the debate over the relationship among free
markets, political power, and community vitality and what all that has to do
with the future of nature in the West. Here is where the plot thickens—both
on the pages of this book and in the halls that ring with environmental debate all over the country.

≈

Perhaps more than in other regions, the public lands of the West seem to
have spawned a growing legion of "free-market environmentalists"—those
who seek to use instruments of the open marketplace (best understood as instruments of voluntary exchange, not simply money) to solve environmental
problems previously addressed through regulation and other forms of coercion. If this book has an intellectual home, it is surely within the debate between free-market and (dare I use this term for a movement we can date only
to 1970?) traditional environmentalists. Perhaps the text that did the most to
set this debate in motion was Randal O'Toole's *Reforming the Forest Service*
(Island Press, 1988), which presented a scathing analysis of the tree-cutting
mentality of the modern USDA Forest Service, explained how that mentality
came to be embedded in an agency with the deepest conservation roots, and
then offered a strong prescription for reform. It's probably safe to say that
most traditional enviros were with O'Toole up to the point of his reform
proposals but then parted ways with him, for he had the temerity to suggest
that the national forests would be far better off environmentally if the Forest
Service were run like a business instead of a political organization.

Skeptical of the role of environmental ethics in an agency dominated by
its own bottom line, O'Toole ruled out the possibility that the Forest Service

could be reformed merely by replacing the agency's old wood-butcher buffaloes with young, committed eco-freaks. His analysis cuts against the "better people" theory and focuses instead on the cold logic of incentive structures within an agency—and in the case of the Forest Service, O'Toole set out to prove that the agency's internal system of rewards was heavily weighted toward "getting out the cut." "Even good people," he says, "will do the wrong thing if their incentives are wrong."

Free-market environmentalism continues to garner adherents, yet the merger of economics and ecology still seems to attract wrath wherever it goes. It's an alien language to old-fashioned conservationists and environmentalists, schooled as they were on the writings of scientists-turned-philosophers such as Aldo Leopold and Rachel Carson. Moreover, most enviros had read their Thoreau, noting his antipathy toward the dismal science. While at Walden growing beans, Thoreau loathed the bean counters, made light of all "pecuniary considerations," and blasted his agricultural neighbors for their swinish tendencies toward base self-interest. He sought laws higher than economic ones; he seemed to believe that economics and spirituality had nothing in common and were in fact antipodes.

Not surprisingly, environmentalists have grown to believe that the only check on the depredations of private enterprise is government intervention—and the more checks, the better. Now come the free-market environmentalists with their claims that the best way to ensure environmental quality and sound land use is to appeal to self-interest (read "greed" if you prefer a balder term), reduce or eliminate the emphasis on bureaucratic management of natural resources, reverse financial incentives so that environmental protection becomes a source of profit rather than of penalty, and, in many cases, seek to localize more decisions about environmental management.

The battle lines between the old and the new are easily drawn, and on this last point—the devolution of power to more local levels—they are becoming especially sharp. Traditional environmentalists rely primarily on central government as a force to create and sustain environmental protection and sound land use (at least on the public domain). They remain skeptical that local people in the West will ever seriously buy into strategies to preserve wilderness or protect wildlife habitats that include robust populations of predators. They believe in the essential value of agencies such as the Forest Service, the National Park Service, the Bureau of Land Management, and the Environmental Protection Agency—precisely because these agencies are supralocal, supposedly above the fray of resource-dependent communities, and, in theory at least, populated by well-informed professionals. If these agencies aren't doing their jobs well, they believe, the solution is to get better, more committed people involved. Ditto for environmental legislation: eco-traditionalists value it; they see legislative action (especially congressional action) as the primary pathway to solving nearly all problems of environmental management, from pollution control to wilderness protection to improved management of federal forests, grasslands, and waterways.

Free-market environmentalists are skeptical of all these approaches. They like to point out that legislated pollution control has been, at best, a disappointment and that the public lands have been poorly managed no matter who has staffed the federal agencies, not because agency people are venal or incompetent but because bureaucracies tend to internalize and act on patterns that have more to do with agency self-perpetuation than with accomplishment of the agency's mission. Moreover, they point out that command-and-control regulatory strategies, running counter to commonly held principles of American liberty, will always engender fatal opposition. Most important, they like to talk about incentives, especially economic ones: give managers, investors, and developers the right incentives to do well by nature and they will, but simply tell them what they cannot do and they'll find the means to circumvent your restrictions. Especially offensive to many is the free-marketeers' tendency to turn governmental conservation on its ear, likening it to the gross failures of the Soviet bloc.

Why, then, should environmentalists pay any attention to the free-marke-teers, in this book or in any other venue? One good reason comes from Aldo Leopold himself, the patron saint of modern environmentalism. In what may have been the first attempt in the United States to apply a broad environmental ethic to principles of governance, business, and land use, Leopold offered this now-famous advice in *A Sand County Almanac* (1949):

> Examine each question in terms of what is ethically and esthetically right, as well as what is economically expedient. A thing is right when it tends to preserve the integrity, stability, and beauty of the biotic community. It is wrong when it tends otherwise.[1]

That's the Leopold beloved by every environmentalist today. Yet we tend to overlook the prologue to the ethic articulated above. We forget that even though Leopold spent his entire professional life in the service of government agencies, he foresaw limits to what he called "governmental conservation":

> There is a clear tendency in American conservation to relegate to government all necessary jobs that private landowners fail to perform. Govern-

ment ownership, operation, subsidy or regulation is now widely prevalent in forestry, range management, soil and watershed management, park and wilderness conservation, fisheries management, and migratory bird management, with more to come. . . . Most of this growth in governmental conservation is proper and logical, some of it is inevitable. Nevertheless, the question arises: what is the ultimate magnitude of the enterprise?[2]

In an essay that predated *A Sand County Almanac* by seven years, Leopold partially answered his own question:

To analyze the problem of action, the first thing to grasp is that government, no matter how good, can only do certain things. Government can't raise crops, maintain small, scattered structures . . . or bring to bear on small, local matters that combination of solicitude, foresight, and skill which we call husbandry. . . . Husbandry is the heart of conservation. The second thing to grasp is that when we lay conservation in the lap of the government, it will always do the things it can, even though they are not the things that most need doing.[3]

To Leopold, "the things that most need doing" called for a three-part approach. You needed appropriate government (but not more), sound economics, and a "land ethic" to guide both private and public action. It was folly, in Leopold's eyes, to make central government bear full responsibility for conservation.

That's an important theme in many of the essays in this volume. These writers—all but one—challenge the progressive vision of the West and everything it has spawned, which is an almost complete reliance on agencies of government to "perform conservation," thus relieving individuals and local communities of substantive environmental responsibilities. Collectively, the authors in this book call for an end to subsidized exploitation of the West; an end to governmental mandates that try to legislate "good" environmental outcomes (no matter what the people are doing and thinking); and increased reliance on the democratic institution known as the marketplace—which includes the marketplace of original ideas, voluntarism, and voluntary exchange as well as the conventional marketplace of barter and sale—to solve important environmental problems. Several also call for a renewal of face-to-face, Jeffersonian democracy in arenas that give citizens decision-making power in public resource management.

These authors do not all agree on specific policy recommendations or outcomes; in fact, one essay openly criticizes free-market environmentalism.

And although these writings do not contain many specific policy recommendations, they do comprise a cogent matrix of reflections on what has gone wrong in the American West of the twentieth century. They point ahead not to a New West of cappuccino cowboys, Internet worship, and some ambient, simpering sense of "the public's willingness to embrace environmental issues" but to a Next West based on the renewal of environmental politics, experiments in local and supralocal control of public lands, and the use of markets at least partly to replace the political allocation of natural resources. In the words of Daniel Kemmis, former Montana legislator, the Next West may simply be "the Sagebrush Rebellion done right."

We have divided this volume into two parts. The first part, titled On the Ground, offers some flavor of what it is to live in the West and practice environmental awareness—whether it's political awareness per se or the broader sort of politically tinged awareness that comes simply with maintaining good relations with the neighbors. These essays deliberately range all over the map in at least two ways. First, they represent a wide geographic dispersion—from the Sangre de Cristo Mountains to the forests of the Pacific Northwest to a single valley in Wyoming to an out-of-the-way corner of rural New Mexico. Second, they range across a panoply of issues: the birth of the recycling industry on the streets of Seattle; the management of a fabled mountain range; the "new forestry"; hunting, falconry, and ranching; the leasing of federal coal. These issues and settings may seem disparate, yet they manage to hang together on a common frame. Each of these writers is speaking out against a perceived idiocy, and each of these idiocies is an idiocy du jour—the kind of foolishness spawned by adherence to convention, correctness, sanctimoniousness, or a simple refusal to accept responsibility. All the essays are about paying the bills—something the environmental movement has often ignored.

The second part of the book, titled Old Traditions and New Ideas, is more theoretical and is grounded more in concepts than in specific places. You'll see these writers engaged in combat not with fictitious foes but with the all-too-real demons that command center stage in the politics and economy of the great American West. The demons in question are not persons but notions—mythologies, if you will, that have guided so much of life in the West for more than a century. Montana writer William Kittredge speaks of these mythologies as "stories we tell ourselves to let us know who we are" and points out that mythologies, like horses, wear out after a while and need replacing.

Many of the ideas presented in this book are apt to upset those who still expect the prevailing regime of centralized governmental conservation to work; they will upset even more the folks who simply can't tolerate the notion of humans meddling at all with wild nature. To my most radical deep ecologist friends, almost any hard-core political or economic approach to our egregious environmental problems seems only to douse the conflagration with kerosene. I, and perhaps most of the writers represented here, have some sympathies with that sentiment, and we may agree over a beer or two that in a very important sense the problem with the environment is environmentalism—that we have objectified, desacralized, and trivialized nature even through the invention of the very words *environment* and its instrumentalist cousin, *environmentalism.*

Still, I counsel caring readers to remember that decisions about the things we love in nature are being made at every moment of every day, and they aren't about to stop. Right now, there's a gray wolf in somebody's gun sight, an ore body about to be exploited in the heart of a wild place, a smokestack wafting toxic fumes into the homes of the least advantaged. Nothing we've done so far has helped much. "Just say no" turns out to be little more than a slogan.

NOTES

1. Aldo Leopold, *A Sand County Almanac, and Sketches Here and There* (New York: Oxford University Press, 1949), pp. 224–5.
2. Ibid., p. 213.
3. Aldo Leopold, "Land-Use and Democracy," *Audubon* 44 (September 1942), p. 264.

PART ONE

On the Ground

The first five essays in this anthology take a ground-level view of several important environmental issues affecting the West and, indeed, the world. The settings and issues shift a great deal, but the theme remains the same: the implications of paying the bills. Although none of them uses the term, these five writers all seem to be struggling with the concept of an "appropriate economics"—an "earth household" well adapted to the natural environment.

In his short essay "Struck with Consequence," Stephen Bodio offers a passionate personal statement on the ethics of living in nature. The setting is Magdelena, New Mexico, a little town in a little county, far from the New Age hubbub of Santa Fe and Taos. Bodio values his adopted neighbors and their traditions, which include stocking the family larder with fish, game, and homegrown meats and vegetables. He suggests that the only life that matters is the sensual life rooted in such reality; he decries the threats to this life posed by newcomers who want of nature a place to have fun, a place to feel wholesome and pure, a place free, finally, of nature's own processes. In Bodio's view, if the Next West is to survive as a true and real homeland, it must continue to be a land in which living well involves the bloody drama of predator and prey.

Idaho's Rocky Barker changes scenes abruptly. In "New Forestry in the Next West," he examines the pressures now forcing timber companies in the Northwest to adopt sustainable forestry practices on both private and public lands. This journalistic essay echoes with Aldo Leopold's urgent proclamation in the 1940s that conservation must become the key motivator for farmers, loggers, landowners, and businesspeople, not just for conservation agents of government. Barker seems cautiously optimistic that an age of "new forestry" is dawning and that the results could be dramatic.

Around 1980, executives of Whitney Benefits—a financial trust in Sheridan, Wyoming, known mostly for giving hundreds of college scholarships to local youth and donating millions of dollars to support the Sheridan YMCA—decided to develop a federal coal lease the trust owned along the Tongue River. Thus begins "The Bizarre and Unsettling Saga of Whitney Benefits," Samuel Western's wry account of the federal government's attempts to protect an "alluvial valley floor" in north-central Wyoming. What ensued became a classic case of governmental ineptitude caused by a combination of conflicting environmental values, shifting personnel within the Bureau of Land Management, and the absence of accountability and clear incentives to operate with the public interest front and center. In late 1994, a federal court awarded Whitney Benefits and its partner, Peter Kiewit Sons', a staggering sum of money in compensation—for a deal that should have cost the federal treasury next to nothing. In Western's view, this case demonstrates the absurdity of a public lands management regime that exempts agents of government from any real responsibility for their actions.

The West's role in promoting solid waste recycling is not well-known, but for Jim McMahon, the story is imprinted in his bones. In "Closing the Loop," this pioneer of the recycling movement in the United States recounts his early days of smashing cans in Seattle and wonders how the movement went wrong. What started out as a cost-effective, market-based effort to save energy and materials and reduce solid waste has been transformed into a feel-good enterprise dominated by political correctness, economic inefficiency, and the accelerated waste of everything recycling set out to save. The culprit, according to McMahon, is the entry of government-mandated recycling targets, lobbied into place by wrongheaded environmental groups and opportunistic politicians. The local has been supplanted by the global, to the cheers of some environmentalists, who do not care to examine the perversity they have helped to create.

Colorado's Sangre de Cristo Mountains offer some of the greatest species diversity of any range in the West, but they have also been pounded by human greed, by humankind's desire for dominion over the earth, and by the shifting whims of a local population and economy. When a large portion of the Sangres was finally designated as federal wilderness in the mid-1980s, environmentalists cheered; these much-abused mountains, they believed, were finally safe. Not so, says environmental historian Tom Wolf. In "Blood and Cotton," Wolf argues that what the Sangres need is active restoration; wilderness designation has frozen into place a kind of "nature freak show" in part of the Sangre de Cristos. Vastly increased recreational use, spurred by the wilderness designation itself, is accelerating the deterioration of this extraordinary range. Using many of the ideas discussed in part II of this work, Wolf suggests a management concept appropriate to the ecological needs of the Sangres.

CHAPTER ONE

Struck with Consequence

STEPHEN BODIO

A Canadian journalist recently wrote that people like me—
"male writers and artists"—live in the West mainly because things stay the
same there, because what you loved one day you could be forgiven for loving
the next. I don't think the motive is ignoble or restricted to males. I have
lived for almost fifteen years now in a determinedly unchic western town
whose charms are obscure, austere, sometimes even squalid, and so far I
have been forgiven for all that I love. But I like another of this journalist's
quotes better: "The wilderness reminded him that everything he did had a
consequence."

∽

We fell in love with the country first. For coastal people, the Real West is
wilder and fuller of marvels than they can imagine without living in it . . . or,
often, even when they do begin to live in it. The heart of the West will always
be the big, dry, blue blocks of Forest Service and Bureau of Land Management land, cut into areas the size of New England states by highways and
New West boomtowns. Off in their centers, invisible to travelers, are whole

worlds. But there is so much going on at the edges that it takes a while to get to them. In my first months, I saw a bobcat in my yard and picked up the skull of an unfortunate adolescent lion in the arroyo that flowed through town. I flushed golden eagles from the highway's edge and climbed to falcon eyries that overlooked pavement. Ravens, in my other life rare denizens of the coast of Maine, were now rarely out of sight. Rattlesnakes were a common summer nuisance; every other week or so, I'd remove a prairie rattler from my yard and release it behind the town dump. Antelopes and scaled quails came to my fence by day; deer and elk crossed the road by night. I had never lived in a place so full of wild creatures—not just managed species like deer and elk but also raptors, songbirds, an ark of reptiles, javelinas, coyotes, three species of fox, lions, bears, and rumors of wolves.

That we hunted, just like everybody else, was at first a source of amazement to our neighbors and then a road into the country and new friendships. My partner, Betsy, who took all things as she found them, had the easier way; that she could ride well didn't hurt, either. I was solitary and set in my ways, a falconer, bird hunter, and naturalist who had a social and aesthetic dislike of such things as deer drives: in short, a bit of a snob, though I didn't realize it. She had no such problems. Once she got a job with the local paper, reporting on rodeos and fairs and traveling seventy miles to town meetings, there was no holding her back. It wasn't until after her death that I realized how friendships with western country people transcend even death. Her friends had become mine.

We had known a few ranchers while she was alive. John, a young landowner who lived where he was born, thirty miles south of the pavement, had shown up, after a cryptic preliminary call, with a goshawk on his fist. It was not an imprinted modern falconer's servant with enough paper to license a liquor store but a wild, old bird that had gone through about twenty fifty-dollar fighting-cock chicks before John livetrapped it with a set of monofilament snares and decided to ask the advice of the only falconer in the county, fifty miles away. I don't know who looked more feral that day— John, a pale caballero slumped in my chair wearing denim, snakeskin boots, and a black tractor cap, with a raptorial nose and an Okie-sounding twang at odds with his land-grant surname, or the hawk. The gos was an old breeder, a "haggard" in falconer's terminology, with eyes that had darkened with age past ruby to garnet. Although he wasn't much bigger than a pigeon, he was as spooky up close as an uncaged leopard and as elegant as an ancient engraving of death. Except for his eyes and legs, he was a study in monochrome, with the black back of the Sierra Madre 'Apache' race and eyebrows and front of filigreed silver. He gripped John's work-gloved fist with spidery yellow toes and watched our every move but made no attempt to fly.

I was impressed by their cool. "Looks like you've already got him manned."

"I ain't done much. He's not stupid."

"What do you expect to do with him?"

"I don't know. Put him back and let him make more, I guess. Seems a shame to keep him . . . "

"What about your chickens?"

"He's worth fifty damn chickens."

I was amused and a little shocked. "Then why'd you catch him?"

"He was so neat, I just sort of wanted to see him up close."

A lot of the older ranchers would not have agreed; they were fond of poisons and shot every rattlesnake they came across. But after Betsy died, I began to meet backcountry people who shared John's sentiments. Sis, ranch-matriarch-in-training, heiress apparent to a four-generation ranch established by an Italian–Swiss family in the 1880s, team roper, bartender, and community activist, wouldn't kill a snake, though she always carried a .38. She collected snakes live for the university, and she once sketched for me on a bar napkin the crucial difference in labial scale count between the Mojave and western diamondback rattlers. Her brothers, who ran a guide service and hunted with a pack of hounds but disliked the sometimes necessary killing of lions, had snapped Polaroids of virtually every local lion, each perched defiantly on a tree or a ledge, and could tell them apart by their tracks. Still later I met Windy Will, a slightly older man who ran a small ranch in the badlands to the north and read Edward Abbey, grinning and shaking his head ("I approve of the sorry-ass son of a bitch at least half the time"), and argued against designating a local peak as wilderness only because it would then fill up with people from Albuquerque.

Something that should have been obvious dawned on me slowly. First and foremost—contrary to the claims of those who portray ranchers as profit-hungry, greedy exploiters interested only in squeezing the most out of the land, monsters who somehow manage to combine the worst characteristics of capitalist consumption and welfare abuse—ranchers love their land.

They love *all* their land, deeded or leased. The majority of ranchers, who live on it—the notion that most ranchers are absentee landlords is a slander—know every inch of it as well as you know your backyard. (And if you care enough to read these words, I suspect you know your backyard better than 80 percent of the populace.) They've ridden over it more times

17

than they could count and will probably die on it. They attach stories and song lines to it: here's where Uncle Pancho was shot by those sons of bitches in 1918; here's where the bobcats den; a hawk nests up there; here's where Billy damn near cut his hand off with the chain saw in '75. Some of them are even good stewards. In time, they have been transformed from Europeans with a fear of all that is wild to people with a quirky affection for all those strange things out there: the singing coyotes, dark, ominous eagles, and invisible mountain lions—all those fellow inhabitants that you have to put up with but that finally make your home a very different place from the suburbs of New York City.

They also love work—hard work—on that same land, though not routines. I've rarely met happier people than cowboys who have work, nor ones who hate "regular hours" more, which may point to one reason ranch folks are hard for outsiders to understand. Urbanites, yuppies, suburbanites, call them what you will: they are all "middle class," bourgeois; they have jobs and routines from which they escape to an increasingly intricate web of pleasures. Ranchers and cowboys, whether owners or workers, stand outside this twentieth-century structure. They control baronial amounts of land, but their customs and language seem working-class to intellectuals. They have the frugality and generosity, the clannishness, the sir-and-ma'am manners of the plain people of the South, from whom their culture descends. They are emotional, contrary to the John Wayne image, and can be moved to tears. But they don't show their tears to strangers.

A Montana friend pointed out a real difference between "modern" and country people. She said that urbanites tend to see all people who work with the soil and nature—farmers and fishermen as well as ranchers and cowboys—as people who are losers in the professional race, people "too dumb to be yuppies," too unintellectual to have real jobs. Because of this, they can be pitied but hardly consulted on important issues. And ranchers and landowners who are in the employer class must be out to make money off the land, to rape it as long as they are allowed to—why else would anyone live voluntarily in W. H. Auden's "desert full of bigots?"

There are consequences here, all around.

I came to romanticize ranchers a bit, a fact that didn't much interest them one way or the other. Defending them against a compulsory multiculturalism in which European-descended whites were the new inferior class, I forgot the true lessons of multiculturalism: that we're all equal, equally screwed, European and Indian and African and Mexican; that even a dog is capable of cruelty; that some sort of original sin exists; that Buddhism demands compassion for a reason. I dreamed of a place where the best of the Old and the New West would come together, where longhaired cowboys and tough, literate cowgirls and sensitive hunters would stand together against the exploiters and Californicators, the miners and vegetarians.

The wave crested when I joined forces with a ranch couple my age and vowed to secede from the larger county and form our own, with guns blazing for ranchers and hunters, readers and rattlesnakes. I started a book on the strength of such euphoria, intending to produce an explanation of ranchers for people on the coast, a manifesto for environmentally sound ranching, and I don't know what else. It collapsed. Feelings were hurt; money was lost. People for the West!, that cynically funded exploiter of legitimate paranoia, claimed my friends. *Environmentalist* became a swear word and spotted owls a joke. I wrote a novel instead.

My town still looks the same. There is no skiing here and no blue-ribbon trout water; we're a hundred miles from the nearest city with jobs. And yet, in the past year, we have elected a mayor who has lived here three years. Two galleries have opened, both selling "southwestern art." A woman who believes herself to be a reincarnated priestess of ancient Egypt and whose new four-wheel-drive vehicle sports an incomprehensible vanity plate has my late partner's job on the county weekly. She has a "vegetarian" dog that roams unfettered. There is talk of a leash law and trash fees; the dump now is routinely referred to as the sanitary landfill and has business hours. You can no longer leave dead animals there. Of course, People for the West! is stronger than ever; the bumper sticker of choice reads "Bobbit Babbitt."

A rumor circulates that goes like this: a lion "stalked" a kid from a new family up-canyon. There's a consensus: everybody wants to kill it, but the Christians and the "new people" are the most fervent, even though the new people say they're reluctant. In the old days, the cat might have been killed but not talked to death by hypocrites. Of course, the lion probably doesn't care much about the various rationales.

I contemplate moving: Provence, Chihuahua, Thailand. I hear John's gone to Belize.

The old people, the old cultures, knew something about consequence that the new ones don't. The new ones, both born-again and politically correct (two faces of the same coin, or hydra, eerily similar in their self-righteousness) are, of course, sure they know, surer than the old ones ever are. Luigi Barzini, an Italian journalist, once wrote of such people that "they lack the humble skills of men who have to work with lackadaisical unpredictable nature, the skills so to speak of sailors, fishermen, farmers, horse-tamers, the people who must at all cost avoid deceiving themselves and must develop prudence, patience, skepticism, resignation, as well as great fortitude and perseverance."

What the old ones knew in their bones was that death exists, that all life eats and kills to eat, that all lives end, that energy goes on. They knew that humans are participants, not spectators. Their work and play and rituals affirmed and reinforced this knowledge.

The new ones all want to evade death and deny it, legislate against it, transcend it. They run, bicycle, network, and pray. They stare into their computer screens and buy their vitamins. Here, they want the street drunks locked up, cigarettes banned, drunken driving met with more severe penalties than is armed assault. They fear guns, cowboys, Moslems, pit bulls, whiskey, homosexuals, and freedom. Strong smells offend them.

In my town, the new people are disgusted by the *matanzas* of the old Spanish culture. Who but the Spanish and Mexicans would call a joyous fiesta celebrating pork a *matanza*, a killing? The new ones hate dangerous hard work. Who but a cretin would voluntarily work on horseback, rope cows, unroll miles of barbed wire? Or, for that matter, cut trees, stack bricks, fish out of sight of shore in winter, plow, balance on high steel?

They fear solitude and people who don't babble. When they are alone or silent, thoughts of death or meaninglessness come flooding in. Who would be alone? For this reason, they fear real leisure and distrust anyone, rich or poor, who has too much of it.

They like games but don't know how to play. They dislike the idea of skill, the notion that anyone might do anything better than anyone else. They distract themselves with endless, interchangeable electronic fantasies, none too different from the others or too disturbing. Real novels deal with hard things—a woman I once dated told me they were all about dysfunctional families—and must be assimilated in solitude, so nobody reads. They raise their children on Nintendo.

New people say the word *spiritual* a lot. They have never looked long into any void. They prefer Paradise Valley to the Red Desert. They pray for angels, extraterrestrials, the Rapture, rescue, intervention. They believe in recovered memories but have few real ones. They think they are victims, but they are conquerors.

According to an article in *High Country News*, "an important regional representative" from a national conservation organization said in a meeting in Aspen that "the role of environmental groups is to save the Colorado Plateau from the people who live there."

The new people disapprove of, and cannot comprehend, hunting. How could anybody but a sadist cause death voluntarily, again and again? That they also do so escapes their tender consciences and consequence-free brains. Curiously, they condone and even celebrate catch-and-release fly-fishing. Some of its practitioners are what environmental writer Ted Kerasote calls "fossil fuel vegetarians." I know a woman who persecuted—not too strong a verb—a fellow worker because he had taken out a permit to hunt wild sheep and backpacked into and out of a remote wilderness area with the sheep's head and meat. She is so devoted to nouveau fishing that she had a beaver dam on her property dynamited. As Dave Barry says, "I am not making this up."

The "instinct to hunt," whatever that is, must be strong, else why would a bunch of death deniers spend the budget of a medium-sized third-world country on chic equipment for what a colder mind might call fish torture? They think they are innocent and brag that they do not eat fish. They leave their fingerprints on the river, their footprints on the gravel; many leave uneaten fish floating downstream. The "greener" among them are merely self-righteous and maybe, to use a phrase I usually avoid, in denial. The more egregious offenders in the same army squeeze whitefish, bash carp, and fight the return of river habitats to native coarse fish because they prefer brown trout.

I have fly-fished since I was four; I still do. I tell people that "pure" catch-and-release fishing is playing without consequence, date rape, politically correct torture for the sentimental. I get some odd looks.

Gary Snyder says: "Life in the wild is not just eating berries in the sunlight. I like to imagine a 'depth ecology' that would go to the dark side of nature . . . the ball of crunched bones in the scat, the feather in the snow, the tales of insatiable appetite." Too abstract? He continues: "The other side of the 'sacred' is the sight of your beloved in the underworld, dripping with maggots." Can you live with the thought of those consequences?

Buddhist hermits, nurses, and cowboys see death as real, horrible, inevitable, necessary, unimportant, and sometimes funny. One night when my partner was still alive, we got to drinking hard with John and his wife, Becky. I believe it was after a cockfight fiesta and a meal of Burmese-style curry with cinnamon and chiles and black Chinese mushrooms. Gradually conversation turned to what we later referred to as "dead animal stories" . . . absurd deaths, horrible ones, hilarious ones. From there, inevitably, we progressed to human death tales. There was chill outside the ring around the woodstove and fire in our bellies. I doubt four people had ever laughed harder. There were tears in all our eyes, and my sides hurt. I could barely sit in a chair.

The evening after Betsy died, John and Becky materialized outside the house in Albuquerque where I was staying, a square bottle of brown whiskey in John's hand. Betsy's oldest sister, Jane, China born, silver haired, and impeccably Episcopal, was staying there as well. We sat around all evening, passing the bottle—not "killing" it but transforming its substance to story, using it to retrieve memories, to offer them with more than our usual eloquence. We told "Betsy" stories, and one of them was about the night of dead animal stories. Then we told dead animal stories. All of us, including Jane, laughed so hard and so inappropriately that we horrified our proper hosts. Telling stories of life and death that made us laugh and weep was exactly the right way to mourn. But for the fact that there was a gaping, ragged-edged hole in my life, it might have been one of the best evenings I had ever spent.

∼

Eagles. Right now I'm writing a book about golden eagles. How can somebody proper, somebody hedged in by written rules, somebody who has never taken his or her food from the ground or brought it down from the air, have even a chance of understanding an eagle? They are so *other*—almost as old as dinosaurs, with eyes bigger than their brains, which nevertheless contain an intelligence as eager as a dog's. They weigh ten pounds yet can inflict thousands of pounds of pressure at their talon points. They kill their siblings and then stay absolutely loyal to their mates for thirty years. They can pick a grouse out of the air at 200 miles per hour or, in a harsh winter, tear at an antelope's side until it totters in circles and falls dead. What might they think of us? That we eat dirt and stones and things that do not move, crawl in slow motion on the face of the earth, and kill at a distance? How can sentimentalists make them little people in bird suits or moralists make them evil?

On the other hand: I was cutting wood with a friend, an old Comanche from Oklahoma, a couple of years ago when a coyote came down the hill and barked at us. I went up to put a little sensible fear into him—not all humans find his kind as amusing as Leonard and I do. He came closer and barked again. Finally, I pulled off my hat and ran straight at him, whooping. He trotted off, looking over his shoulder. When I returned, Leonard was muttering something about goddamn stupid Eyetalian Yankees.

"What, Leonard?"

"Forget it."

"I'm serious. What's the matter?"

He finally permitted himself a smile. "Well, anyway, he was talkin' to *you*. I don't know why I was worried . . . it's all on *your* head."

"What?"

"Either money or a death. We'll know when we get back to town. Shut up and load."

As a matter of fact, it was money—a book advance, as we found out when we got to the bar. I should add that I don't believe this story. What's money to a coyote?

So again, what? I am the one without solutions. We're all screwed, remember? We all await death where we are, playing or not, seeing or not, accepting consequence or denying it. It is easier to be awake, easier not to be a somnambulist, in some places than in others. The phrase "last best place" scares the piss out of me. Use it and lose it—besides, what does "last" mean? Still, I had hoped we might grow a different kind of culture here.

Doing what, exactly? Maybe living with and in, not off or beside, the land and its creatures. Christians kill predators. The purist greenie thinks he or she kills nothing and is deluded. Better to eat and respect. Consequences. Those who avoid or deny those choices think evolution, or God, got it wrong. I don't. "And as for small difficulties and worryings, prospects of sudden disaster, peril of life and limb; all these, and death itself, seem to him only sly good-natured hints, and jolly punches in the side bestowed by some unseen and unaccountable old joker." A hermit monk in the foothills of the Tien Shan? No, Herman Melville.

Eat and respect. Cultivate your garden, on your hands and knees. Eat weird things like lion and hawk; taste the wild; save roadkills. Eat a cow raised by a good rancher; know who the good ranchers are. Eat deer constantly. Hunt mushrooms. If you are female, hunt. If you are male, hunt with, and converse with, those outside the fraternity. Dogs are a start. But how about your wife, children, falcon, horse, ferret, neighbors? Befriend your weapons and tools and the people next door.

The West we inhabit, the Next West we will, should not be a suburb or a text or a landscape photograph, all glossy and flat, but the Real West, an intricate mosaic in motion whose uncountable facets are rocks, birds, mammals, rivers, people, ourselves. It has a meaning apart from us, which we can only partly comprehend. Its history is full of heroism, pain, and horror, like all history; its future is unknowable. We can save the parts, but we can't freeze-dry it or edit it. Living in it beats watching it. Releasing a trout still leaves a mark on the river.

That Real West is something wild and edged; like life, it makes us sad just at the moment we think we've caught it, the moment at which we are most struck with its beauty and consequence. Sooner or later we must leave it all, and the knowledge breaks our hearts. We can live with this knowledge and celebrate it; it keeps us honest. But if we treat the land as a television set or a backdrop, if we fail to see it and its myriad inhabitants, from deer mouse to rancher, as real, then it will first bore us and then leave us behind . . . even as we slap down another payment on the lease. Haven't we done this enough times already?

CHAPTER TWO

New Forestry in the Next West

ROCKY BARKER

Stieg Gabrielsen cruises through a lush mixed stand of pines and firs south of Athol, Idaho, his boots sinking into the moist forest floor. Sunbeams slice through the thick canopy of tall white pines towering over fifty-year-old Douglas and white firs.

There is a sense of majesty in these older trees. Their branches slacken the winds and form a homelike enclosure that keeps the competing fresh pine scent and musty odor of decomposition near. An assortment of sprouting lodgepole pines and other young trees rises from the forest litter of mossy dead logs and branches. Moving through the lush growth a few paces behind Gabrielsen, I find a few huckleberry bushes where the canopy has broken, spilling in sunlight like water from a broken dike. Several snags remain standing; birds have chipped out little caverns in them for nests. As we walk into a thicket of young lodgepoles, Gabrielsen spooks a small buck.

This is the kind of mixed-stand forest that typifies the ideal of forestry promoted for decades by conservation groups and embodied in the concept of "new forestry," which popped up in the wake of the bitter forest wars of the 1980s. Here the forester is a steward who is rooted in the land just as solidly as if he himself has come out of the soil. Gabrielsen, a tall man with an erect bearing and a black mustache, wearing the forester's traditional plaid work shirt under a down vest, controls thousands of acres of forest for the Crown Pacific Corporation, a timber-manufacturing company, and he readily admits that not all his stands look like this one. This place is special. For more than twenty years, he has marked each tree for harvest. Instead of taking the most valuable trees, he leaves those that will grow the fastest. Moreover, he leaves the land and the forest's other plants and animals as undisturbed as possible.

When Gabrielsen began his forestry career, there was no economic or scientific motivation for such special husbandry of the deer, owls, and forbs that fill in the forest between the trees. Beyond their aesthetic value, which was not useful to his employers, these forest inhabitants were economically benign. A forester who paid more than a minimum of personal attention to these resources didn't advance in the world of corporate forestry. But then, the forester who dallied in the luxury of any hands-on management at all was viewed as an eccentric who would never be able to meet the fierce demands of the mill managers when they made their call for wood.

Even in the public forests, where profit purports to take a back seat to the public interest, the demands of politics, economics, and efficiency discouraged the tree-by-tree, acre-by-acre ideal toward which Gabrielsen and other foresters like him strive. Fish and wildlife were valued only where politics demanded it. A good hand on the computer was worth more than a good eye for standing board feet.

Today, the science and practice of forestry are undergoing a transformation like nothing seen since forestry's beginnings, in the late 1800s. Thunderous controversy over the protection of endangered species, water quality, and aesthetic values of forests has made foresters in industry and on public lands reexamine their methods, their science, and even their values. Foresters now recognize their jobs as protecting the integrity of the entire forest ecosystem, not just growing one generation of trees. This paradigm shift was born in the West, and it is here that the effects will be seen the most.

The Resource, Today and in the Early Days

In seventeen western states, including Hawaii and Alaska, forests cover 356,354,000 acres. Of those, 132,449,000 acres are rated as commercial timberland, capable of growing at least twenty cubic board feet of timber per acre per year. The USDA Forest Service controls the majority of this timberland, 63,562,000 acres. Private, nonindustrial timberlands total

36,531,000 acres. States and other public agencies own 17,124,000 acres, and the forest products industry has 15,232,000. The West accounts for roughly half of all U.S. forests, one-fourth of all commercial timberland, and three-fourths of the National Forest System. Most of the region's timber comes from the Pacific Northwest and the northern Rocky Mountains.[1]

Before Europeans came to North America, its forests provided Indians primarily with fuel and structural support for their homes. The numbers of natives were relatively small, and their demands were minimal. But they affected larger areas of forest by setting fires to drive game or by causing random accidental forest fires. The extent of their impact is a subject of growing debate in forest management. The fact that foresters even care about it demonstrates how much forestry has changed since its beginnings.

Since the first settlers pioneered the United States, our society has depended on forests to provide wood and fiber. Americans carved their way west through the pre-Columbian forest, which in many cases was ancient and extensive. The industrial revolution allowed the harvest of timber to be made ruthlessly efficient, and by the middle of the nineteenth century, the demands of a growing nation had made forest liquidation highly profitable.

Industrial foresters mowed bare the deep and seemingly endless old forests of the Midwest's North Woods in a capitalistic orgy lasting for one generation. Thousands of acres of 400-foot-high, 12-foot-thick white pines, cedars, and even inferior hemlocks were creamed. The logs were either piled high on poorly engineered railroads or dumped into rivers like the Flambeau, which were dammed and then released to allow a flood of water and logs to rush down to the mills and markets below. Both practices loaded northern Wisconsin's rivers with muddy sediment that still bleeds red into the Great Lakes after a minor rain shower.

By the end of the nineteenth century, the effects of unbridled capitalism on America's forests were beginning to be recognized as one of the ills of a society that needed the guidance of experts and technicians to save itself from its own excesses. Foresters such as Bernard Fernow and Gifford Pinchot were at the vanguard of a progressive movement that sought to spread the benefits of America's bounty more fairly through the economic strata and over the generations.

Fernow, trained in Germany and responsible for the establishment of forestry schools throughout the United States and Canada, preached the concept of sustained yield, the basis of the science of forestry. It was really more engineering than science. Forestry was based on the idea that silvicultural technology was a universally applicable science that could be applied to all forest sites to provide biologically sustainable forests. Foresters saw themselves as stewards of the forest much as farmers see themselves as husbands over their dominion. Naturalness had little value. Indeed, in the eyes of many foresters even today, nature is a poor forester. Forestry pioneers advocated cutting down old "decadent" natural forests that grow slowly. These tangled messes were replaced with man-made, carefully propagated forests that grew faster and were easier to manage. Fire was one of the foresters' major enemies and had to be extinguished as quickly as possible. Pinchot, trained in forestry in France, added to Fernow's teachings the utilitarian ethic of "the greatest good for the greatest number over time." Eventually, because of his more political role in the development of national forests, he added the concept of multiple use, which allowed the powerful ranching interests and growing hunting lobbies to get their piece of the forest pie.

Foresters saw recreation values and wildlife habitat as desirable offshoots of their work, but only secondary to the scientific and economic task of growing trees for homes. Even these forest engineers were viewed as idealists by the corporate powers who employed them. From the beginning, many timber executives viewed sustained-yield forestry as an ideal rather than a mandate. Economically, sustained-yield forestry was always a marginal endeavor that many corporate foresters privately ignored. Instead, corporate goals or simple sawmill demand shaped the harvest and reforestation schemes of all but the most fervent forest companies. Forest harvests on private lands, which remained mostly unmanaged until the 1940s, peaked in 1950, just as the postwar exodus to suburbia was driving a new growth in wood demand. Seeking the next great woodpile, the timber industry looked to the national forests. Now foresters had the chance to show the benefits of their work. By then, they themselves were dividing into two separate camps. Aldo Leopold, who began his career with the Forest Service in 1909 under Pinchot, described these camps in his landmark essay *The Land Ethic,* published more than forty years ago:

> Group A is quite content to grow trees like cabbages, with cellulose as the basic forest commodity. . . . Group B, on the other hand, sees forestry as fundamentally different from agronomy because it employs natural species and manages a natural environment rather than creating an artificial one. Group B prefers natural reproduction on principle. It worries on biotic as well as economic grounds about the loss of species like chestnut and the threatened loss of the white pines. It worries about a whole series of secondary forest functions: wildlife, recreation, watersheds, wilderness areas. To my mind, Group B feels the stirrings of an ecological conscience.[2]

Troubles in Modern Times

Gabrielsen looks back on his own education as a forester to trace the roots of both of these ideas in his own work. He tells how the tree-by-tree approach was espoused by his professors as the ideal on which foresters should judge themselves ethically. Later, he was taught that if a stand was beyond saving, whether because of a mistake or poor past practices, drastic measures could be used. These might include clear-cuts.

Unfortunately, the pressures of growing demand and politics favored the Group A foresters. Ultimately, the mills needed to be fed, and the system that could best meet that demand was going to win. Clear-cuts and massive land manipulation became normal practice. The height of the power of the Group A forest engineers came in the 1960s. Foresters learned they could maximize growth in most forest types by clear-cutting the old, slow-growing trees, burning the slash to release nutrients, and either replanting or allowing natural regeneration to take place. What was first proposed as an emergency measure became standard practice.

Practicing such intensive forestry in the Rockies required unique equipment such as the Idaho Jammer, a combination hauling truck and loader that required the construction of many parallel roads across steep mountain slopes. Even in the best conditions, these roads carried tons of mud into nearby streams. In the worst conditions, entire mountainsides were destabilized and flowed like lava into prime salmon and trout streams, causing serious, permanent damage. In 1965, the banks of the South Fork of the Salmon River gave way, loading hundreds of thousands of tons of silt into the river, one of the most important spawning streams for chinook salmon in the Pacific Northwest. The salmon population never recovered, and even today mud covers much of the river's former spawning gravel.

Some foresters went even further, carving terraces in steep slopes with bulldozers in an attempt to make tree growing easier and more orderly. In some cases, such as in the Bitterroot National Forest in Montana, such massive intervention still wasn't enough to allow trees to regrow on the harsh, high-altitude sites chosen by professional foresters. To defend their unbridled efforts to cut every forest they could, foresters warped the Forest Service's call to protect watersheds, defending thousands of acres of clear-cuts as a prized method for increasing water flows in downstream rivers. They knew irrigators would respond favorably to increased flows.

The abuses in the Bitterroot and in national forests across the West led Congress to pass the National Forest Management Act of 1976. The law required the Forest Service to take into account the effects of its logging on other resources in a systematic public planning process. This was the beginning of the age of computers, and the foresters and road engineers who ran the Forest Service embraced this new technology as a tool to improve their efficiency in cutting and managing timber. They adopted the language of computer programs, calling actions that limited timber harvesting, their main job, "constraints." They paid lip service to protection of fish and wildlife habitat and even to protection of biological diversity. But chain saws continued to chew through ancient forests at an unprecedented pace, peaking in the National Forest System in the late 1980s. Clear-cuts in Idaho's Targhee National Forest carved a straight line along the boundary of Yellowstone National Park, so distinctive that the border could be seen from space.

The election of Ronald Reagan to the presidency in 1980 put a sympathetic administration in the White House, which accelerated timber harvests on public lands. Moreover, Wall Street's leveraged buyout frenzy sparked a massive liquidation of timber resources in states such as Montana. Group A foresters tightened their grip on both private and public forest management. They bulldozed thousands of miles of roads, clear-cut millions of acres of pristine forest, and sullied countless miles of streams.

By the end of the decade, the most obvious features of the Pacific Northwest and the northern Rockies to jet passengers were the extensive clear-cuts spread across the mountainsides like open sores. Yet these scars were only symptoms of a more serious ailment: the systematic breakdown of the biotic communities of entire watersheds and ecosystems. Environmentalists faced a long and often lonely battle to expand the view of foresters beyond the pursuit of marketable timber. They continue to fight in court and in the forests to move public foresters from an emphasis on cutting trees toward one of protecting forests, fish, wildlife, and other values. Their success has been the impetus behind the forest industry changes seen today. Lawsuits over protection of the northern spotted owl's old-growth habitat, based on the federal Endangered Species Act, brought the timber harvest on federal land to a dramatic halt in the early 1990s in Oregon and Washington. By 1994, lawsuits over water quality problems, the disappearance of Pacific salmon, and other issues had sharply reduced inland harvests. In Montana, the Plum Creek Corporation and the Champion International Corporation had clear-cut most of their private lands. In the Southwest, protection of the Mexican spotted owl and changing pressures on federal land managers also began to limit the harvest in the early 1990s.

Foresters and the timber industry had argued for years that clear-cut forests were no different from farm fields furrowed by the plow. They thought that through education and propaganda they could convince the public of their higher wisdom. David Adams, a forestry professor at the University of Idaho, says that this thinking turned out to be flawed: "We are now finding that no matter how knowledgeable the public may be, they still don't like a lot of what they see."[3]

The Beginning of the Great Shift

At the same time some environmentalists were winning in court, others were winning the hearts and minds of the foresters themselves. A new generation of foresters, educated after the first Earth Day, had studied ecology and read Aldo Leopold's *Sand County Almanac*. They identified more with the Group B foresters Leopold described. In the Forest Service, they were joined by a growing number of fish and wildlife biologists, hydrologists, and plant ecologists who had originally been brought in to collect data necessary to allow timber sales to go forward. Increasingly, though, their data were used by opponents to stop timber cutting.

Jack Ward Thomas, a thoughtful and politically astute biologist, largely shaped the management plan for forests west of the Cascade Range in the early 1990s. He headed the team that wrote the first scientifically defensible spotted owl recovery plan, in 1989. Then, in 1993, he led the Forest Ecosystem Management Action Team, which wrote the plan for the Cascade forests that carried the federal government out of the courtroom and back into its forests. In late 1993, he took the helm of the Forest Service and immediately prompted a major reshuffling of staff and priorities within the agency, which had lost its consensus on forest management. More important, it had lost public confidence.

Until recently, most foresters were not seeing the forest for the trees. Today, foresters, even in the timber industry, are beginning to recognize forests not simply as stands of timber but as living, interconnected ecosystems. Spurred on by the research of forest ecologists such as Jerry Franklin of the University of Washington, they are focusing their attention on the wide scope of forest organisms, including fungi, fish, and fowl. Scientists today agree that widespread use of clear-cuts has fragmented wildlife habitat and in extreme cases has threatened the long-term productivity of the soil. Ultimately, this makes a site less productive even for tree growing, the very activity foresters wish to promote. Franklin argues that leaving old trees standing and leaving much of the woody debris on the forest floor preserves the fungi and other organisms that contribute to the natural ecological processes necessary for forest health. Forestry no longer is a simple case of applying engineering techniques to enhance tree growth. Inherently, it must include maintenance of the forest's biological diversity, processes of energy transfer, water cycle, and natural fire intervals. "New forestry isn't any one thing," Franklin wrote. "It's an evolutionary way of looking at and managing forests for both ecological and commodity values. While it incorporates the beginnings of big picture science, it does not eliminate any of the old tools such as clearcutting, herbicides and fire management."[4]

Management in these terms, according to forest ecologist Chris Maser in *Global Imperative*, "means engaging in a balancing act between nature's stresses and humanity's cultural stresses. We can manage an ecosystem for products on a sustainable basis," he wrote, "if we are careful to remain within the stress threshold in which the ecosystem is self-repairing and self-sustaining in the sense of being able to once again approximate its condition at the time humans disturbed it."[5]

Such an approach takes a larger view than has previously been considered. Care is needed in maintaining single stands such as those Gabrielsen manages, but foresters also must husband landscapes along natural boundaries such as watersheds and even bioregions. Because trees take years to mature, forestry has always been a discipline that tends to look to the long term. Today, it is necessary to think in even longer time frames, such as the historical frequency of forest fires.

The old battles between timber cutting and wilderness preservation remain, but the arrogant belief that humankind can control all of nature's forces has been tempered. Suppression of fires resulted in unnaturally high levels of fuels in the forests. This left them vulnerable to larger, even more intense fires that threatened natural and man-made entities. Even environmentalists who want less manipulation of the landscape support some level of prescribed burning and thinning to remedy this unnatural condition.

To restore the public respect it once had, the Forest Service will need to change the budget-driven incentives and mix of expertise it calls on to guide public forest management. Ecosystem integrity should be the agency's bedrock value, but it also must become more responsive to local communities' needs. Most important, rangers will need to be in the forests and the communities more and in regional offices and behind computers less.

Jaded by the clear-cut scars they saw throughout the country they were trying to protect, environmentalists have been unable to recognize how successful they have been. The new reality in forest management incorporates many of the concepts of even the most radical environmental voices of the early 1980s.

Recognition of the need to preserve the integrity of ecosystems and to protect biodiversity will mean reduced timber harvests throughout the West. It won't, however, close down the timber industry, and it shouldn't. The industry will be an important player in the Next West, just as it was in the Old

West and the so-called New West that followed World War II. Encouraging its potential to play a positive role, instead of expecting the worst, can promote partnerships rather than polarization.

To be sure, there remain significant unreconciled differences in values. Battles over water quality issues and over how much of the remaining roadless areas should be designated as wilderness will continue to generate controversy where science cannot provide answers. The wilderness debate in particular will challenge both sides to go beyond philosophy and science to reach a satisfying resolution. If ecosystem management programs are truly successful, many roadless areas can be managed to protect wildlife and biodiversity without official protection of wilderness. However, the spiritual, aesthetic, psychological, recreational, and intrinsic values of wild country still are best protected by the Wilderness Act of 1964.

The Slow Grip of a New Reality

In some areas, foresters foolishly hold on to old goals and values, hoping to ride out the passing fad of biodiversity protection and ecosystem management. But in others, especially the inland Northwest, they are accepting the new reality. Craig Savidge, resource manager for the Louisiana-Pacific Corporation's plant in Sandpoint, Idaho stopped all clear-cutting on his company's 45,000 acres of timberland in 1993 in favor of mixed-stand management. Better than anyone, he understands that his decision raises the costs of harvesting and allows a lot of valuable timber to be left in the stand, but he sees his move as a good investment for the future. "I'll always have options out there," he says. "When you clear-cut, you lose options." Mixed-stand management, the method most of the forest industry is moving toward, can also preserve diversity of species, canopy cover, and habitat for wildlife. "What we're basically doing is treating the land less as a factory and more as our backyard," Savidge says.[6]

Barry Rosenberg, an activist with the Inland Empire Public Lands Council, led the fight to reform forest management in northern Idaho. Still, he points to the efforts of Savidge and others in the timber industry as examples of good stewardship. He even takes Gabrielsen and other like-minded industry foresters with him when he meets with Forest Service officials to try to persuade them to consider alternatives to clear-cuts. These discussions may be the basis for a new consensus in forest management.

This isn't the first time the timber industry has changed direction in the face of public pressure. In the beginning, the industry and the western senators who represented it fought Pinchot and President Theodore

Roosevelt in their expansion of the National Forest System, and the timber industry was slow to accept even basic forestry measures beyond fire control. In the 1930s, the Roosevelt administration's discussions about nationalizing forestlands prompted Philip Weyerhaeuser to push the industry toward sustained-yield tree farming as an alternative to cut-and-run lumbering.

A general consensus regarding forest management built on the concept of sustained-yield management survived well into the 1960s. Only the clearcutting binge and a growing understanding of ecology ripped it apart. The opportunity for a new consensus centered on ecosystem integrity is out there waiting for good-faith managers to prove its worth.

Unfortunately, some of the current changes appear to be mostly window dressing. Representatives of Plum Creek Corporation, which liquidated the timber on thousands of acres of its land in Montana in the 1980s, went to Jerry Franklin to learn how the company could use "new forestry" techniques. Today, Plum Creek manages only 15 percent of its land using his techniques but calls its timber practices on the remaining lands "environmental" forestry.

Other companies, however, appear serious about changing the way they do business and have restructured in order to do it. Once one of the most intransigent timber companies, the Potlatch Corporation has embarked on a landscape management program on its 665,000 acres of timberland in Idaho. Using its computer-based geographic information system, it is one of the first of the large owners of forestland to practice ecosystem management on its own land. If it successfully integrates its management programs with those of other landowners in the area, it could break through the polarization of the current forest debate, help move the West to a new consensus on forest management, and bring back stability such as was in place from the 1940s through the 1970s.

Contrasting land management goals, private property rights, and varied degrees of scientific certainty make the necessary coordination challenging. Owners of private timberland seek to grow and harvest trees at a profit, whereas federal landowners have a wide variety of goals, including wildlife protection, fisheries enhancement, and timber harvesting.

At the heart of Potlatch's stewardship initiative is a recognition of the advantages of managing at a landscape level—10,000- to 20,000-acre units instead of the traditional stand of 10 to 200 acres. Within these landscape units, goals and objectives are set for timber, water resources, and wildlife resources. Overall, Potlatch seeks to have a mosaic of stands for timber, wildlife, biodiversity, and stream quality, according to the company's resource manager, Kevin Bohling.

Potlatch's geographic information system, developed in 1985, provides a detailed inventory of information for each of the company's 7,900 timber stands. This revolutionary new tool provides digitized information on elevation, topography, hydrology, soils, precipitation, roads, and ownership patterns in map form. Potlatch's database provides resolution on the ground to thirty feet. With this information and additional data provided on tree growth potential, wildlife habitat needs, locations of sensitive species, water quality, and other factors, Potlatch foresters can predict how the forests will look over time. This allows the company to set objectives—for timber harvest, water quality, or wildlife habitat—over a larger area and a longer period of time. Potlatch hopes it can meet its timber harvest goals and at the same time comply with increasingly strict regulations to protect wildlife and water quality.

The company now benefits from the efficiencies of sustained-yield forestry, a practice Bohling acknowledges it had ignored until 1991. Instead of deciding when and where to cut primarily in response to mill demand, the company established detailed silvicultural plans to take advantage of the growth potential available on its lands. What was left in a stand became more important than what was removed.

Bohling acknowledges that Potlatch is only beginning the program and that it intends to continue to clear-cut 30 percent of its lands. Many of these clear-cuts were made necessary by poor harvest decisions in the past. Through better stand management, fewer and fewer clear-cuts will make sense even for this corporate forest company.

On one of its landscape units, Potlatch is working to develop a landscape management plan in cooperation with the Forest Service. If the company can develop a plan that meets its own needs while meeting the Forest Service's goals for its public lands, it could advance ecosystem management efforts throughout the region.

But there are limitations. Timber companies themselves are limited by antitrust laws in how much they can cooperate, especially in such activities as timing of timber harvests that could affect markets.

Jim Caswell, supervisor of Clearwater National Forest in Orofino, Idaho, sees great potential in cooperative arrangements such as these. But he predicts that public lands will for the most part be used to offset the effects of activities on private lands. This "mitigation management" role for public lands, though preferable to past land abuse, is a raw deal for the public.

When the Forest Service loses its ability to reap marketable timber from its own lands in a given watershed but private foresters can continue cutting with fewer limits, the public loses. To be fair, all owners of forestland in a watershed should share equally the costs of protecting the integrity of the natural ecosystem.

Ross Gorte, a natural resource specialist with the Congressional Research Service, warns that companies owning land in pristine watersheds may decide to harvest all their timber to ensure that water quality restrictions or other limitations fall on other landowners, not on them. "That allows the large landowner to impose substantial costs on society, like limiting its ability to cut timber for twenty years," Gorte says.[7]

This is why cooperative approaches such as Potlatch's are so important to ecosystem management, for both the industry and the public. "The public has to decide: do we do it cooperatively, or do we approach it regulatorily?" Gorte says. "My feeling is that if we don't approach it cooperatively, we *will* approach it regulatorily."[8]

Perhaps the greatest challenge to this new approach is the poor condition of many forest watersheds. Poor logging and road-building practices and other activities have left many watersheds filled with sediment or washed out and containing little fish habitat. Fisheries have suffered, and major restoration will be necessary to return them to health. That means building fewer roads and reclaiming thousands of miles of roads already built.

Although water is universally recognized as the most important resource in the West, there is no general agreement about the quality of water and streams in the national forests or about how to protect and restore them in the future. To complicate matters further, although the water itself is often pure and clean, many watersheds are severely damaged, with their biological and physical systems sick or out of balance. Complex hydrologic processes will be required to determine scientifically the health of these water systems. The problems are most apparent to the public in the declining population of bull trout, cutthroat trout, and salmon over wide areas of the forested portions of the northern Rockies.

What also is clear is that concerns over water will play a decisive role in determining where, when, and how logging will take place in many of the region's forests. The amount of timber placed for sale by the Forest Service in the Clearwater and Panhandle National Forests has been cut dramatically due primarily to concerns for and protests over water quality. Efforts to protect salmon spawning streams have reduced or slowed timber sales throughout the Salmon and Clearwater basins.

Efforts to shift forest management toward ecosystem management inherently shift more attention toward water and watersheds. Simply thinking bigger in space and time changes the focus toward managing watersheds as systems instead of responding only to individual activities.

Restoration Forestry

When the first loggers and miners entered Idaho's Coeur d'Alene River basin in the late 1800s, the river channels in the steep terrain were diverse and stable. Trees as wide as six feet choked the channels, slowing the flow and forcing the streams to snake through canyons in a meandering fashion. Vast forests covered the surrounding mountains, storing water and shading the snow so it melted slowly, lasting into late spring.

Today, mining, logging, and residential development have opened up the canopy over large areas of the watershed. Roads running alongside streams have limited and straightened the streams' channels. Placer mining in earlier days and the practice of damming rivers and then opening the dams to wash logs downstream have scoured out the channels.

During the 1960s and 1970s, Forest Service officials inadvertently exacerbated these problems and created two new ones. First, they removed woody debris from the streams in a misguided attempt to improve fish habitat. Today, many of the streams in the Panhandle National Forest can barely support fish. According to Edward Lider, a Forest Service fisheries biologist in Wallace, Idaho, "Right now we have such simplified channels that when we get high water we have massive movement of material downstream."[9]

The second problem is more complex and less obvious. A combination of factors in a watershed—including loss of forest canopy, building of roads, and removal of woody debris in streams—leads to increased flooding, especially during the frequent rain-on-snow storms that hit northern Idaho and western Montana. This flooding moves heavier rocks and gravel downstream, replacing a watercourse's natural series of pools and riffles with long, scoured-out runs. Pools and riffles provide most of a stream's fish habitat and serve to slow down its flow. In a healthy stream and watershed, the stream channel reaches an equilibrium among its runs, riffles, and pools, according to Forest Service scientists in the Panhandle National Forest.

Since the early 1960s, these hydrologists have watched as many of these channels have lost their equilibrium, according to Al Isaacson, a former Forest Service hydrologist. And though timber industry scientists don't disagree about the seriousness of the problem, they rightfully worry about imposing restrictions with a broad brush. "I don't think you can generalize," says Dale McGreer, a hydrologist with Potlatch. "I would want to make an analysis watershed by watershed. You may find [that roads and canopy removal] are significant and need to limit development in some, while in others it would be insignificant."[10]

Both Isaacson and McGreer agree that removing roads and placing big logs in the streams can help, but Isaacson believes that some watersheds need to be left alone until significant cover returns. Still, he says that logging can continue in some affected drainages if most of the overstory is left, using techniques of adaptive forestry such as Louisiana-Pacific uses on its own lands.[11]

Forest Service teams are currently ripping out old roads and punching large logs back into stream channels. They are using a variety of conventional and exotic equipment to tear out old culverts and to reslope former channels to their natural contours. The major problems they face are the miles and miles of roads left from years of logging and mining. In some watersheds, road densities are as high as nineteen miles of road per square mile. Few of the roads are necessary for current logging operations, and they contribute to both sedimentation and, more important, heavy spring runoffs. Restoring all the damaged watersheds in the Panhandle will cost millions of dollars.

One bright spot is that many of the people who built the roads will now be employed in dismantling them. One local contractor had received part of the $180,000 the Forest Service spent for equipment use in 1993. His crew removed 170 miles of road and restored 700 acres of damaged stream channel. The timber industry has proposed and endorsed adding watershed restoration projects to existing timber sales so that ongoing sales can help pay the enormous costs. Environmentalists say that the industry must rectify its old mistakes before they will support new timber sales. "It doesn't make sense to be adding impacts to these watersheds at the same time we're putting in rehabilitation projects," says Al Espinosa, a retired Forest Service fisheries biologist from Moscow, Idaho.[12] The answer lies somewhere in the middle.

Careful harvesting can recover timber without further damage to the watershed. David Cross, a fisheries biologist with the Panhandle National Forest, says that in healthy streams he tries to "ensure that the ecosystem processes that produce good fish habitat are sustained." In streams that are damaged, he works throughout the watershed to restore their health. "When working to restore watersheds, a certain level of patience has to be factored in," Cross says. "That doesn't mean you have to stop activities; it means you won't necessarily see the improvement on the ground for years."[13]

Addressing sediment problems is more straightforward but no less controversial. Sediment enters a stream primarily from poorly built roads, clear-cuts, old railroad grades, or other soil disturbances. Increased sedimentation covers stream gravel used by trout and salmon for spawning and fills in slower-flowing stretches used by fish, especially juveniles, as holding and resting areas. Sedimentation also increases filtering costs for drinking water, interferes with irrigation systems, and increases flood potential.

Better-engineered roads with careful landscaping can reduce siltation dramatically. The timber industry has supported laws requiring antisedimentation practices. But environmentalists question whether roads and clear-cuts can be engineered well enough to prevent sedimentation in some soil types and in streams already heavily damaged by past logging and road building. Science probably won't completely answer their concerns.

Often in water quality and watershed issues, there comes a point where scientific uncertainty will remain and values must take over the process. The timber industry wants to ensure that all avenues are studied before logging is prohibited in a particular watershed. Environmentalists want risks removed for fish, especially in already degraded areas, until rehabilitation takes place. "Otherwise the best we can hope for is a stable system, not improvement," says Espinosa. If the past is a guide, environmentalists say, we should err on the side of the fish. That in itself should goad the industry to advocate strong monitoring and protection measures.

Forest Health Insurance?

Another great challenge to a new consensus in forestry lies in what foresters call the growing forest health crisis. Throughout the inland Northwest and the northern Rockies, forests are in decline, demonstrated by rising tree mortality and reduced growth rates. Large areas of forests in southern Idaho and eastern Oregon are dying faster than they are growing. Even in northern Idaho, eastern Washington, and western Montana, where forests are among the most productive in the nation, root diseases and white pine blister rust are threatening the timber potential. There is widespread agreement about the cause. Decades of misguided fire suppression, harvesting of only valuable tree species, and introduction of blister rust have changed the composition of tree species. Firs, especially grand fir, have replaced ponderosa and white pine as the dominant species in many stands now overcrowded with trees competing for water and nutrients. Years of drought have caused massive die-offs of stressed trees. Increased fuel buildup from a century of fire suppression has led to fires of unnaturally high intensity.

Such fires have burned hundreds of thousands of acres of forest that could have provided timber for the economy and habitat for wildlife. Unfortunately, in many of the same areas, watersheds have been damaged by poor road-building, mining, and logging practices. Water quality and biological diversity have suffered, adding to the poor health of forest ecosystems. The challenge of forest managers, especially on public lands, is to remedy both forest health problems—excessive fuel buildup and watershed degradation—without exacerbating either one.

A wide variety of cures have been proposed. In the Boise National Forest, the Forest Service has begun salvaging thousands of acres of timber killed by fire and insects in an effort to reduce fuel that continues to cause huge fires. It also proposes extensive thinning of dense stands and the use of prescribed fire to return the forest to the natural short-duration fire cycle that fostered massive stands of old ponderosa pine. Removal of root rot–susceptible species such as grand fir and replacement with blister-resistant white pines are proposed for forests in northern Idaho.

Neil Sampson, executive director of the American Forestry Association, believes that there is little time left to restore stability to the region's forests. Unless restoration is begun soon, the more or less even-aged stands will be replaced by yet another generation of even-aged stands, leaving little chance to restore natural diversity for several generations. "We have a reasonably short window in which we can do something—probably only fifteen to thirty years," he says.[14]

Others argue that rash, sweeping prescriptions, which include huge timber salvage programs, may cause more problems than they cure. "The current health situation is not a crisis but a normal ecological event," say forest pathologists Arthur Partridge and Catherine Bertagnolli. "There has been considerable mortality; but concurrently, ecological reinforcement has been replacing the dying trees with genetically superior, resistant species that historically populated the area."[15]

Sampson says that because fire suppression and high-grading of timber have transformed the forest ecosystem so drastically, nature can't balance itself in a manner that provides for both ecosystem and human needs. "We've got to get away from the age-old notion that if you leave the forest alone, everything will be all right," he says.

Steve Mealey, former supervisor of the Boise National Forest, has evidence to support Sampson's approach. Neighboring lands to the Boise, owned and managed by the Boise Cascade Corporation, are not suffering the growth problems taking place on public lands. On those lands, extensive thinning programs and uneven-stand management have led to healthy forests resistant to insects, drought, and even fire. Many foresters say that the best way to determine an appropriate balance is to look back at forest history, using studies of tree rings and other methods to determine the "historical range of variability" of forest conditions. If current conditions or predicted future conditions are outside the historical range of variability, they can be considered unnatural. Such a guideline would place the conditions in the Boise and Payette National Forests and other dry ponderosa pine forests of Idaho outside historical ranges. But the verdict is not so clear for northern Idaho's forests, which are now declining primarily because of root rot.

The obstacles to the "emergency room forestry" Sampson advocates are public policy and public trust. An increasing segment of the public no longer trusts the Forest Service to protect the public interest. The only way forest health will be addressed is to ensure that wildlife, water quality, and other forest values are protected. That means dramatically less clear-cutting, more uneven-stand management, and a move away from managing forests simply for timber production. The forests' problems can't be cured if the agency worries only about how much timber it will harvest. Instead, it must decide how many acres will be treated, whether by cutting, thinning, or using prescribed fires. This concept must take into account more than simply trees and must acknowledge values beyond commodities.

Penelope Morgan, a fire and plant ecologist at the University of Idaho, says that restoring and preserving variety in the forest is the key to meeting one of the fundamental goals of ecosystem management: preserving biological diversity, or the sum total of life, from genetic material to species. "If we are careful to maintain a mixture of habitats and patterns within landscapes, we have a better chance of preserving biodiversity," she says.[16]

Also standing in the way of a wise forest health policy is the public's aversion to forest fires. Foresters themselves are only beginning to take a more enlightened view of fire, as demonstrated by the fires that burned in the Payette National Forest in 1994. The Blackwell and Corral fires burned more than 100,000 acres: most of the trees lost were spruces that had been killed by bark beetles. Prompted by safety concerns and stretched fire-fighting resources nationwide, Payette's forest supervisor, David Alexander, declined to put firefighters ahead of the blaze to stop it. The Yellowstone fires of 1988, which burned nearly a million acres, taught an entire generation of Forest Service firefighters that they can't always control nature. But the forest ranger who allows a fire to burn still takes a great risk with his career. Firefighters spent $120 million to fight the Yellowstone fires—ten times the park's annual budget—because no manager wants to say he didn't do all he could to stop the "destruction." Only when forest supervisors' careers are threatened if they don't use a forest fire to its full advantage to restore the forest's health will wise fire management take place.

The Struggle for Sound Incentives

Changing the personal and professional incentives for forest managers is fundamental to the drive toward a new consensus in forest management. For most of the 1980s, environmentalists fought below-cost timber sales and subsidized roads as their major thrust toward changing the economic incentives that drive the Forest Service. Randal O'Toole, author of *Reforming the Forest Service*, called for sweeping changes in the agency's budget policy to reward managers for protecting natural and recreation values. He pointed out that managers are rewarded for timber harvesting and road building in the form of higher budgets and additional programs, but they are not rewarded for forest protection. At the heart of his proposal is requiring all forest users, not just commodity users, to pay user fees. Overall, to protect forest ecosystems, preserving ecosystem integrity must become the top budget priority. The measure of each employee's worth must take into account that employee's efforts to protect the land base even as he or she carries out other responsibilities.

Economic incentives on private and state lands also do not reward managers for protecting ecosystem integrity. New tax programs and more far-sighted management directives for state lands will be needed to foster new forestry. State lands are managed to maximize returns to the state for schools. Some states, such as Washington, interpret this mandate loosely, recognizing that forests have values beyond their commodity uses, even for schoolchildren. Others, such as Idaho, read the mandate as requiring as much logging as possible within the constraints of the sustained-yield concept. State land managers must be given the ability and the directive to work closely with other landowners in each watershed or larger ecosystem to protect ecosystem functions. These need not conflict with their prime mandate. Improved wildlife habitat and water quality can bring in paying customers for hunting and fishing. Even so-called nonconsumptive users can pay in the form of annual fees or passes, already required in some states for forest access or recreation.

Tax policies on private forestland have generally allowed landowners to defer some property taxes in exchange for wise forest management. Unfortunately, the "wise management" usually under discussion has been sustained-yield forestry of the kind that ignores the forest ecosystem. And sadly, even these incentive programs reach only a fraction of the forestland owners. A new woodland tax incentive program would not throw out the old incentives but instead would add attractive new incentives for forestland owners to cooperate with others in landscape management programs covering watersheds and other natural boundaries. Those whose lands are home to particularly rare plant or animal communities would be given the highest incentives to preserve them. Water quality credits could be shared and marketed throughout a watershed to allow market forces to more fairly distribute limited harvest opportunities.

For ecosystem management to succeed on any land, management practices must be ecologically sustainable, economically feasible, and socially acceptable, according to Mark Brunson, a forestry professor at Utah State University.[17] The new forestry consensus in the West must be built to meet the needs of people and the rest of the life community. We must recognize that there is a place in new forestry for both plantation forestry and wilderness. Each has its benefits and costs to society and the environment. Plantations may not be as diverse as natural forests, but at the same time, wilderness areas may become centers of disease and fuel buildup for catastrophic fires. As Penelope Morgan says, "We have to recognize the consequences of the choices we as a society have made."[18] Wilderness and tree plantations are both manifestations of human values. The new imperative in forest management requires that both be measured on a site-by-site basis against their effects on the entire ecosystem.

Advances in scientific understanding of the complex and varied forest ecosystems of the West will keep bringing westerners closer to a new consensus on forestry. But the demand for wood and fiber will continue to pressure both the marketplace and the political arena. There will always be those who want to cut more trees than the forest can provide and still sustain its ecological integrity. Short-term gain has often won out over scientific concerns about just how much wood an acre or a watershed can deliver. Thus, new foresters cannot look solely to new science for their salvation; they also need to look back to Aldo Leopold for inspiration. We all need more walks through the forest with men like Stieg Gabrielsen. Our forests will not thrive if they are run by computer foresters who crunch numbers instead of twigs beneath their boots. True husbandry, whether on private land or public land, demands a personal connection, a relationship greater than that dictated by occupation or profit. The success of foresters and of forestry in the Next West will depend on the strength of their land ethic and on the involvement of all of us.

NOTES

1. U.S. Forest Service figures.

2. Aldo Leopold, *A Sand County Almanac* (San Francisco/New York: Sierra Club/Ballantine Books, 1973).

3. David Adams, interview.

4. Jerry Franklin, "Toward a New Forestry." *American Forests* (November–December 1989): 37–44.

5. Chris Maser, *Global Imperative: Harmonizing Culture and Nature* (Walpole, N.H.: Stillpoint, 1992).

6. Craig Savidge, telephone conversation.

7. Ross Gorte, telephone conversation.

8. Ibid.

9. Edward Lider, interview.

10. Dale McGreer, telephone conversation.

11. Al Isaacson, telephone conversation.

12. Al Espinosa, interview.

13. David Cross, interview.

14. Neil Sampson, telephone conversation.

15. Arthur D. Partridge, and Catherine L. Bertagnolli. "Pathogens and Pests-Engines that Drive Succession." *Inner Voice* (March–April 1993): 3–4.

16. Penelope Morgan, interview.

17. M.W. Brunson. "'Socially Acceptable' Forestry: What Does It Imply for Ecosystem Management? *Western Journal of Applied Forestry* 8, no. 4 (1993): 116–119.

18. Penelope Morgan, interview.

CHAPTER THREE

The Bizarre and Unsettling Saga of Whitney Benefits

A Federal Parable

SAMUEL WESTERN

In the tale of Whitney Benefits, I ask the reader to set aside class rage and, possibly, to think mean thoughts about the public interest. Poet Nikki Giovanni wrote that it is the responsibility of writers to "have as much sympathy for the rich as for the poor; as much pity for the beautiful as for the ugly; as much interest in the mundane as in the exotic." In the case I am about to describe, it may be best to have some sympathy for the devil.

As a writer covering the West, I often see interpretations of the public interest, from both environmental and extractive industry organizations, blocking the possibility of a good relationship with federal agencies. Equally prevalent and common is various groups' practice of associating the stridency of their cause with the public good. For example, several western environmental groups I know of take pride in *not* negotiating with the federal government, and they proclaim that their very recalcitrance supports the public interest. In the long run, however, this adherence to dogma will fail them, as will the conviction of "wise use" groups that their stridency and Abrahamic sense of land is embraced by the general populace.

But the same limitations could be attached to the federal agencies, the official interpreters and vehicles for dispensing the public interest. If we are to have a sense of community in the Next West, we'd better have more responsive federal land managers. This prosaic pronouncement calls forth the obvious question: when has the West not wanted more responsive federal land managers? In the past decade, an entire "collaboration" industry has sprung up trying to get the federal government to be more responsive to community needs. Furthermore, as public policy battles over federal land intensify, conscientious Forest Service and Bureau of Land Management (BLM) employees find themselves cast as political pawns, tugged and swatted, reviled by locals and ignored by Washington. This hardly encourages originality or the manifestation of conviction.

Yet nothing can excuse the god-awful job the BLM did in carrying out the wishes of Congress in the case of Whitney Benefits, a legal-political coal-leasing morass that has dragged on for more years than any sane person wishes to count. In this instance, the BLM, in the name of "the public interest," squabbled over matters on which only bureaucrats have time (and money) to spend: Who has jurisdiction over what? What should the application cost (in pain as well as dollars)? How much sympathy can we generate by whining and complaining about how complicated the new rules are? Furthermore, the Department of Justice, defenders of the BLM, played its case to the highest court in the land and lost. For years the Department of Justice refused to abide by the verdict; eventually, however, they paid $200 million, the largest takings award ever handed down by the U.S. Claims Court. It is a case of almost breathtaking bungling and obfuscation on the part of our federal government—the kind of case that can give enemies of federal landownership ammunition for a thousand battles.

But I'm getting ahead of myself. Let's head for the scene of this slow-motion event and start all over again with the facts, as well as a bit of background.

∼

Sheridan, Wyoming, sits on the eastern flank of the Bighorn Mountains, twenty miles south of the Montana border. Even the most jaded of scenery seekers call it lovely. But its virtues extend beyond appearance, for in the past thirty years Sheridan has probably enjoyed more constant prosperity than most towns of its size in the West. Its sawmill, community college, Veterans Administration hospital, Forest Service office, and ranches, as well as its proximity to historic sites such as Little Bighorn Battlefield National Monument, all provide jobs to an increasing middle class. The town is blessed with opportunities for the economic diversity that has become much cherished in the growing West.

Sheridan also has a preponderance of coal and lawyers; although most of the coal is located across the border in Montana, the coalfields are almost entirely serviced by the Sheridan community. This situation has proved both lucrative and troublesome. A bitter local coal strike, which provided work for lawyers and mediators but not many others, divided the community in the 1980s. It's fair to say that the volatile mixture of low-sulfur coal and local lawyers probably had a lot to do with starting the battle over Whitney Benefits.

The battle centers on a parcel of land about fifteen miles northeast of Sheridan, alongside Route 338 and about a mile below the Montana border. To look at it on a hot August day, the parcel could be placed almost anywhere in the lowlands of the northern Rocky Mountains. The rolling hillsides shimmer in the heat with brome, Russian and Canadian thistle, sage, and alfalfa struggling to compete with the grasses. Fence lines, power poles, irrigation ditches, and haystacks dot the horizon. The Tongue River, small as rivers go, has been reduced by drought to a flow of 100 cubic feet per second. A tall man could wade it in under ten steps and hardly get wet past the knees.

The parcel under dispute is also small, as Wyoming strip mine sites go: a mere 1,327 acres, or about two square miles. The Decker Coal Mine, right up the road from this parcel, works a federal lease covering 10,000 acres. But the Whitney land is privately held, a fact that explains in part why it was ever the proposed site for a strip mine. In 1972, the Department of the Interior, worried about environmental damage and giveaway prices for coal, placed a moratorium on all federal coal leases. Then, in 1973, the oil embargo sent coal prices to record highs. Coal operators scrambled to compete for the sixty private coal holdings in the West. The Whitney site was one of those, and it happened to be one with spectacular potential, for under its 1,327 pastoral acres lie six seams containing 140 million tons of coal. Although the land looks unsuited for controversy, the coal underneath it and the river flowing next to it combine to put this property at the center of the storm.

The story begins on November 19, 1917. Edward A. Whitney died that day in a room above the Sheridan Banking Company, an establishment he founded. He was seventy-four years old, rich, and eccentric. He had probably received some of his money from his wealthy Eastern family, but a good deal of it had come from his own skill in finance. Banking in Sheridan, Wyoming, had been good to him, and apparently he had decided to give something back.

His will stipulated that his estate, valued at $750,000, should be applied "towards aiding the needy and deserving young men and young women in attaining, through education, such positions in life as may appeal to them as best suited to their individual needs and capacity." At a time when the American ethos focused on growth and industry at any cost, Mr. Whitney wrote this in his will:

> It has been my belief that while bequests for purely education purposes have their place in the world's economy, there is often great danger in opening up before the youth of a nation only such paths as lead to so-called professional pursuits.

Clearly, he had sympathies for what we today would call vocational education.

In the three surviving photographs of Edward Whitney, he refuses to show his face. He is turned to the side or has his face down, invisible to the camera. Although Mr. Whitney was eulogized as a pillar of the growing city of Sheridan, he must have been an atypical citizen. Litigious as well as camera shy, he was involved in no fewer than seventeen lawsuits during his time in Sheridan. A former diplomatic counselor, Whitney once boasted that he had "traveled through every country with the exception of Iceland." He belonged to no church but believed in a future life and praised the idea of God, "if there is a God." He stipulated cremation upon his death. Half of his ashes were deposited in Mount Hope Cemetery, outside Sheridan, with the following epitaph: "What man really believes seems to him to be really true, but that does not make it so, except to his mind."

He directed that the other half of his ashes be placed in front of St. Martin's Church at Vevey, Switzerland, on the shore of Lake Geneva, and deposited in such fashion "that nothing shall obstruct the view of the [Dents du Midi, a mountain range] on the other side of the lake." Here was a man who appreciated beauty as well as utility.

For reasons unexplained, it took ten years to probate Whitney's will and set up his foundation, Whitney Benefits. By December 9, 1927, the estate of Edward A. Whitney was worth $928,103, equal to about $7.1 million in 1994 dollars. Whitney Benefits plodded away, survived the Great Depression, and grew in size. In 1956, it made loans totaling $53,113 to 101 students; in 1966, 169 students went off to college on $116,400 in Whitney monies; in 1993, it extended 73 loans, worth $439,000. In its sixty-seven years, it has given out 3,646 loans, valued at $7 million.

But Whitney Benefits did much more for the town of Sheridan. It helped found Sheridan College and later built what is acknowledged as one of the finest YMCA facilities in the nation. Because banks and cash were in short supply, the trust also gave "investment loans" at competitive rates to ranchers and the business community (this was discontinued in the 1960s). How a 1,327-acre ranch along the Tongue River found its way into a portfolio that includes bonds from Switzerland and the Kingdom of Norway no one knows. The best information available says that the land once belonged to a rancher who owed Edward Whitney money. The rancher defaulted, and Whitney took the ranch. Whether he knew how much coal lay beneath the parcel is open to speculation, but there were "wagon mines" on the property, where settlers hand-dug coal close to the surface.

A man as astute as Edward Whitney could not have failed to notice that a booming coal trade was under way just a short distance from this ranch. In fact, Sheridan's first underground coal mine opened in 1892; then a series of coal camps and towns sprang up northwest of town along Big Goose Creek, about four miles above where the creek joins the Tongue River. Omaha, Nebraska, was the major market for Sheridan coal; not surprisingly, Omaha businessmen began coming to Sheridan.

A 1902 document shows a freight and price agreement between the Sheridan Coal Company of Omaha and the Chicago, Burlington and Quincy Railroad. On August 6, 1904, the Sheridan Coal Company held a banquet in Dietz Mine No. 1 (named after one C. N. Dietz of Omaha) for fifty Nebraska and Omaha coal dealers. By 1908, the coal town of Dietz, near Sheridan, had a population of 3,000. But like most energy booms in the West, the prosperity was short-lived. The mines began to close in the 1920s, and with the installation of a natural gas pipeline into Sheridan in 1940, the few mines that remained struggled to supply local coal. The town of Dietz—complete with tipple, power plant, brownstone offices, churches, schools, hotels, and its own brass band—vanished. Not a house or a remnant of track remains. Black Angus now graze over what was described in a 1901 *Sheridan Post* headline as "A Busy Little Town."

Homer Scott sat on the board of Whitney Benefits in 1973, and it was probably through his influence that Peter Kiewit Sons', an Omaha-based mining and construction corporation, bought the right to mine the coal on the Whitney Benefits property. The company had come to Sheridan in 1941 with an interest in producing coal for the Nebraska market. Observing the near-surface deposits found in northern Wyoming, Kiewit modified its construction equipment and began strip-mining. Its first coal shipment out of Wyoming was in 1943. Ten years later, Kiewit expanded its Wyoming holdings by buying out one of the last remaining underground mines, the Sheridan Wyoming Coal Company.

Scott worked for Kiewit during these formative years in the coal strip-mining business. He did well by his company, and his company did well by him. Scott eventually bought the Padlock Ranch and made it one of the largest livestock operations in the country, owning or leasing about 450,000 acres. Like Whitney Benefits, the Scott Foundation has given millions to Sheridan, and Scott, who died in 1993, is remembered as a shrewd operator and a philanthropist.

At a public meeting on November 16, 1973, Kiewit submitted the highest bid for a coal lease covering Whitney's 1,327 acres. A year later, Kiewit signed a five-year lease agreement and wrote a check to Whitney Benefits for $581,789 for advance royalties. Engineering studies showed there were about 140 million tons of recoverable coal, which would bring Whitney, depending on the price, somewhere between $10 million and $15 million. In March 1976, after spending approximately $1 million on tests, Kiewit filed for a mining application from Wyoming's Department of Environmental Quality (DEQ).

The application had its detractors—among them were a local conservation group, the Powder River Basin Resource Council, and the University of Wyoming Water Resource Research Institute. Mr. and Mrs. Gerald "Digger" Moravek, who owned agricultural land near the proposed mine site, filed a formal objection, claiming that not enough was known about the mine's potential environmental effects. Furthermore, they claimed the mine would destroy prime agricultural land near the Tongue River. The Moraveks withdrew their objection, however, after Kiewit threatened to file a $14 million lawsuit against them. Gerry Spence, perhaps the most famous litigator in the West, represented the Moraveks and the Powder River Basin Resource Council.

Mr. Moravek, who died on June 29, 1994, eventually sold his land to Kiewit. According to the *Powder River Breaks*, a publication of the Powder River Basin Resource Council, the Moraveks endured a lot of hardship for their opposition. In remembering those days, Mr. Moravek said, "We weren't too worried [about the suit threatened by Kiewit] because you can't get blood out of a turnip. But it sure hurts while they're squeezing." Still, despite the removal of their objections, the Moraveks managed to get Kiewit to withdraw the application because the company had failed to properly notify adjacent landowners of the mine. Kiewit said it would reapply.

During the sale and testing of the Whitney coal, mining was a hot topic in Congress. The federal Surface Mining Control and Reclamation Act of 1977 (SMCRA, pronounced "smack-ra" by the cognoscenti) seemed to be approaching passage, and Wyoming's Washington delegation became aware that the law, if passed in its then-current form, would prevent mining of the

Whitney coal. The problem was that the Whitney site lay near enough to the Tongue River that it could be considered an "alluvial valley floor" (AVF). Environmental regulations applied to modern mines are especially stringent in protecting sensitive areas, and AVFs are surely sensitive in the West. They are the moist zones adjacent to rivers and streams where the stream itself has deposited most of the soil (alluvium). The National Academy of Sciences had offered to Congress plenty of evidence that mining of alluvial valley floors anywhere was unwise. The coal-rich piece of land in question, near Sheridan, Wyoming, was a classic AVF, a combination of clay, sand, and gravel essential for storing and channeling water in dry summer months. A river runs through one side of the property; mining of the coal would have undoubtedly disrupted surface and subsurface flow.

During debate on SMCRA, Wyoming congressman Teno Roncalio, concerned about possible lawsuits in cases involving environmentally sensitive mining areas—cases just like Whitney Benefits—spoke to the body of whole, saying:

> I do not propose to think that we can write a bill that will eliminate all litigation to take place in every State of the Union where coal may be strip mined in years to come. I do hope—and believe that is the intent of this bill—that we can fashion a law which will permit the State licensing authorities to govern where their reclamation permits are more stringent.[1]

The problem of impending lawsuits was partially resolved by Wyoming Congressman Malcolm Wallop and his staff assistant at the time, Rob Wallace. As Wallace described it:

> We were sitting around a conference table with Cliff [Senator Clifford Hansen, a Republican from Wyoming] and Teno's staff, trying to figure a way around the possible problems concerning Whitney and Kiewit. Malcolm gave me the OK to float the idea of a land exchange. I'd written the idea down on a napkin: the BLM would lease a piece of federal coal property with any coal company who had begun mining, or made financial commitments to mine, a piece of ground with an Alluvial Valley Floor. Teno came back from lunch. He saw the napkin. "What's this?" he asked. I shoved it across the table. He liked it and showed it to Mo Udall, who was also sitting at the table. He liked it, and it became the foundation for the Wallop amendment to SMCRA.[2]

It is important to note, however, that the Wallop amendment was further altered in committee to say that the secretary of the interior shall exchange coal with any operator who has actually begun mining before August 3, 1977, or made "substantial financial and legal commitments" before January 1, 1977. The command *shall*, written into the amendment, would later boggle the minds of BLM officials; it was an inedible spice, distinct and sharp in the starchy and bland stew of "the public interest." SMCRA passed on August 3, 1977.

On October 20, 1978, Kiewit reapplied for a mining permit, which was denied by the State of Wyoming on grounds that the proposed mine lay under an alluvial valley floor and was therefore in violation of SMCRA. Four months later, Wyoming's DEQ wrote to Cecil Andrus, then secretary of the interior, and recommended that Whitney and Kiewit be declared eligible for a land exchange under SMCRA. Because the companies had been denied the right to mine on private lands by federal law, the DEQ judged that they were indeed entitled to compensation by such an exchange.

The BLM disagreed, declaring the DEQ's determination insufficient; the federal Office of Surface Mining Reclamation and Enforcement would have to see for itself whether the Whitney piece qualified as an AVF. This action set the stage for conflict: the BLM would subvert the meaning and intention of Congressman Roncalio's proposal that state agencies play an active role in SMCRA. In effect, the BLM had declared the state ineligible to determine whether the Whitney site constituted an alluvial valley floor.

A frustrated Whitney Benefits, weary of waiting for its revenue, filed an inverse condemnation claim against the state for $231,920,187, alleging that its coal had been taken for public benefit without just compensation. James Griffith, the state auditor, consulted attorneys and thought about the matter for three months. On May 1, 1979, he wrote a five-line letter that stated, simply, "I am herewith denying your Inverse Condemnation Claim against the State of Wyoming, as made by Whitney-Benefits."

So the wait began.

~

At this point, it must be said that Peter Kiewit Sons' could easily be perceived as another private corporation at the public trough. Kiewit is a mining and construction conglomorate that has become, as Kurt Vonnegut might say, "fabulously well to do" on its holdings in Wyoming and elsewhere. As a private corporation, it discloses no assets or earnings, but, as one writer put it, "it is a company so vast in the kinds of work it does and so solid in financial resources that it stands alone in its field." Kiewit's own estimates suggest that its contract coal sales from properties in the Sheridan area will surpass $10 billion by the year 2000.

At the same time, no one suggests that Whitney Benefits, the owner of the coal in question, is unworthy of revenue or royalties; its primary mission is to help Sheridan County students meet college costs by offering them interest-free loans. Both of the primary actors in the Whitney Benefits case are private parties with deep, vested interests in the outcome of the case.

From the public's point of view, the dispute surrounds the question of financial relief. It offends our civic and taxpayer sensibilities that public funds should be used to pay a company for *not* mining a coal tract that was probably unsuitable for mining in the first place. Mining of that coal, in the eyes of many, would have constituted a classic nuisance, "injurious to the health, morals, or safety of the community," as the legal lingo goes—in the same category as a bootlegger of popskull whiskey or a factory that dumps heavy metals into the public drinking water supply. It should be squashed without any thought of compensation.

But the Fifth Amendment to the U.S. Constitution says that no property shall be taken for public use without just compensation. An awful lot has been written lately about takings, mostly unworthy of rehash. But the reader needs to know that for a century, takings were a fairly straightforward proposition: when government took land by eminent domain for an army base or a road, it paid for it. But as the nation and population grew, so did the regulations and the definition of property. In 1922, in a U.S. Supreme Court case involving coal mining in Pennsylvania, Justice Oliver Wendell Holmes said, "The general rule is that while property may be regulated to a certain extent, if regulation goes too far it will be recognized as a taking."

L. S. Klepp, a writer who follows literature and philosophical trends, once observed that "people like to be mystified: nearly impenetrable prose draws crowds for the same reason that nearly impenetrable nightclubs draw crowds." So it goes with impenetrable law topics. Law and environmental journals are crammed with articles and commentaries on takings. The topic of regulatory takings, said Yale University law professor Carol Rose, "draws young legal scholars like moths to flame. There are a number of reasons why every sensible person should stay away from this subject." My reasons are manifold for avoiding yet another impenetrable explication, the least being sloth and a reluctance to pulp any more our nation's dwindling supply of forest products for legal matters.

However, this much needs to be said: Congress, packed with lawyers, hoped to avoid the takings morass when it passed SMCRA. To mollify and quell any Fifth Amendment issues, Congress offered an exchange package: any title holder already mining a piece of coal that qualified as an AVF could swap parcels with the government. Simple. The government would take control of the condemned piece—for the purpose of protecting it from mining—and the coal operator could mine on a more suitable piece of ground. Again, the primary reason for passing the law with that proviso was to avoid Fifth Amendment issues. So in the case of Whitney Benefits, all the BLM had to do was agree that that little 1,327-acre site was indeed an AVF and proceed forthwith to exchange the parcel with a federal parcel of roughly equal value. The exchange would quiet any takings claim before it emerged.

But that's not what happened.

~

On July 6, 1981, one and a half years after the Department of the Interior rejected the DEQ's claim that Whitney qualified for an exchange, the federal government finally agreed that the parcel did indeed involve an AVF. Furthermore, it told Kiewit to draw up a short list of federal coal parcels for an exchange. Kiewit showed an interest in the 4,370-acre federal lease known as Ash Creek, also located in Sheridan County and, in January 1982, formally proposed the exchange. The *Federal Register* published the proposal that same month; Kiewit and Whitney were told a decision would be made by March 15, 1982.

By April, no decision on the coal exchange had been made. The Casper, Wyoming, office of the Bureau of Land Management told Whitney Benefits that the federal government now had doubts that the exchange would be in the public interest. The BLM wrote to Kiewit and asked for another year to make a decision, saying that the exchange was "one of the more difficult realty transactions with which the Bureau must deal." The letter went on to say, "We cannot guarantee specific dates because of the many uncertainties and variable factors involved with the coal exchange process." In May, Maxwell Lieurance of the BLM's Cheyenne office wrote to Rebecca Thomson, an attorney representing Whitney, stating that the BLM needed to decide whether to lease coal land outright to Kiewit or exchange it. This was another stall. Two years before, the U.S. District Court's decision in *Texaco v. Andrus* had declared that the "congressional intent appears to favor a mandatory fee exchange program."

On April 24, 1982, the federal government changed its mind. Nine months after agreeing that the Whitney parcel qualified for an exchange, Paul Arrasmith of the BLM's Casper office told Kiewit that it was not eligible for a swap. He listed three reasons: no substantial investment had been made prior to January 1977, the AVF constituted only part of the property, and the land was not significant to agriculture. Five months later, Marla Mansfield, regional solicitor for the Department of the Interior, declared the exchange "improper." She wrote that only "322 acres of the North or East tract (of Whitney) cannot be mined."

Months passed, with Whitney, Interior, and the State of Wyoming squabbling about AVFs, a term that had begun to take on almost mystical significance. Wyoming's DEQ had to fight for the right to determine the size and scope of the Whitney AVF. Then James Watt, a Wyoming native, took the helm at Interior. One might have thought that between two Wyoming politicians, Watt and Malcolm Wallop, who is from the Sheridan area—both with strong leanings toward commodity development in the West, both in high places (Wallop was then in the U.S. Senate)—the exchange between Whitney and Interior would have been rapidly consummated. Instead, Wallop expressed reservations about the exchange. He confessed to Sheridan attorney Henry Burgess in 1977, "I cannot support national legislation which will throw open the door to mining in these areas simply because there was an investment." Meanwhile, when Watt became secretary of the interior, he wrote to Wallop: "Please be assured that we will process the Whitney application as expeditiously as possible."

This was not to be. In November, Interior wrote that if the exchange did take place, the administrative cost would be borne by the applicant. In this case, the cost was $36,000; if the bill were not paid within thirty days, interest of 1.18 percent, compounded monthly, would be added. However, on January 27, 1983, the BLM's Casper office said that any exchange would be at least a year to a year and a half away. The Minerals Management Service, the arm of Interior that monitors federal mineral leases, informed Kiewit that the Whitney coal was "uneconomic to mine."

In May 1983, Wyoming's governor, Ed Herschler, wrote a letter to Watt, stating, "I would very much appreciate your attention to this particular exchange. . . . For whatever the reason this exchange request is four years old, and far from complete." The same month, Paul Arrasmith of the BLM said that within two weeks, the federal government would declare the entire parcel of Whitney coal available for exchange, but not for the Ash Creek parcel, which now had other leasing interests. Instead, the BLM offered a new lease, called Hidden Water. Kiewit responded that Hidden Water had been mined in the 1940s and 1950s and therefore was not suitable for an exchange. Spencer S. Davis, Kiewit's manager of engineering and estimating, later said that he did not "recall any specific response or any rebuttal to (Kiewit's) conclusion concerning Hidden Water."

The government changed its mind again and said that because Ash Creek had been dropped from the competitive leasing circuit, it was now available for an exchange. Both parties worked through the summer of 1983 in an effort to exchange the Whitney Benefits parcel for Ash Creek. Kiewit was told that it must acquire an exploration license to drill on Ash Creek and that processing of the paperwork would take as long as three months.

At that point, Whitney, led by its head legal counsel and board member, Henry Burgess, decided that the government had no real intention of ever exchanging coal and that the "exchange provision [had] been rendered illusory." On August 2, 1983, almost six years to the day after passage of SMCRA, Whitney filed a lawsuit in the United States Claims Court stating that its coal had been taken by the federal government and that therefore the company was due just compensation of $300 million.

In Washington, D.C., the court dismissed the takings lawsuit, saying that an exchange must occur and be unsuccessful before a taking could be found. Whitney and Kiewit filed an appeal. In the interim, Donald Brabson of the BLM's Cheyenne office estimated that the exchange would take at least another year and that an environmental assessment, economic evaluation, and consideration of the public interest must be examined before the exchange could take place. Whitney and Kiewit, worried about their appeal, began working the courts from a different angle. SMCRA provided for "citizen's suits" to be filed against "the United States or any other governmental agency . . . which is in alleged violation of the provisions of this Act." Whitney and Kiewit decided to file a second lawsuit, this time against the State of Wyoming. The case would be heard in the federal district court in Cheyenne. Although the companies did ask for a monetary award of $232 million, the real reason for filing the claim was to get the State of Wyoming to push for an exchange.

On January 9, 1985, a major breakthrough came in favor of the Kiewit-Whitney partnership. The United States Court of Appeals reversed the lower court's ruling, claiming there had been a taking of Whitney coal. It rejected the United States Claims Court's argument that "an exchange transaction must occur and be unsuccessful before a taking can occur."

"Actually," wrote Judge Philip Nichols Jr., speaking for the majority, "the exchange transaction is a method of ascertaining and paying just compensation for a taking, which may be negotiated and agreed upon either before or after the taking itself, and is optional with the claimants, who may reject any exchange and pursue a money award under the Tucker Act" (the statutory regulation encompassing the Fifth Amendment to the U.S. Constitution).[3] Nichols remanded the case back to the U.S. Court of Claims. This verdict stunned the Justice Department, which began appealing.

~

Twenty-two years have passed since Peter Kiewit Sons' successfully bid on Whitney's coal. The exchange process was put on hold pending the outcome of the takings case. Part of the Ash Creek coal tract was swapped in 1989 for the Rockefeller family's 1,006-acre JY Ranch, located in the middle of Grand Teton National Park. The Rockefellers donated the proceeds from the sale of coal to the Sloan-Kettering Institute for Cancer Research. On October 13, 1989, when the U.S. Court of Claims ruled that a taking had occurred, the Interior Department and the Justice Department took the case to the U.S. Supreme Court, but in 1991, the Supreme Court declined to hear the case. The government still owed Kiewit and Whitney the value of the coal plus interest: $60.3 million.

Thwarted at the highest level, Interior and Justice attempted a variety of legal gymnastics to escape payment. First, they declared that the United States Claims Court lacked jurisdiction over any claim in which the plaintiff had the same obligation pending in another court. Whitney and Kiewit, they said, could not have the same case at both the United States Claims Court and a federal district court—the citizen's suit—at the same time. The complaint was dismissed, with the U.S. Claims Court declaring that "the government appears to seek a 'Heads I win, tails you lose' position."

Then Justice claimed that Whitney and Kiewit had violated the Anti-Assignment Act. This claim, although dismissed, was inspired by the untoward behavior of Whitney and Kiewit, which had engaged in an impolitic legal punch-out on how the spoils were to be divided. Kiewit claimed it was entitled to 96 percent of the award. Whitney disagreed. They eventually settled, but the quarrel gave the Justice Department what it thought would be an out, for the Anti-Assignment Act "prohibits the assignment or transfer of any part of a claim against the U.S. until the claim is allowed, the amount of the claim is decided, and a warrant for payment of the claim has been issued."

Then came more suits about the money. From the beginning, the government had fought the valuation formula of the Whitney coal and sued to have it adjusted. The U.S. Claims Court declined to do so. Then a fight ensued over whether interest on the award should be calculated as simple or compound; the court decided that in order to "accomplish complete justice the award should be compound." In 1994, the federal government, convinced that both the Anti-Assignment Act and valuation were still live issues, asked for a new trial "in order to prevent the perpetuation of an injustice against the United States." The United States Claims Court refused, saying that the issues had "already been addressed at the Appeals Court." Wrote Chief Judge Loren A. Smith: "The court has seen no evidence or other material submitted by any party that casts even the slightest doubt upon the original findings of the valuation trial."[4]

As to the Anti-Assignment Act allegations, the judge wrote:

> None of the defendant's briefs on this issue adequately explains how such an assignment took place, and the court does not find the existence of such an assignment. The court notes that defendant makes its present claim based on the Anti-Assignment Act in the eleventh hour, having failed to press this claim during the first nine years of this litigation.[5]

The Interior Department attempted questionable leveraging techniques. In 1987, it unabashedly tried to strong-arm Kiewit into settling the Whitney case by canceling an unrelated coal sale in Sweetwater County, Wyoming. Robert Burford, then director of the BLM, told Dean Skalla of Kiewit that its highest bid on a federal coal lease near the Black Butte mine would be canceled unless Whitney and Kiewit agreed to settle the Whitney coal case. Both Kiewit and Whitney protested this action, but Interior refused to "decouple" the Whitney coal from the Black Butte coal.

Whitney Benefits became a showcase of stalling, with the taxpayer footing the bill. Finally, on May 18, 1995, the Justice Department paid Whitney Benefits and Peter Kiewit Sons $200 million, thus far the largest takings claim ever awarded by the U.S. government. The Justice and Interior Departments themselves had little incentive to settle. The award did not come out of their own departmental budgets. Congress, in its habit of largess, paid it out of the "judgment fund" from which it pays any award found against the government. In other words, individual departments such as Interior and Justice are not held financially accountable for their legal actions.

≈

This saga pertains to a dispute between private and governmental actors, but it also illustrates a fair portion of what western communities often believe they are up against and why their complaints against the federal government are growing so strident and loud. It reveals, in painful detail, how a federal agency, without ever saying no, can thwart the plans of Congress. All the conferences and roundtables on "collaboration" between public land managers and communities, or discussions of "the new Western economy," won't amount to a sparrow's chirping among a murder of crows unless the government is able to do one thing: keep its word. And it won't be able to keep its word unless it stops fooling itself about "the public interest." It is sorry common knowledge that the public interest is rarely more than a collection of special interests.

In the case of Whitney Benefits, the BLM managed, year after year, to weasel out of its responsibilities by questioning whether the coal exchange was in "the public interest." But Congress had already decided that it was in the public interest and mandated an explicit exchange provision in the surface mining law. If the Next West is to have a sense of community, the government had better think hard about modifying the "public or national interest" clause in all federal land statutes. Every time the phrase "public interest" appears, a legal lacuna opens, making way for a lawsuit or some other roadblock that questions not how but whether the federal land manager is to do his or her job.

To protect the public interest is to keep the earth habitable. Clean air and clean water are the ultimate and final goal of environmental public policy. The case of Whitney Benefits does not portend a major assault on the pillars of federal environmental legislation, as some critics claim, nor does it spell doom for the government's ability to keep the countryside reasonably clean. This case is one of a handful, maybe more, in which the government got hammered and failed to learn much. And just what was the lesson it neglected to absorb? When you pass a law restricting commodity development, do it in phases, and monitor the effects of the legislation. Grandfather, at least temporarily, those with well-established rights, primarily property rights. It may look suspect and smarmy on the statute books, but in the end it's the simplest and most economical way to keep our air and water clean, for ourselves and for that "thousandth generation" Thomas Jefferson spoke of. That is why these laws were passed in the first place.

As a legal case, Whitney Benefits is often dismissed as extremely complicated, which it is, but its fundamental story is a simple one. Twenty years ago, two Western entities, a Nebraska mining company and a Wyoming charity, made a good-faith deal. Federal law prevented consummation of the deal but provided for a form of relief. When it came time to provide that relief, however, the government proved unwilling and hid behind the veil of "public interest." With no incentive to do better by the taxpayers, the involved agencies of government refuse to this day to comply with congressional or court orders.

Environmentalists, community advocates, and just plain citizens interested in justice and environmental quality in the West and elsewhere ought to take interest in this case because it provides us with such a clear cautionary tale. Ultimately, it is in no one's interest, least of all environmentalists', for the government to demonstrate that its word is not good. For if the federal government can so readily subvert the legitimate claims and interests of two cooperating companies in the West—regardless of how rich those companies are or what anyone thinks of them—then whose claims and interests will ever be safe?

NOTES

1. 123 Congressional Record, House 3735, April 28th, 1977.
2. Personal conversation, June 2, 1994.
3. *Whitney Benefits, Inc. v. United States* 752 E. 2nd 1554 (Fed. cir. 1985).
4. 31 Fed. Cl. Ct. 116 (1994).
5. Ibid.

CHAPTER FOUR

Closing the Loop

JIM McMAHON

I often wonder how the recycling movement first lost its way. What started out as a noble idea, driven by activists disgusted with excessive consumption and material waste, has been lost to a perversity of political correctness and greed. Instead of saving materials, energy, and landfill space, the recycling model that has emerged feeds on consumption and the gross waste of energy; it fails to accomplish what it originally set out to do. When I think of these things, I am drawn to my own roots and an evening forever etched in my memory.

The year was 1975, and it was one of those cool, gray, drizzly nights Seattle is known for. I remember the month as January or February, but only because of the weather. On this particular evening, there was a closeness, a peculiar intimacy, created by the reflection of the antique streetlights against the gray, low-hung clouds so typical of the Pacific Northwest. We'd just closed down the shop after another long, hard day. Armen Stepanian and I ran a nonprofit recycling center, one of the first in the nation. Back then, that meant crushing glass in steel barrels by hand with a pipe and flattening tin cans one at a time with a hammer. Every scrap of material had to be begged from an unwilling public, and every piece was processed for market with a reverence deserving of a resource taken from nature.

When you live in Seattle, you grow ambivalent to the rain. It becomes a part of you. Armen and I were standing on the corner, unaware of the mist, reflecting on the day's accomplishments, when a long, black limousine drew up to the curb beside us. Our conversation was stilled by the electric hum of the rear window sliding down. In the velvet black where the window had been, we saw the pale, shrunken face of a thin old man. It was my first and only look at him. We leaned down and peered inside.

"You're wasting your time," Josie Rozore said flatly. Rozore, old as he was, remained the kingpin of the Rabanco Companies, Seattle's local garbage collectors. This was the same man who in 1938, as president of the Diamond Tank Transport Company, had submitted the low bid for a five-year garbage collection contract with the City of Seattle. His bid was not only the lowest but also lower than the previous year's cost for the same service—this in spite of well-publicized labor demands for an increase in wages. After he won the contract, Rozore announced that he would lose money on the deal and successfully negotiated an additional $100,000 in annual revenues. He'd owned the contract ever since.

Rozore's blunt comment poked at our efforts to instill a recycling ethic in both the local neighborhood and Seattle's city council. In Rozore's eyes, garbage was garbage. Why didn't we find something constructive to do? We argued that recycling was important to building a sustainable future. We must integrate our use and reuse of resources into the way we manufacture consumer goods. We must reduce consumption and save resources for future generations.

He looked at us queerly. His eyes said we were fools. In turn, I thought him the fool for his failure to understand the urgency of our cause. Here was a man who could help us, help the world, if only he understood. We argued our case with a vehemence becoming of the times, but still he dismissed us as the window rose again and the limousine pulled away, its occupant unconvinced.

Those were heady times. There were only a handful of recyclers in the entire country, but we were consumed by the importance of our cause. The idea of recycling was not new. At one time recycling had been the norm, but the country had strayed as it reveled in economic growth and the postwar boom, and as it did, consumption became the driving force of economic growth. Life in America was good, and we measured that goodness in sales of washers and dryers, new cars, and houses and in our consumption of material goods at a rate unprecedented in history. Waste stood as a sign of our success, and the tiring task of recycling became an unnecessary burden on a growing society.

Our goal was to right this obvious wrong—to place limits on consumption and to reinvent recycling. We wanted a revolution in the way our country valued and utilized its resource base and produced its consumer goods. We knew in our hearts that it was only a matter of time until we'd win, that the country was certain to come around to our way of thinking. This belief drove us as we pounded each steel can and as we flailed away at the glass, crushing it into loads heavy enough to transport to market.

The work was tedious. First, I went door-to-door in the Fremont District of Seattle and asked each person to sort recyclable materials and set them out on the doorstep once each month; we would pick them up for free. "We don't use that much," they would respond. "Our little bit can't possibly make a difference," they'd say.

"It all adds up," I would tell them. "Please, just give it a try and let's see what we can do," I'd plead. Some agreed; most did not; but we slowly built a clientele.

Working with the material was equally difficult. It came to us dirty and unprepared for market, in spite of the neat little directions we provided. Picking up a bag full of recyclables, we'd shudder when an unfinished can of pop or beer drained out on our hands and clothes. Cigarette butts soaked in beer would spill out on the sorting table. We handled each piece by hand, sorting it by type or color. As we crushed the glass, small fragments would fly around the room, smacking our faces and lodging in any available crevice. Each type of material had a separate market, and each had to be prepared to specification before we could sell it. The work was dirty, but it built both muscle and resolve because of the vision that drove it.

We went home each night exhausted and rank with spillage and sweat, fragments of glass in our hair and clothes. Our goal was to save energy and resources. Our labor could be renewed each day, whereas the planet held only so much tin and aluminum.

~

Recycling may have been reborn beneath the gray skies of the Pacific Northwest, but the region's two principal states took oppposite approaches. In 1972, Oregon passed its infamous "bottle bill," mandating the return of beverage containers to grocery stores. Industry in Washington State countered with a bill of its own, the Model Litter Control Act, which attacked litter, the most obvious and politically sensitive sign of waste, but did nothing to promote recycling.

Taking Washington's action as their cue, industry groups assembled to fight a proliferation of bottle bills across the country by focusing on litter. It was clear to industry that if we could hide the symptoms of waste, the public would be appeased. Times were good, and America, both industry and the people, didn't want to stop wasting resources if the issue could be "solved" in some other way. Leave it to the P.R. guys to figure that one out.

Industry in Washington went a step further, however, when the region's unique collection of local breweries established a voluntary effort to buy back their own beer bottles for refilling. The nation's major aluminum companies enhanced that effort by offering to purchase used aluminum beverage cans. Newspapers had been recyclable for many years, and a network of wastepaper dealers already existed throughout the country.

As markets for used containers spread, a recycling industry began to evolve. Entrepreneurs opened private recycling centers in neighborhoods throughout Washington State. Slowly, these centers grew in number, from perhaps six in 1974 to several hundred by 1984. When another partner and I established Seattle Recycling, Inc., in 1976, we recovered in one day what Armen and I had accomplished in a month. We were onto something.

Then I met Harry Leavitt. Harry is an environmentalist who has learned how to be true to himself and the ideas he holds dear. We had met before, but we became staunch friends after he asked me to help him with a problem. Seattle had mandatory trash service. Each home was allowed to set out as many as four cans and eight bags of trash each week. But Harry had no trash; therefore, he hadn't paid his trash bill for months. After several warnings, Seattle's Solid Waste Utility had placed a lien on his house. Harry felt pure, but his wife was livid. Still, he would not pay that bill. We formed a plan.

With hearings on trash collection rates coming up, the city planned to review the need to raise rates, but no one in city government expected to meet the likes of us. We searched Seattle and found twelve other people who, like Harry, had no trash. Together, we formed the Zero Can Club. This was not some ragtag band of young environmentalists but a coalition of older folks who had started recycling and composting along with their victory gardens during World War II and simply had never stopped. The Zero Can Club attended the rate hearings and requested that Seattle's mandatory trash fee be replaced with a variable fee, charging for what a home actually set out and including an exemption for those who worked to have no trash at all.

Seattle's Solid Waste Utility scoffed at the idea. Preposterous. A nightmare to administer. People will dump trash in the streets. It will never work. But we persisted: We packed the city council chambers. Harry poured one month's worth of his trash onto the podium. Armen insulted the council's Solid Waste Committee chairman as deserving of that role because he was "both solid and a waste." Sensing a revolution, the television cameras rolled.

Councilman Paul Kraabel heard what we were saying, however, and invited me in to his chambers to discuss the idea. A reporter from the *Seattle Times* sat in on the meeting. Everything was off the record, but I explained the inequities, the possible solution, and the closed-mindedness of the Utility staff. Although nothing from that meeting ever appeared in the *Times,* we gained an ally in the press, and the Utility went on the defensive. From then on, everything it said, every assumption it presented, was attacked. Seattle changed forever the way it dealt with its trash.

Claiming that variable rates were too risky to endorse outright, the city council decided to put the idea to a test. The SORT (Save Our Recyclables from the Trash) project was an eighteen-month pilot program affecting twenty different trash routes. Once a month, a truck would collect recyclables from the homes on these routes. Half of these and another ten routes not provided with collection service had variable trash rates instead of the flat rate that existed elsewhere in the city.

SORT was a mixed success. Recycling rates proved to be tied to demographics, with the wealthy recycling the most. Variable rates had a clear and positive impact on recycling, but neither recycling nor variable rates seemed to influence how much trash was discarded.

Meanwhile, the city's trash woes mounted. Its two landfill sites were filling, and alternative sites were scarce. The city created four staff positions to develop energy recovery and recycling strategies aimed at solving the disposal problem. I went to work for the project under the auspices of the mayor's Office of Energy Conservation, charged with developing a recycling strategy for Seattle. This turned out to be one of the most disappointing experiences of my life.

Mayor Charlie Royer's commitment to the project was mixed at best. The Utility engineers, long accustomed to big solutions, favored incineration as an alternative to disposal. It was a high-cost, high-profile plan that carried the attractive moniker of "energy recovery" (since it would create electricity), but it was also highly controversial. Waste incineration would require expensive new air pollution controls of unknown effectiveness, and it would not eliminate the need for landfills because the ash and sludge created by combustion would still require disposal. At first, the mayor seemed to favor these high-tech alternatives. Recycling, never seen as the solution to anything, appeared to be merely a way to get environmental groups to buy into the city's overall scheme.

Of course, I didn't know this at the time. I went to work for the city with a zeal that reflected my love of the place. I lived in a Capitol Hill apartment on a bluff overlooking the freeway and downtown. Each night when I came home from work, I would sit in the bay window, watch the cars speed by, and feel the pulse of the city. As I watched, an orange sun would sink slowly behind the collection of skyscrapers framing my view, reflecting bright red on the frigid gray waters of Puget Sound, and then disappear behind the Olympic Mountains far to the west. I was captive to the beauty of the place.

So when I went to work for Seattle, I threw my heart into the effort. I was not prepared for the apathy that was the norm in Seattle's civil service. Foolishly, nor was I prepared for the enmity of the Solid Waste Utility. As a person of logic with scientific training, I believed that the place to start was a database. What was going on in Seattle already? How much trash did we generate? How much recycling was already being done in the private sector, at no cost to city ratepayers? But when I sent a memo to the Utility requesting solid waste volumes, instead of data I got a memo asking whose budget was going to pay its staff to look in the file to "research" this information.

The game continued with each request. The Utility staff's tone turned brazenly derisive. Any request for information we made was denied, in spite of the fact that we all worked for the same person, the mayor of Seattle. It turns out that there is a certain job security in civil service, an immunity that allows one to remain firmly esconced regardless of what the political leadership or the citizenry may want. The Utility staff scoffed not only at us but also at the city council itself. I remember when someone in a leadership position at the Utility described the city council to me as nine people in a canoe rowing blindly down a stream, each thinking that he or she was steering. This was my first lesson in government, and it did not fit with my perception of Seattle as a well-governed metropolis of exceptional beauty.

We developed a recycling strategy without the help of the Utility, whose staff continued to taunt us at every turn. The constant bickering , combined with a lack of support from the mayor, gave me an ulcer. It was inside the walls of Seattle's Municipal Building that I first learned I literally did not have the stomach for government. Nor did I have much respect for those who endured. The key to longevity in Seattle civil service was a low profile and a distaste for change.

In spite of all this, we endured long enough to produce a significant recycling strategy. We found that the city enjoyed a recovery rate of some 14 percent of its waste stream, due entirely to the efforts of the private recycling industry in Seattle and the Pacific Northwest. I crafted a strategy that would build on this effort and enhance it by encouraging the public to get involved. Variable trash rates became the cornerstone of the strategy. They provided a direct financial benefit to those who reduced their waste and a cost to those who did not. Along with the new financial incentive, we launched an educational effort to raise awareness citywide. Our goal was to increase recovery from 14 to 22 percent within five years and to set up a means to measure the recycling rate periodically.

We exceeded the goal. By 1987, recovery had increased to 24 percent. The cost to consumers was almost nothing—perhaps $100,000 per year plus a small added cost to administer the program and monitor voluntary compliance with the variable rates. The strategy relied on private efforts; government played only a supportive role. For Seattle, this was a local and appropriate solution that worked well. The strategy achieved all it needed to, and it did so with a high benefit-to-cost ratio. To my knowledge, Seattle's original recycling strategy is unmatched to this day in cost-effectiveness.

Our original strategy dismissed curbside collection of recyclables as too expensive. Some private residential collection efforts continued, but their effects were minuscule. The bulk of recovery came from drop-off programs in grocery store parking lots, the purchase of recyclables by retail recycling centers, commercial collection programs by trash companies, and office paper collection programs.

Each of these, shepherded along by a variety of private companies, continued to grow and evolve from 1980 to 1987. A healthy and profitable private recovery system was emerging as a new feature of the city's and state's economies. At the same time, the trash disposal problem became more and more serious. Seattle's two landfills, now full, were declared Superfund sites by the Environmental Protection Agency. Trash disposal was about to become dramatically more expensive due to the costs of remediation and the enormous expense of finding a replacement site.

City councils across the country spent millions studying energy recovery as a means to rid themselves of increasing trash volumes, but with little effect. The combination of high costs and the sudden proliferation of NIMBY ("not in my backyard") groups that opposed incineration sites crushed the engineers' dream of energy recovery. Meanwhile, recycling proved increasingly effective at recovering material throughout Washington State. It had begun to spring up throughout the rest of the country as well, though the effects were minimal in comparison with those in the Pacific Northwest.

Recycling as it emerged in Washington was a product of the people and the place, and it made excellent economic sense. Markets grew as large manufacturers became more comfortable relying on secondary materials as a feedstock for their production processes. While most cities remained enchanted with their dreams of big engineering systems to combat the solid waste crisis, we in Washington were growing our own solution through a combination of individual action and good business. Our success was based on an understanding of what a market really is: one person convincing another to try something new and foreign, to enter into a transaction for mutual benefit despite past experience and objections. Individuals were working together to achieve that original goal of integrating postconsumer resources back into industrial processes. Small, local solutions were netting good results.

As an example, we recycling activists met with the president of the local glass bottle manufacturing plant to find ways for him to take more used glass, to develop systems to clean it, and to receive it in ways that would accommodate the growing number of small recycling companies. We also met with the manager of the local detinning plant, which was geared entirely to recovering canning plant scrap, to get him to accept higher levels of contamination from food waste and paper labels, to take smaller loads, and to pay more.

These efforts took time and initially were met with skepticism and resistance. Individual purchasing agents representing large corporate manufacturers were often pushed beyond their comfort zones by our requests that they accept postconsumer waste. But as they agreed to try recycling and then witnessed the growth in volume, they eventually learned that recycling provided a new growth opportunity. This is market development in its purest form.

While we in Washington were building a recycling industry from the ground up, Oregon, the other recycling mecca of the Pacific Northwest, spawned a completely different approach. The differences in these two original approaches continue to be relevant today.

In Oregon, a legislated mandate, the "bottle bill," required the return of beverage containers to grocery stores. The bill did not address markets, but it managed to create them by fostering a cheap supply of materials, which had to go somewhere. Independent recycling companies did not emerge in Oregon as they did in Washington because the economics of the marketplace did not support them. What emerged instead was a network of nonprofit recycling centers that focused on recovery of the nonlegislated and less valuable recyclables, such as tin cans and nonbeverage glass. Recycling centers in Oregon never had the economic vitality of their counterparts in Washington because they were deprived of the opportunity to handle the more valuable beverage containers—aluminum and glass—which the law mandated would go elsewhere. Thus, the Oregon recycling centers had to be supported by subsidies.

The two states provide a sharp contrast between mandates and incentives. Oregon's bottle bill rapidly led to recovery rates of 85 to 90 percent for aluminum cans and beer bottles. The aluminum was recycled, and the beer bottles were either washed and refilled, if they came from local breweries, or recycled as scrap glass. In Washington, with financial incentives in place, a private industry operated by individual entrepreneurs slowly emerged in response to the creation of markets for materials. Recovery rates for aluminum cans and beer bottles reached only 65 to 70 percent, but recovery rates for nonbeverage glass, tin cans, and paper were significantly higher, simply because these materials were all collected at the same place. Washingtonians enjoyed the convenience of recycling everything at once. In Oregon, on the other hand, although the recovery rate for beverage containers was higher, the bottle bill weakened the recovery of other materials. Oregonians were faced with the inconvenience of returning beverage containers to grocery stores and everything else to the state-subsidized nonprofit collection centers. The strong governmental mandate aimed at fostering recycling actually suppressed it.

In Washington, consumers benefited from a more diverse network of recycling centers that paid them for materials. Private recycling markets provided a solid economic base that spawned an entrepreneurial response: the emergence of an entire network of recycling centers. Thus, Washingtonians enjoyed a lower-cost recovery network. Instead of costing consumers money, it actually paid them for materials.

As far as I am aware, this is the first example of the demonstrated effectiveness of mandates versus incentives in crafting solutions to environmental problems. Mandates achieve the desired end rapidly, leaving no doubt as to their effect. Incentives, on the other hand, take time to achieve the same ends, but they do so at a fraction of the cost to consumers, relying as they do on individual entrepreneurial activity to create private business opportunities. Markets are natural mechanisms. They mimic evolution in natural systems in that they spur unpredictable and beneficial results as individuals attempt to survive economically within the system. The resulting solutions are more efficient than those achieved by mandates because they reflect individual action, the purpose of which is to thrive economically by being efficient at earning a livelihood. These same issues are pertinent today as we increasingly debate the best ways to achieve environmental objectives and a sustainable economy.

In those early days of recycling, when the Pacific Northwest seemed a world apart and Ernest Callenbach's Ecotopia felt imminent, there was an altruism driving the creation of the recycling movement. Under those gray northwestern skies we reminded one another, with an almost religious fervor, that it was our goal to spur a movement, to change the world. And when we'd achieved our ends, we would each step aside and let the big businesses carry forth our ideas. I don't know what the hell we thought we'd do to make a living at that point or how we imagined the world to be such a gracious and giving place. Just the opposite was about to occur in the peaceful setting of the Pacific Northwest.

One might attribute the next spurt of activity to our sleepy mayor, Charlie Royer. He seemed just to wake up one day and tell a reporter that it was time for Seattle to develop a curbside recycling program. His reasoning was based on the fact that he was from Oregon. Royer often seemed to govern that way, and he told a good joke, but neither his awareness of an issue nor his interest appeared to extend much deeper than that.

No one could have predicted the impact of Royer's sudden announcement. Individuals had staked their investments on a nascent recycling industry, and now the government threatened to intervene. The natural competitiveness among companies—normally a benefit to consumers—turned perverse as recyclers fought to stave off the city's intervention. Instead of banding together to publicize the progress of Washington's young recycling industry and to point out the hard-won gains of a decentralized recycling system that relied on the creation of industrial markets to digest postconsumer waste, the industry diffused its energies in internecine battles. Discomfort over the prospect of working with their competitors caused local recycling companies to stand apart, fighting government intervention as separate entities. As a result, they lost ground to the overwhelming enthusiasm that was to spur a new era in recycling in the Pacific Northwest.

The city's Solid Waste Utility, by then under new and progressive management, proceeded to decide what sort of curbside program it wanted and, in the summer of 1987, published a request for proposals. City management had traditionally split Seattle into two areas for its trash-hauling contracts, and it did so again for recycling. Waste Management, Inc., won the contract in the north section of the city; who else but Josie Rozore's Rabanco Companies would win in the south.

Although Seattle was one of the first cities in the country to implement citywide curbside recycling, San Jose, California, had preceded it, and Waste Management's bid was based on the collection model established there. What was different about Seattle was the overwhelming public response. In the north end of the city, where the demographics were more conducive to curbside collection and Waste Management provided weekly service, the participation rate immediately approached 90 percent. Seattle's streets were dotted with yellow-and-green recycling bins set at the curb in a different neighborhood every day of the week. The visual effect of the bins resulted in a kind of mania. Participation continued to skyrocket.

No one involved had anticipated a response of this magnitude. On the first day of the program, Waste Management needed six more trucks than it had purchased in order to handle the unanticipated volume of material. But more important, Seattle became an instant national celebrity. Its recycling program gave the city something it had never much experienced, the national spotlight. Suddenly, this quiet, remote city, known only for its rain and the Space Needle, became the nation's environmental torchbearer.

Seattle's success spawned a sort of mindlessness. The whole country became aware of its recycling program, and people from other cities came to take a look. What they saw when they came to the shores of Puget Sound were those yellow-and-green recycling bins lined up at the curb, at house after house. What they failed to see were the infrastructure and the very special sense of place underlying this superficial visual image.

Seattle's overwhelming response to the curbside program had grown from the years of effort that had gone into building a recycling ethic in the Pacific Northwest. The city was well aware of its unique recycling centers. Its citizens had been hearing about recycling for fifteen years, and during that time, Seattle had developed an outdoor and environmental ethic that was unmatched in the nation. It was nurtured by the rain, the setting, and perhaps by the city's growing reputation as a hot spot for progressive young environmentalists. Recycling worked in Seattle because it was a local solution to a real problem, based on an emerging local ethic.

So when recycling came to the front door and knocked, people set out their recyclables as asked. Seattle's success spewed out across the nation as other cities copied its efforts. From 1988 through 1990, the number of recycling programs nationwide grew from 2 to more than 400; from 1991 through 1994, to more than 6,000. Of these, not a single city that implemented curbside recycling has demonstrated awareness of any component of Seattle's recycling infrastructure other than the curbside program and the variable trash rates, which had apparently spurred such a dramatic proliferation. What all the copycats missed was this: Seattle's curbside recycling program managed to recover some 11 percent of the waste stream at a public cost of $1 million per year. But before the curbside program hit Seattle, the city had been recovering 24 percent of the waste stream for a mere $100,000 per year. The rest of America got the icing but missed the cake.

This failure had to be due in part to the Utility's own misunderstanding of what had occurred in Seattle. And part of the blame lay squarely on the leaders of the recycling industry, who never effectively conveyed their own story. When visitors came to view the curbside program—and they came in droves—they learned little about the underlying private infrastructure that supported the vast majority of recycling. Had these outsiders taken the time to study recycling in Seattle carefully, they would have seen in the periodic surveys the graphs showing that the bulk of recycling took place in the private sector.

Perhaps some did see the massive effect on solid waste from private recycling, but Seattle's hugely successful recycling industry posed two great problems for public sector employees. First, to develop such a system would take knowledge, skill, and time. Second, it would require a sharp focus on markets, something the public sector knows little about. And frankly, the public wanted recycling right away. People weren't asking for quality or depth; they wanted the stuff picked up at the door.

So, between 1988 and 1994, a recycling mania swept across America. Curbside collection programs popped up everywhere. Along the way, recycling became chic. Those in the industry constantly reminded politicians that without markets, recycling could not succeed, but both politicians and environmental activists chose to ignore their advice. This had little consequence for them but has resulted in consumers paying far more for recycling systems than those systems are worth—for in almost every instance, curbside recycling relies on public subsidies.

It became cool for politicians to endorse recycling. The public wanted the convenience of curbside collection. And former recycling activists, who barely understood recycling themselves, suddenly became highly paid executives at big trash companies and solid waste consulting firms. People who had lived on less than $1,000 per month a few years before were now earning $70,000 per year.

Recycling, in an economically stupid form, took hold. The rapid growth in curbside collection created a vast surplus of materials, and existing markets were suddenly saturated. With materials in vast oversupply, the industries quite naturally lowered their prices. North American collection programs went on to saturate markets in Asia and Europe. The cost to consumers spurted still higher because of the low prices now being paid for recyclables.

Perhaps the best example of recycling run amok occurred in California, which implemented its own version of a bottle bill requiring the return of beverage containers to grocery stores and the payment of fees for recyclables. But the value of the materials themselves could not support California's dispersed recovery network, a system that now resembled Oregon's. With the state mandate in place, the costs of recovery soared dramatically higher than when private recycling centers had bought waste from the public. California responded with subsidies to support its notion of a convenient recycling system. The cost of this system is far in excess of any benefit derived from it. Consumers pay the price when they buy the product.

There's nothing wrong with the notion of adding the cost of recycling to the purchase price of a product, but in California, recycling advocates backed into this notion by establishing first in their minds and then on the ground a system based on a bureaucratic notion of convenience. That system has turned out to be highly inefficient and costly. Had California chosen to spur markets instead, it might have accomplished the same level of recycling at a much lower cost.

The notion of subsidized recycling ignores any responsibility to the public to provide recovery systems at a reasonable cost. The cost should match the benefit derived or the effort should be postponed until it does. Recycling has taken hold nationwide, but what has been implemented is a shadow of what we could have had at a fraction of the cost. Had the nation, politicians and recycling advocates in particular, exhibited some patience, an entire recovery system could have been developed that would have cost the public almost nothing at all.

In the case of recycling, subsidies are the usual result of mandates, and mandates probably grow from impatience. Pass a law demanding statewide recycling and you get a solid response overnight. But it's often a shallow response, and it's always a costly one. Mandates may be well-intentioned, but they create the wrong results. The very concept contains an implied misevaluation of the cost to consumers. Mandates say that we want to achieve a specific objective, regardless of cost. They create actions that are fixed through time. They stymie rather than encourage the natural evolution of markets, which will arise and endure only through efficiency. Is that really what we want—recycling at any cost? Even when the recycling systems use more energy than they save in collecting materials and shipping them thousands of miles to distant markets?

In the suburbs of Denver, for example, trash collection goes unregulated; as many as four to six recycling trucks may travel down the same street offering recycling services to residents. Fuel is burned by each truck. The material collected by these trucks all goes to one of a few processing centers, where it is prepared for markets. These markets, with the exception of the Adolph Coors Company, which buys glass, are either in the Pacific Northwest or overseas. So these materials are shipped long distances, consuming fuel once again. The potential energy savings of recycling in the first place are marginal. Glass recycling saves only 10 percent of the energy it takes to manufacture bottles from raw materials. Newspaper recycling saves little energy but does lessen our reliance on forest products. When shipped across the globe by truck, train, and freighter, however, recyclables create net losses of energy.

So what is the point? To instill a recycling ethic? Advocates of recycling at any cost say that once the public is accustomed to recycling, the markets will follow. To some extent this is true. An overabundance of cheap materials may encourage investors to create markets. But the two could be brought on-line together, in regionally sustainable systems that would optimize the use of resources. The truth is that politicians often don't want to think that deeply or deal with challenges that difficult. It is much simpler to give the public recycling in spite of its negative environmental impacts. And that is precisely what has been done, across the nation.

Go back to the roots of recycling. Its purpose is to conserve energy and materials, a task accomplished through the efficient reintegration of postconsumer waste into production processes. To be energy efficient, the reintegration should take place at the regional level. The strain on virgin resources should be lessened; secondary materials should replace or augment the virgin source.

Our recycling systems today don't meet these standards. Recycling has become politically correct; its focus has shifted to appearance rather than function. Our politicians have given us systems that look great but lack depth. The result is that regional markets only occasionally exist, materials are shipped across the planet to any market that will take them, and the recovery systems cost us more than they are worth, burning energy to drive votes instead of saving it in the name of conservation. Recycling has become a palliative that eases the guilt we feel for our consumptive ruin of the planet. It serves no other purpose.

Natural ecological systems provide the perfect contrast. In natural systems, the economy is primarily a local one. The sun and rain provide inputs into a system, which otherwise depends on local resources to sustain itself. Sustainable human systems are also local or, more precisely, regional. In a sustainable economy, many of the consumable products would be produced from materials present in the bioregion, whether virgin or secondary. Imports would be minimized and would be treated as opportunities to develop substitutes via new business enterprises.

The notion of a global economy and an ever expanding universe is an illusion based on the erroneous assumption that humans can continue to outmaneuver natural systems. We become increasingly reliant on a geographically expanding production system to bring us the resources we need to survive. As we do, we become less aware of the constraints of the natural community in which we live. If this is not obvious today, it will become so as we try to expand infinitely.

In the case of recycling, we have built collection systems that ignore market demand. Our approach to markets has been either to strong-arm the big multinational companies into using recyclables in order to sell products or to rely on markets that require us to ship recyclables thousands of miles. We are building the recycling model to complement our global production model, which itself is the cause of many of our environmental problems. This "bigger is better" mentality is precisely what is wrong with our economic model in the first place.

~

On a chilly October night in 1993, Harry Leavitt, the intrepid challenger of Seattle's mandatory trash collection fee, stood huddled with me on the bow of a ferry plowing through the frigid water to Vancouver Island, British Columbia. It was an unusually clear night, and the sky was full of stars. The scent of fresh cedar hung in the air as a barge hauled its load of chips past us on its way to some market. We were making the crossing to visit Clayoquot Sound, where more than 750 activists had been arrested that summer in their defense of old trees. We wanted to see those trees, and we planned to lie on the road in front of logging trucks ourselves if the spirit so moved us.

Others were there with us. We spoke casually with a former colleague of Timothy Leary, from back when Leary promoted mind expansion and the environmental movement was in its infancy. That touch with the past reminded Harry and me that our activism had been born during those years of hopeful experimentation. We had learned then that the point of living is to have an open mind and to work aggressively for a saner world. Our conversation on the ferry that night set the tone for our journey into the heart of the old growth.

The controversy in Clayoquot (pronounced "Clakowit" by the locals) centers on the largest remaining stand of temperate rain forest in North America, a forest stretching from the coast of Washington State through British Columbia and Alaska. Environmentalists want the remaining trees in Clayoquot Sound left standing. The lumber companies and their massive labor force want to continue the tradition of a timber export economy. Their jobs, livelihoods, and communities are at stake.

The road across Vancouver Island to the sound amply shows why so many people are distressed about logging in British Columbia. The road winds through the ruins of once-great stands of timber that were butchered fast and hard and then burned, with the help of diesel fuel, to accelerate the cycling of nutrients back into the soil so the cutting could proceed again. From the charred stumps and underbrush, the rot and the waste, you would think you were driving through a war zone.

On occasion, the ripped-up hillsides are highlighted by messages activists have scrawled on highway barricades in red and blue paint. As we continued west toward the coast, we felt the rage I'm sure many feel. The loggers stupidly lost this battle when they chose to cut trees so openly, so callously. With greater discretion—with some attempt to hide their butchery—they could have continued the "harvest" a while longer. All they harvest now is travelers' hostility.

When we arrived in the fishing village of Tofino, we went directly to The Common Loaf, a bakery that serves as unofficial headquarters for the fight against logging. We read the news clips, drank rich, black coffee, and got a feel for the battle. Afterward, we visited the office of Friends of Clayoquot Sound. We met the leaders, discussed the issues, and saw the maps of what was left and what was being cut. A road blockade was planned for the morning. Would we join it?

Before we committed ourselves, we wanted to take a look around. Impressed by the enthusiasm and political daring of the ragtag band of young environmentalists, we walked toward the bay to see a display that had been put together by MacMillan Bloedel Ltd., the Canadian timber giant responsible for what we had seen. We spoke with the attendant, who showed us detailed information on the extent of the planning process that determined which trees would be cut and which areas preserved.

The Clayoquot Sound forest plan, created under the direction of a diverse group appointed by the provincial government, is the key to the coastal forest puzzle. The plan endorses continued harvests but calls for sustainable yield—something relatively new to British Columbia—and sets aside specific watersheds from harvest. Environmentalists were invited to participate in the planning and initially did so, but the process of compromise necessary in every planning effort led them to abandon the group. They chose to stand firm in their opposition to any more logging anywhere around the sound.

Harry and I agreed that the Clayoquot Sound controversy is the epitome of the problem confronting the environmental movement everywhere. Immense tracts of land have been clear-cut to produce wood products—products that have created income, supported communities, and provided materials not for British Columbia homes but for American and Japanese homes.

When MacMillan Bloedel cut those trees, it was not solely responsible for the way it logged. Its society had endorsed those harvests as a means to drive the economy of the province. The people of British Columbia must share the guilt and shame of those plundered forests, which were unlike any we had ever seen in the United States. Those hillsides had been left barren not for some pointless enterprise but to drive housing starts in the United States and Japan—houses for people who similarly participated in the destruction, whether they knew it or not.

We cannot expect to save trees if we never address the need for wood. In the United States, we measure our economic health by the number of new homes being built. Our fixation on endless growth, and on housing starts as a key indicator of growth, forces the cutting of trees. Where are those trees to come from?

Harry and I rented a boat and crossed the water from Tofino to Meres Island. We walked through the tangled web of old twisted and gnarled giant cedar. We spent a good part of the day on the island, walking the shoreline and cruising the bay. The activists are right: this is a very special place.

But we did not lay our bodies in the road, on that day or any other. The environmentalists had erred in not staying on the planning committee; their call for an abrupt end to logging of the coastal rain forest is unrealistic and naive. British Columbia's economy, once driven by natural resources, is in the midst of a transition to a new economic base. The provincial government must ease the pain of that transition by slowing the harvest of trees and refocusing economic development. But it cannot simply stop logging, for too many communities still depend for their survival on the export of trees and the import of cash. Long ago, British Columbia bought into the international marketplace for timber and became dependent on it, and now it can only do its best to wean itself away. Environmentalists must participate in that process. They must work face-to-face with their neighbors—loggers and shopkeepers, mill workers and truck drivers—to create new enterprises based on economic solutions that make sense on their wet, tree-haunted island. This battle is not about who is right and who is wrong. It's about living in community with other people and other species. Harry and I could not support the cry to just say no. It is too simplistic.

The travesty in Clayoquot Sound is not a separate issue from recycling in the United States. Like all things in natural systems, they are interconnected. In the United States, we measure economic success using housing starts as one factor. At the same time, we set aside timber in wilderness areas. We do not consume less timber; we simply freight it in from farther away, preferably from places less visible to consumers and activists. As with recycling, our participation in an international market for the products we desire insulates us from the truth of what we have helped to create. Politically correct recycling makes us feel better as long as we don't have to face the fact that our governmental mandates subvert the original purposes of the effort. Taking trees out of the lumber market by designating wilderness areas, parks, and preserves merely pushes the cutting to some other place. Wild places continue to fall before the plunder of our consumption, but as long as those places are far away, our efforts to preserve the forests here at home seem ever so correct.

The perversion of recycling and the destruction of rain forests both underscore two great problems: runaway consumption and the drive to build endlessly larger economic machines. We cannot use consumption as a gauge of our success and still live sustainably on the planet. We cannot continue to feed raw natural resources into the engines of faraway corporate bureaucracies and still have any semblance of a livable home where the resources exist. As long as the bottom line of a Chicago-based corporate headquarters drives the timber harvest in the forest surrounding a stud mill in South Fork, Colorado, or Libby, Montana, we can't expect much more than plunder and dependency in those little towns.

Our success in developing a recycling strategy and a high recovery rate in Seattle was based on individuals working together as neighbors in a community. In the name of caring about the place we all loved, we called on others to extend themselves beyond what they might otherwise do. Both the manager of the local mill—which might have cut trees to make paper—and the environmentalist—who hoped to convince him to use wastepaper along with wood chips—had to stretch to create new ways of doing business. In so doing, we created new markets. This ethic and our willingness to work together toward a mutually acceptable solution resulted in success.

You can't legislate such sentiments through governmental mandate. What recycling mandates do instead is replace one set of stakeholders (those invested in virgin extraction) with another (those invested in supplying recyclables). In either case, the stakeholders will subsequently work to preserve and protect their own economic welfare. When we enter into this cycle, we're repeating the error we made when incentives to mine or cut virgin resources were not hard-wired to come to an end once our goal of settling the West was achieved.

In a successful economic system that mimics a natural system, it will not matter greatly whether a mill manager uses virgin or secondary resources on any given day. The manager should do whatever is appropriate to the place and time and should do so by free choice and in response to the needs of the community, not because of a mandate to do so regardless of the cost to the company or the customers. Any governmental incentives set in place to drive entrepreneurs to integrate secondary resources into product manufacturing should expire once they have accomplished that goal.

When I ponder these things, I am always drawn with some remorse back to that misty evening in Seattle so many years ago. Twenty years have passed, but what has changed?

We've built a recycling system based on politics instead of conservation. Recycling has become a placebo that assuages our guilt and blinds us to the consumption of resources, which if left unchecked will be the ruin of our planet. We continue to measure our economic health by housing starts and retail sales. We've saved some trees but have left unfettered the markets that consume them, so deforestation continues around the world. The trees we use just come from far enough away that we don't see them.

The environmental movement and its political allies have deliberately chosen to take a mindless approach to the creation of solutions. It's all about stakeholders, political might, greed, and appearing to solve problems without asking anyone to change. I am reminded of the early industry attempts simply to remove the litter along the roadside. Were they right? Is it true that all we want is to hide our impacts from our own view? If so, perhaps Josie Rozore was right. We were wasting our time. All that matters is making money and getting ahead, by whatever means necessary, including deceit.

I see in my mind's eye the taillights of that black limousine moving slowly down the rain-swept street. I see the antique streetlights reflected in the glare of the wet pavement. I can see and feel the low, gray clouds closing us in. I recall, as though it were yesterday, Rozore's ominous words. I feel the mist and the sweat and the grimy bits of broken glass clinging to my skin. And I wonder now, who was the fool?

Blood and Cotton

TOM WOLF

Looks Like a River, Sounds Like the Wind

Extremes of water and wind make and break the San Luis Valley side of Colorado's Sangre de Cristo Mountains. A constant drainage of cold air from Poncha Pass down to Alamosa renders the valley one of the coldest places in the country. The prevailing wind from the southwest never seems to cease. When it does, it wheels about and blows even harder from the northeast.

If water comes at all, it comes all at once. The valley itself averages just seven inches of moisture per year, yet snowmelt from the Sangres makes it one of the wettest places in Colorado. If you drive the valley's rifle-barrel highways, you can speed past the Sangres in a few hours; the valley is only the size of Connecticut. Determined drivers can circumnavigate the island-like Sangres in a day.

If, however, you leave the beaten path, then water and wind become more engaging traveling companions. Then you can experience how they connect the valley's environmental history with that of the Sangres. It is not a straightforward tale. No, the approach to the crooked timber of the Sangres teems with fantastical crooks and characters, meandering and turning back on themselves and on one another, appearing and disappearing, expanding and contracting.

Approach Cotton Creek by car from the north, via Salida and Poncha Pass. If you stop at the top of the pass, you may imagine how different the San Luis Valley must have appeared in earlier times, when the valley floor was thick with forests of Douglas-fir or when the Arkansas River flowed south from Salida to join the Rio Grande.

If his luck and his orienteering had been better, Zebulon Pike might have found gentle Poncha Pass in his explorations of the region. Had he wandered to the upper Rio Grande flyway in the fall, Pike might have noticed many different species of waterbirds, especially whooping cranes and sandhill cranes, coming and going in their annual migrations along the Rio Grande.

If Pike had crossed Poncha Pass rather than Medano Pass (south of the Great Sand Dunes), he might have escaped more than starvation and frostbite. He might have traversed the west side of the Sangres, crossing Cotton Creek and Rito Alto Creek and ending up near the former mining town of Crestone. Had he taken the Poncha Pass route, he would have taken the path of least resistance. Some fifty years later, former beaver trappers led explorers John W. Gunnison and John Frémont along Pike's route through the valley and across the creeks just described in search of the golden gateway to the West.

Pike, Frémont, and Gunnison could have learned a simple ecological lesson that less empire-crazed, more sensible civil engineers and road builders like Otto Mears soon grasped: rails should follow trails—if the trails are the seasonal migratory paths of bison. For there is something about a bison that resembles a steam locomotive. Both will ascend only so far up a steep slope. It is this limitation, along with extremes of wind and water, that has made of the Sangres an island in the sky: their sheer steepness.

After you top Poncha Pass, coming from Salida, you can see the last lodgepole pine on the west side of the Sangres, slyly hiding beside the highway. Something there on the west side of the valley loathes lodgepoles—something sinister, perhaps, for the lodgepole loves disturbance. Whatever else the forests of the Sangres are, they are disturbance forests. On your descent, you can observe the northern valley's last sagebrush, which yields to greasewood and to no fewer than six different species of rabbitbrush. Both are more salt tolerant than the pungent sage, which does not appear again until you round Blanca Peak, escape the soggy soils of the lower valley, and head either east up La Veta Pass or south to San Luis and then to New Mexico.

It all seems simple enough. But in the Sangres, there is always a catch. Although Pike reported the sand dunes to be naked of vegetation, Gunnison found them dotted with sagebrush that do not exist there today. No one knows why—no more than we know why the brusque, aggressive, prolific lodgepole suddenly turns cagey and finicky when it hits the Sangres on its way south to Colorado's southernmost Fourteener, Culebra Peak, above the village of San Luis. There the lodgepole vanishes while sagebrush surges far down the Rio Grande.

If you had traversed Poncha Pass in Pike's time, you might have seen other migrations as well, such as those of the bison and the Indians as they moved west out of the valley and over Cochetopa Pass (the name means "gateway") or north over Poncha Pass and into South Park. The Denver & Rio Grande Railway followed this latter route in 1890 when it drove a narrow-gauge line from Mears Junction, above Salida, over the pass and down the valley to Alamosa. In 1891, a branch sprouted from Villa Grove, to the east, to the Orient Mine, not to be lopped off until 1942.

From the top of Poncha Pass, visitors today can also peer south into four canyons on the west face of the Sangres: Orient, Valley View, Cotton, and Rito Alto. The adventuresome can turn off on any of the roads that lead to the four-wheel-drive track over Hayden Pass, an obvious low point that separates the northernmost part of the range—Salida's Sangre—from its midsection—Westcliffe's and Crestone's Sangres. Those who like mechanical challenges can attempt Hayden Pass, once a small mail route and a main wagon thoroughfare and stock driveway through the Sangres, like Mosca Pass far to the south.

Birders know that the high-altitude spruce forests accessible from Hayden Pass echo with the calls of some mighty fancy owls. Some of these may be boreal owls, which evolved in today's Canada, as their name suggests, and then left for the south, working their way from peak to peak as they followed the lofty belt of cool, moist forests. Isolated on peaks far to the south in New Mexico, boreals have been absent from the Sangres for a long time. But now they may be on the move again. If the supersensitive boreals are indeed headed back north, following the chain of the Sangres to cooler, wetter climes, they may confirm the Sangres' key position in debates about global warming.

The Orient

Those who don't give a hoot about fancy owls or broken axles may commit their vehicles to the labyrinth of roads leading south from Poncha Pass

toward the great fault that fractures the west face of the Sangres. Old photographs show this flat, treeless plain bristling with cottonwoods that lined
creeks and irrigation ditches. Although most of the trees are gone, you still
see hawks and golden eagles perched menacingly on roadside power poles.
They don't look grateful, but they wouldn't be here if not for our roadkill
and the fact that our agriculture spins off lots of succulent rodents and seed-
eating songbirds.

Because the roads in the valley are so straight, distances and reference
points deceive. As you approach the Sangres, you probably won't notice the
changing grade, any more than you might sense how an earlier,
Pueblo–related history played itself out here in local place-names: Steel,
Lime, Black, and finally Orient Canyons run down the range. In the last
canyon rest the remains of the Sangres' greatest industrial enterprise, the
Orient Mine.

The Orient was discovered in the late 1870s during the great mineral
boom that centered statewide in Leadville and locally at Bonanza, west
across the San Luis Valley. By 1880, the mine employed forty men and the
town boasted two restaurants, a saloon, a milling company, and several small
businesses. By 1900, 400 people called Orient City home. About 60,000 tons
of ore made the 155-mile trip to Pueblo that year. The Orient averaged
40,000 tons annually through its half-century existence. That's a lot of rock.

It's also a lot of action, considering today's stone-still canyons. Yet just
over the crest of the Sangres, related ore deposits at Cloverdale and Rita Alta
mock the recent designation of the Sangres as official wilderness, for their
development could bisect the range, thereby slitting the Sangres' long, thin
jugular.

Veins of limonite, a very clean iron ore, drew the railroads over Poncha
Pass, down-valley to Villa Grove, and east right up to Orient City. When
Pueblo-based giant Colorado Fuel & Iron (CF&I) took over in 1892, the Sangres got a taste of the mining business that still burns on the tongue of
Cotton Creek, especially where it mouths out in vain toward San Luis Creek.
San Luis Creek drains the whole upper valley into the Closed Basin, where
water goes in but is not supposed to come out. Sometimes San Luis Creek
looks like a river. Sometimes it disappears. Sometimes it sounds like the
wind.

By 1900, the Orient was booming as the largest working iron ore deposit
in Colorado. Three thousand feet above the mine and the town, above
today's private homes, you can still see the remains of a reservoir, but that
source never provided enough water for both industrial and domestic needs.
Mine workers faced an even more serious hardship than an inadequate water

supply, however. Toiling thousands of feet underground in the dank, dark slopes proved extremely dangerous, since the company consistently refused to use wooden mine props. Even today, fatality figures remain buried in company files.

Could it be that a local source of suitable timber no longer existed? Records show that the forests of every canyon but one on the west face of the Sangres burned in the 1870s and 1880s. Most of these have regenerated, though sometimes not to their previous timber types. Eroded and heavily grazed former ponderosa pine sites have proven particularly vulnerable to colonization by piñon, a hardy raider from Chihuahua. And sometimes no trees return. The lonely slopes around the mine remain denuded today. The Orient finally shut down in 1932, not because the deposit was exhausted but because Wyoming ores at Atlantic City on South Pass were cheaper to mine.

Nature abhors a vacuum. When the Orient fell silent, its gaping mine shaft sucked in another sort of colonist who also had followed the Rio Grande north, just as New Mexicans did after 1848 and just as piñon does in our time. Today, the Orient houses Colorado's largest bat colony. Should you approach at dusk or dawn on a July or August day, you might experience the Sangres' single greatest wildlife wonder. It started in 1965, when someone noticed around 10,000 of them. Today, more than 250,000 free-tailed bats come and go from the mine's mouth at dawn and dusk. Watching the hour-long out-flight, an awed biologist once exclaimed, "Looks like a river, sounds like the wind."

When the bats return to their roosts at dawn, they stoop, nighthawk style, dropping like stones from on high and abruptly unfurling their wings at the last possible moment. Once inside their dormitory, they perform in-flight flips that leave their claws hooked into the ceiling. There they sleep in stable temperatures that never vary from the bat-comfort range of 43 to 54 degrees Fahrenheit.

These tiny, pioneering insect eaters winter in the interior of Mexico, a thousand miles to the south. Their migratory range exceeds that of any known bat species. For reasons unknown, 95 percent of the bats present in the mine at midsummer are males. Back in Mexico at this time, the females are pregnant or nursing. Every night is a night out for these boys, during which they consume 30 percent of their body weight in moths, locusts, grasshoppers, gnats, and mosquitoes, netted with a membrane stretched between their legs and tails. Each midsummer night, more than two tons of valley bugs become bat guano.

Why have the bats moved north into the San Luis Valley, where they were not found before? No one knows for sure, but a local wag has suggested a commonsense cause: "Blame us ranchers and farmers! Of course, we're behind it! We irrigate crops and the bugs that go with 'em. We waste as much water here as possible," he said. "We have to, or else the state water engineer will lap it up, or the Bureau of Reclamation will suck it into the Closed Basin. Or our neighbors will steal it. Or some fool will pipe it to Denver. But let me tell you: those bug eaters make life tolerable for humans here in the summer."

Valley View

You can walk or drive south from the Orient to Valley View Hot Springs, where hot pools and springs stretch far up through the piñon-juniper forests, from 8,700 to 9,500 feet. Fireflies abound here, a rare phenomenon in Colorado. (No news yet as to how bats and fireflies get along.) Like so many hot springs and mineral springs in Colorado, Valley View started business as a spa-and-cure resort in the early 1870s, catering to tuberculosis sufferers. Many arrowhead finds tell of occupations from earlier times. It seems unlikely that the Utes wintered here; there were hot springs, milder temperatures, and wintering bison to the southeast, where Cañon City is today.

Valley View hints at the activity along the Sangre de Cristo fault. Like the geothermally driven Alligator and Fish Farm a few miles to the south, it is that rarity in today's San Luis Valley, a sustainable, ecologically sound private business, a self-supporting contributor to the local economy. Modestly and carefully managed to preserve a certain ambience peculiar to the site and the natural resource, Valley View Hot Springs might be a model for other local entrepreneurs to study. For radically different reasons, some would say the same of the Cotton Creek Ranch.

Cotton Creek

Driving south from Valley View, it is not far to Cotton Creek, about twelve miles southeast of Villa Grove. Should you be unaccustomed to the mysterious properties of Colorado water, you will think you are following the flow of San Luis Creek down-valley, the way God and gravity intended, maybe into the Closed Basin, maybe even into the Rio Grande. But you will be wrong.

Earlier in this century, thirsty CF&I pumped sizable portions of Cotton Creek up-valley and uphill to the Orient Mine. And if to the mine, an entrepreneurial soul might ask, why not right back up and over Poncha Pass? Or over Hayden Pass? Why not down into the Arkansas River? There the water could buoy the white-water rafting industry, deepen the experience for powerboaters at Pueblo Reservoir, slake the thirst of Kentucky bluegrass lawns in Colorado Springs, and perform a thousand other odd jobs. But then what would become of your fellow capitalist at Cotton Creek Ranch? You'd see him in court. But would you see him out on the land, irrigation shovel in hand?

If you approach Cotton Creek in a circumspect state of mind, you might pause at the two little roadside cemeteries near Cotton Creek Ranch. Although it is desertlike at first glance, this landscape is in fact not deserted— and certainly not desertified, unlike its besalted, besotted counterparts down-valley. Wheat from Cotton Creek Ranch earns honors in nationwide competitions. The first potato crop in the upper San Luis Valley sprouted here.

Mute witnesses to this precarious fertility, the departed would speak, if they could, about water wars. In one of the graveyards repose the dead with Spanish surnames, former parishioners of the church of San Luis de Cotton Creek. Recently, fifty years after the last legible date on the headstones, someone who still cares cow-proofed the fence and pieced together the cracked concrete tombstones, wreathing them with rusty barbed wire and lashing the engravings into sense with plastic flowers.

As these parishioners slumber, somewhere upstream their church's adobe walls melt back into the soil. Like so much of the story of change in the Sangres, some history is beyond repair. Yet a number of names are legible: E. P. Atencio, Alba Duran, Bernardo Martinez, Frank Martinez, Joe Mordena, Manuel Quintana, and Joe Valdez. As interesting in their own way as the territories and patterns of owl, crane, bat, piñyon, sage, and lodgepole, these boneyards remind us of what we Europeans have made of the Sangres—and why.

If Germans ever rest, just a stretch downstream, at the Mirage cemetery, doze people with names like my own: Niedhart and Hoffman. And far upstream, above Cotton Canyon, there beckons Mount Niedhart (12,863 feet), casting a wary eye over Horsethief Basin. South of Mount Niedhart towers De Anza, named after the Spanish military man who pursued Cuerno Verdo's Comanches up the valley, over Poncha Pass, down the Arkansas, and out onto the plains, finally catching and crushing them near the town of Rye and near the little volcanic cone called the Huerfano.

Unaccustomed to pausing over the past, we may find the citizens of these cemeteries buried in times of hard work beyond our comprehension. We may compare our own kinds of rigor, such as disciplined contemplation or high-country backpacking, with the sweat equity they amassed here.

Or we may compare ourselves with John Mattingly, the imposing presence who ran Cotton Creek Ranch before starting his own Mirage Farms nearby. Mattingly is proof that one can still make money here at farming—through dedication, brains, and backbreaking labor. In the past I never went into the valley without visiting Mattingly, a world-class tinkerer, novelist, and sage. Like home-brew, the headiest philosophy is homespun. Resembling one of his home-engineered irrigation systems, Mattingly unfailingly gushes wisdom and opinion about water politics, pesky bureaucrats, the art of farming in a harsh environment, and most anything else you'd like to know.

And I never go into the valley without the work of historian Virginia McConnell Simmons. On her gracefully written pages, you can learn how Hispanic shepherds and farmers from New Mexico were already reaching northward throughout the valley on a seasonal basis by the late 1840s, when the area south of the Arkansas River became part of the United States. After the Civil War, troops stationed at Fort Garland made the Sangres themselves safe from the Utes, who had hunted in and burned mountain drainages on an irregular basis for hundreds of years.

Taking advantage of the effective military hammer at their disposal, Hispanic settlers began to drive their stock into drainages like Cotton and Rito Alto Canyons. There they wintered and began to farm. In the meantime, similarly land-hungry men were riding cavalry patrols into the north valley. Many of the soldiers at Fort Garland were of German descent. Back in Europe, they had faced desperate economic conditions and conscription in the Kaiser's army; in America, they faced desperate economic conditions and conscription into the president's army.

In America, however, there was land, or at least there might be land, if the Civil War would ever end. In 1864, the Homestead Act helped guarantee that free men and women would work the lands around the Sangres but the act ignored those who were already on the land, such as Hispanics, Utes, bison, and wolves.

The Homestead Act's 160-acre limit doomed many ranching and farming operations to a scale at which land abuse, water piracy, heartbreak, and bankruptcy were inevitable outcomes. Efforts to deal with this acreage limit (such as permits to graze cattle on nearby federal land) sowed the seeds of a persistent, sour love-hate dependence on the federal government. Today, the nettles and burrs of that original cursed crop plague the mix of public and private lands that compose the Sangres. A balky mule of a place to begin with, the Sangres with such pests under their packsaddle perform about as well for their would-be masters as one might expect.

Craving land they could claim as their own, the German soldiers from Fort Garland liked what they saw in Colorado. After the Civil War and after the Homestead Act, they formed a colony under Captain Charles Kerber to settle the northern part of the San Luis Valley. One of the colonists was George Niedhart, who in 1868 homesteaded near the town of Lower Cotton Creek, the Germans' version of the Hispanics' town, named for the patron saint of the church of San Luis de Cotton Creek but commonly known as Upper Cotton Creek.

Horsethief Basin was where you went when you wanted to get the jump on both colonies. As a source of timber, firewood, and forage, Cotton Canyon and Horsethief Basin remained unclaimed. They were the commons, where the only law was: This is a war of all against all; take all you can get as fast as you can get it. Only minerals and water bore more or less enforceable private property rights.

Today, official wilderness or not, mineral claims stretch far up Cotton Canyon and even unto 13,621-foot Electric Peak, the highest of the northern Sangres. As a source of precious water, Cotton Canyon flows with stories of how the Sangres were won for some, lost for others, and never held by anyone for long. While their brothers and sisters to the south at San Luis inherited a legal stake to the Sangre de Cristo land grant, the folk of Upper Cotton Creek remained squatters on public land, betting that someday a deed might be issued. Whereas the San Luisans had the presence of mind to file Colorado's earliest water right in 1851, the people of Upper Cotton Creek had no water rights and, as it turned out, no land rights either, since their coming had preceded the Homestead Act. Their lack of defensible, enforceable private property rights rendered them easy prey for their neighbors at Lower Cotton Creek and, ultimately, for the predatory giant to the north, CF&I.

As demand increased, water became more scarce, more valuable, worth fighting about. Although individuals like Niedhart and Joseph Hoffman filed legal claims on some of Cotton Creek's water in the 1860s, the rest belonged to the German colony's mutual ditch company. Before long, violence flared even among the inhabitants of Lower Cotton Creek. John Frey and Pryor Cloud quarreled over water in the late 1890s. Frey served ten years at the state penitentiary in Cañon City for killing Cloud with an irrigation shovel.

Simultaneously blunt and sharp, the weapons/tools of the Sangres' water wars haven't changed much over the years. During the so-called energy crisis of the 1970s, when panicky Coloradans stampeded to wood-burning stoves, fuelwood demand boomed in the Front Range market served by the Sangres.

The eyes of USDA Forest Service timber planners grew bigger and rounder. A sawmill bloomed at Crestone. Foresters prepared big, bold plans to cut firewood and sawtimber from forests that had been cut a century before for these purposes and for charcoal, mine props, and railroad ties.

The rest of the Forest Service formula was simple. Steep slopes and harsh conditions have always made the timber on the Sangres' west side relatively worthless, even when it was free for the taking. The Sangres came under Forest Service management for watershed protection purposes, to secure and stabilize water quantity. But once the forests return, they inconveniently use lots of water. So why not "produce" more water by cutting the Sangres' timber in snow-catching five-acre patches? There was talk of recovering an extra 100,000 acre-feet of precious water in this way.

There was also talk of building small, low-head hydroelectric dams at the mouth of every creek exiting the Sangres. Power from these dams would pump the Sangres' water wherever there was a market. These proposals fizzled. With one major exception (the American Water Development, Inc., or AWDI, plan of the mid-1980s), they represented the most recent lunge toward industrial development in the Sangres.

The sight of the Sangres' towering peaks and abundant water seems to breed megalomania. If we ever learn to tone things down, we'll have to revise our mythology to reflect the region. Maybe we can take heart in the patron saint of the church of San Luis de Cotton Creek. Originally known as San Luis de Seville and renamed by the denizens of Upper Cotton Creek, San Luis de Cotton Creek got his start in the valley as a Spanish import. He probably felt pretty awkward when he saw his new digs, as chanting parishioners bore his statue into their adobe chapel.

Maybe this modest saint solved his identity problem by going native, by acclimating, melting into the aspen groves that line Cotton Creek. There he remains hidden, looking after the place—or so I like to think. I like to think that San Luis de Cotton Creek keeps a watchful eye on the Sangres.

It would be enough if, grown aspen eyed and beaver toothed, he just walks the rounds at Cotton Creek, punching in on the night shift with the beavers, the deer, and the mountain lions. If he does, if he cares for Cotton Creek top to bottom, rock glacier to wheat field, his midnight encounters will include the looming, shaggy figure of John Mattingly. Mattingly rises in the midsummer nights, when Cotton Creek's snowmelt-swollen waters gather to just the level of greatness needed to drive his clever, simple water and power system.

Short of the primitive earthen dam at Cotton Lake, no one has yet developed a storage facility on Cotton Creek. Mattingly says that a healthy beaver population and blowing snow provide all the storage he needs to work the creek's fertile alluvial fan. Snow blows off the peaks all winter long, icing the rock glacier and the lake and drifting deep into the long, narrow canyon. Cotton Lake itself often remains icebound until after Independence Day, so the Cotton Canyon drainage releases its water more slowly than other west-side canyons. They may produce greater volume, but they do so over such a short period of time that holders of water rights must waste much of the all-too-sudden largesse.

Like water, users come and go, but the source—the Sangres—remains. Eventually, the Hispanics at Upper Cotton Creek were struck down like the ill-fated but wonderfully named Pryor Cloud. In the meantime, however, they prospered, gradually shifting from irrigated farming at the mouth of Cotton Creek to further exploitation of the commons through the timbering and tie hacking that served the newly arrived railroads and the region's many mines. CF&I's records may not yield fatality figures, but they carefully detail ethnic origin. They show that many Hispanics found work at the Orient Mine. Their vital community hit its high-water mark in 1899, when they finally built their own church.

In those days, Cotton Creek may have flowed farther out into the valley than it does today, as one can see from several dry creek channels. By 1870, a water-driven sawmill was already at work on Cotton Creek. There were still beavers in the creek in the 1880s, a rarity after the heavy trapping earlier in the century. Also in the 1880s, tie camps were springing up at Cotton Creek and Rito Alto Creek. The Sangres were booming as they never have since.

As the years passed, the villagers of Upper Cotton Creek become more dependent on the Orient for employment. Forgetting San Luis de Cotton Creek, they renamed their town Las Minas de Ferro (The Iron Mines). As the town grew, it first sat on the mesa and then extended up the creek and into the mountains, roughly where the Forest Service would later establish its ranger station. For reasons unknown, most of Las Minas de Ferro's families remained squatters. Meanwhile, they farmed the meadows of Cotton Canyon, ran a few cows of their own up into the forests, and worked on local ranches and mines.

When the Sangres became national forests around the turn of the century, their west-facing canyons contained many such pockets of humanity. CF&I signaled the end for Las Minas de Ferro in 1914 when it obtained the water rights of the Germans' mutual ditch company. A mile-long steel flume diverted water from the old Cotton Creek channel through three-foot tubes. Every thousand yards, it paused in cement tanks that were supposed to slow it down. The flume moved water down to Lower Cotton Creek; from there, it was pumped to the Orient. Farms along the upper part of the Creek dried up, and people abandoned their homes.

Even mighty CF&I couldn't control Cotton Creek forever. As you approach the Forest Service trailhead at Cotton Creek, you see the remains of the ruined flume to the north. Its design problem is a familiar one to both engineers and beavers: too much water at one time. Once it exits the canyon, Cotton Creek drops so rapidly that it develops a head too powerful for ordinary engineering. You can still see some of CF&I's diversion and settling structures at the mouth of the canyon, as well as the remains of the old sawmill.

Downstream today, John Mattingly has solved the problems that defeated CF&I. The head from Cotton Creek drives twenty-six giant center-pivot irrigation systems. Each one makes twelve revolutions per growing season, distributing one and a half inches of water at each pass. Since the soils of the northern valley are well drained, they could handle such floods, as long as Mattingly applied yet more water in the fall to drive salts back down into the water table. Of Cotton Creek Ranch's 8,600 deeded acres, Mattingly farms 3,100 for wheat, rapeseed, alfalfa, and fancy new crops like canola.

True to local tradition, Mattingly warred fervently with state water regulators over Cotton Creek. They claim he used too much of Cotton Creek. He said that since the advent of irrigation on the alluvial fan below Cotton Creek Canyon, all the water of Cotton Creek has been consumed by farmers, so there have been no return flows to measure. He also claimed that Cotton Lake was improved by the founders of Cotton Creek Water Company, the same outfit (Mattingly claimed) that built the Airline Ditch with its elevated flumes and concrete dissipators. Opinions will differ about the history of local engineering efforts, but the record should note that the state engineer eventually conceded Mattingly's point about return flows from Cotton Creek to San Luis Creek.

San Luis Creek, for its part, is even more ephemeral than San Luis himself. It exists on maps and in law books, but on the land it is a mirage, appearing and reappearing on the surface in bewildering ways, as it flows down into the Closed Basin, where the Bureau of Reclamation "salvages" it— pumps it into the Rio Grande to meet Colorado's water obligations to its downstream neighbors.

Up near the head of it all, Mattingly roars defiance against distant bureaucrats much as earlier Americans resisted far-away King George. Of course his system provides ample return flows from Cotton Creek to San Luis Creek—it's just that no one has ever measured them.

I've tried to coax Mattingly and his son, Mac, into walking with me up to Cotton Lake on July 4 to celebrate Independence Day and to raise a glass of glacier milk to the confusion of the king. But by the time the ice is off the lake, the rhythm of their work year has stepped up along with the flows of Cotton Creek. Short of that, Mattingly always asks me to take along beaver chow and beaver sex stimulants of the kind that the "stink men" must have used in their trapping days. In their nightly dance with Cotton Creek, the hardworking, fast-reproducing beavers remain Cotton Creek Ranch's finest allies.

Rito Alto

The church of San Luis de Cotton Creek may no longer stand, but that hardly renders local gods homeless. If you drive the back roads south from Cotton Creek, you will encounter the valley's most beautiful structure, the church at the Rito Alto cemetery. Still maintained with loving hands, this church was built in 1889 from ponderosa pines cut and milled at Cotton Creek.

Homesteader Harrison Wales donated the twenty acres for the Rito Alto cemetery and church; he was the first person buried there. He lies near his daughter, Abigail Wales Shellabarger, who wrote a spirited history of the San Luis Valley in 1923 at the request of Albin Hamel, the supervisor of San Isabel National Forest. Both of Shellabarger's sons, Walter and Ralph, had worked for the infant Forest Service. Ralph had been San Isabel's first forest supervisor, in 1905.

Shellabarger wrote that the middle to upper parts of every drainage on the west side of the Sangres burned in the 1870s, except for Rito Alto. That was where the Wales and Shellabarger families had their ranches. They controlled fires. There were no beavers or trout in the drainage, so they planted rainbows halfway up the canyon toward Rito Alto Lake. Half a century earlier, mountain man Antoine Leroux had trapped the beaver out. In 1853 (while his old compatriot Kit Carson was changing careers at Fort Garland), Leroux passed Rito Alto again, this time guiding Gunnison's railroad expedition through the Sangres and on to the San Juan Mountains.

Some say the roots of real forestry are German. If so, these German families, whose descendants still work the Rito Alto ranch today, knew the value of intact watersheds for maintaining irrigation water quantity and quality. Even though they had artesian wells, they used Rito Alto Creek to irrigate their 5,000 acres. Those neighboring irrigators whose mountain drainages suffered fire damage were quicker to switch to saltier groundwater. All too often, the result was irreversible salinization of the soil.

Although there is little physical evidence of it today, the town of Cotton Creek operated a post office from 1875 through 1927. After 1895, Cotton Creek was renamed Mirage, perhaps prophetically. Today wilderness separates towns and people, but strange as it may seem, Cotton Creek/Mirage and Rito Alto were on a postal route that connected the San Luis Valley to Huerfano Valley towns like Gardner, Red Wing, and Malachite via Mosca Pass. Ralph Shellabarger was the district ranger at Malachite after he served as forest supervisor at San Isabel.

A Constant Interchange of Growth and Blight

In the second decade of the twentieth century, a fresh-faced Forest Service, eager to make friends, built a nine-mile trail from Goat Park, just north of The Pines, over an inconvenient ridge, all the way up South Brush Creek, over Three Step Pass, and then down through Horsethief Basin to Cotton Creek. For ranchers and sheepherders, the trail served as a convenient stock driveway into the burned-over mid-level mixed conifer forests, through the remnants of the high-altitude spruce forests, and into the alpine meadows. Thanks to such determined early Forest Service efforts on behalf of their politically important grazing clients, modern researchers have found not one accessible square inch of the Sangres' original vegetation left unchanged by grazing.

In those days, since most of the forests had been cut and/or burned and then heavily grazed, catastrophic floods threatened downstream cities. (One flood smashed through the Wet Mountain valley in 1911; another wiped out Pueblo in 1921.) Accordingly, a legitimately worried Forest Service designated the Sangres a "watershed protection forest." Trying to get water-and-soil-holding vegetation to grow, they suppressed all fires. Then they went fishing for allies in ranching and recreation. Buried deep in an old-fashioned olive drab metal filing cabinet at San Isabel National Forest's headquarters in Pueblo, I found the annual reports of J. A. Langworthy, San Isabel's third forest supervisor, who served from 1908 to 1914. Langworthy wrote:

> Grazing is the greatest source of revenue from this forest. The San Isabel is one of the most fully stocked Forests. . . . One important effect of grazing the forage crop has been the great reduction in loss from severe ground fires. . . . One of the most important results of grazing is the favorable attitude to which it had brought the stockmen toward the Forest Service.

Supervisor Langworthy waxed proud over the Cotton Creek ranger station, which had twenty-five acres of pasture to serve the horses of its wide-ranging personnel, ever afield as fire lookouts and range riders. Thanks to the nearby sawmill, the station itself was a six-room frame house with a meeting hall. Even a barn was in the works.

For decades, I passed through the portals leading to Cotton Lake without giving any thought to the role of humans in its environmental history. In fact, it was humans I wished to avoid. Headed for the high and holy country like most backpackers, I never asked myself how the early Forest Service, committed to the restoration of a damaged resource, managed the devastated corridor of forests along Cotton Creek or how the high-altitude fires in the nearly fireproof spruce might have started.

As far as I was concerned, the farther I could get from the valleys and their people, the better. With this attitude, I watched as the Sangres slipped first to de facto wilderness, then to an official wilderness study area, and finally to designated wilderness, safe from humans for all time—or so I thought. As the years paraded a series of congressmen before me, beginning with my local congressman, Wayne Aspinall, I dutifully penned heartfelt letters demanding wilderness, now! (please, Sir) for my beloved Sangres.

And now the sins of my youth return to haunt me. As of 1993, wilderness is upon us, and I suffer from a bad case of buyer's remorse. It used to be that some citizen would regularly blast with a shotgun all the Forest Service signs leading west to the Cotton Creek trailhead from Highway 17. For years, I got lost every time I tried to go there—generally much to my improvement, since that bred an intimate knowledge of a lot of valley backcountry I would have ordinarily ignored, my eyes fixed on "heaven."

Now wilderness will put the Sangres on the map. This means that they are in danger of suffering a second tragedy of the commons in which too many visitors and too little hands-on management may lead us into loving their precious diversity and obscurity to death.

Here is Langworthy again. His logic runs in circles, but there still smolders in his musty report the zeal of the early Forest Service, the heroes of this book: "The San Isabel being a Protection Forest, the question of protection becomes of the utmost importance so our work is planned accordingly. We believe in first taking care of what we have and then going ahead with other work."

What is it that we have in the Sangres? You, too, might walk up the Cotton Creek trail to find out. Unwitting beneficiaries of Langworthy's reclamation efforts, we only dimly sense how the first tragedy of the commons altered Cotton Creek. We see Cotton Canyon as the stable, beautiful gateway to pristine Cotton Lake. But doesn't Cotton Creek's environmental history prompt phrases more disturbing, such as "a constant interchange of growth and blight"?

Sometimes a saying will sum up a host of problems. What do we have in the Sangres? Something we should conserve? Preserve? Protect? Something we should improve? Both? All? Such questions are tough enough for mere mortals—so tough that I suspect they periodically propel our saint southeast, sending San Luis de Cotton Creek over the hill, over the old Mosca Pass postal route to the upper Huerfano, where he and Our Lady of the Grottos can put their heads together at Our Lady's shrine near Red Wing. Or maybe the two of them trek down to the Stations of the Cross Shrine at San Luis. There they may find the answers.

In the meantime, until those two and their allies come up with such answers, here is Langworthy's entry under "Protection Improvements":

> The building of roads and trails is necessary in order that the entire Forest may be made accessible. It will take some time before this can be accomplished so that at present we are opening up areas which contain the largest bodies of timber in need of protection and areas which will net us the greatest returns for grazing, etc., and will at the same time be valuable from an administrative standpoint.

As you walk up Cotton Creek Canyon, consider another episode in its environmental history. Fifty years after Langworthy, the Sangres had become worthless to almost everyone. Heavy grazing during both world wars had rendered cowpunching so valueless that most Forest Service grazing permits fell into nonuse. Ranger stations at places like Cotton Creek were abandoned as the Forest Service administration consolidated and contracted, moving to urban areas. As the agency's attention shifted from growing trees to cutting them, poor timber-producing areas like the Sangres entered a backwater period of neglect from which they are only today emerging.

Yet in the 1960s and 1970s, a new wave of settlers crashed onto Cotton Creek. What one saw there was what one of my grandmothers called Okies, and the other called white trash. They called themselves hippies. Every spring, these colonists circled their battered school buses in the meadows at the mouth of Cotton Creek. There they squatted for free on public land as long as the growing season would allow.

These latter-day itinerants were pursuing the American dream of free land, free love, free drugs, free something, free anything. Where the people of Upper Cotton Creek had grown squash and beans, where the Forest Service had pastured government horses, they diverted the waters of Cotton Creek to irrigate rich-soiled fields hidden in the aspen groves. There they cultivated remarkably fine marijuana.

In the fall, at harvesting, cleaning, and packaging time, they baled the stuff in neat kilogram-sized, plastic-covered slabs. Tensions were high. The work of cleaning required many hands and nimble fingers. A lot of those hands also held guns. And all the hands' and fingers' owners, however connected or disconnected, wired or unwired, systematically sampled the product, falling easy prey to the paranoia that plagues the perpetually stoned.

They knew how to brandish firearms at strangers. Animals, especially deer, that encroached on the valuable fields were poached. If you passed by in the evenings, smells of savory venison stew and wood smoke thickened the air, along with the sweet, piquant aroma of pot. If you lingered, there was casual talk of booby-trapped approaches to the growing crops. Taking their cue from the Vietcong, these pioneers sharpened shoots of abundant local hardwoods like willow and water birch. Then they buried the sticks butt down in the aspen duff, smearing the fire-hardened tips with local supplies of human excrement.

Like the trappers of the early part of the nineteenth century, these frontier folk skimmed the cream off the land and then moved on and on and on. They were hard on the local deer, beaver, and fish populations. Generally longhaired and dirty, they were a colorful, irreverent bunch, beset with scores of towheaded kids and full of scorn for the hapless, terrified Forest Service people who tried vainly to move them on. Then one day in the late 1970s, they fired up their fleet and never reappeared. And so, in time, beavers and aspens, lions and deer returned, as always, even unto the mouth of Cotton Canyon.

Unless you count brain damage, this latest round of utopians did no more nor less harm to Cotton Creek Canyon than those who went before or came after. They simply got something for nothing, as people always have from the Sangres. And today, they are as likely as you and me to visit the Sangres for recreational purposes, still expecting something for nothing.

Cotton Lake

After the hippies departed, for a long time Cotton Canyon was home to a pair of goshawks nesting in a long, lean aspen overlooking the trail. No one puzzled over their territorial or habitat needs. They were simply there. Once in a while, defending her nest, the female would attack hikers and riders at eye level. That nest is empty now. No one knows why. For those few years in the life of the Sangres, and in our lives, the setting was right for some unknown number of goshawks and for some unknown number of humans. Now there are fewer of the former and many more of the latter. Could there be a relationship?

Maybe, but as you walk up the canyon, the abandoned mines on the south slope and the old irrigation ditches of lower Cotton Canyon tell you that off and on there have been many, many more people living and working here. And that somehow, maybe thanks to San Luis de Cotton Creek, the goshawks survived and returned when the beavers and aspens returned, temporarily providing just the right mix of foraging and nesting areas. With the Southwest's goshawk population in serious trouble today, will we be so lucky again?

Before the Forest Service routed today's trail up on the south slope, a friend and I once followed the old four-wheel-drive road that extended right up to the junction of Cotton Creek Trail and Three Step Pass. It is aspen all the way from the mouth of the canyon, as if Cotton Creek only grudgingly admits the narrowleaf cottonwood you would expect in a canyon so named. These aspens sport a gorgeous assortment of blackening scars and galls, as if to confront us with our own ecological status as parasites, agents of change, carvers in soft, inviting hide. Yet we are hardly alone. Territory-minded bears do not spare these trees; nor do mineral-starved elk. What with all the autographs of claws, teeth, and antlers, the corridor's eloquent aspens might as well have been pulped and newsprinted.

Surely there is older news, but the oldest human symbol I have found dates itself to 1938. Could this one, then, have been the biggest tree the shepherd could find? Like the animals, his loneliness evoked artistry in the form of florid claims on sex and territory, in this case carved into wood in *norteño* Spanish. By the end of the 1930s, who else could and would do the lonely, demanding work of herding sheep? And yet now, half a century later, perhaps because they belong to different clones, perhaps because they are on better sites, many other aspens exceed this living relic in size. Every tree we see here either postdates 1900 or was rejected by the sawyers, whose portable mill spared very little that was worth cutting.

As the canopy of the forest corridor opens and closes over the course of a long, gentle walk, you see more of its diversity. Way out of their ordinary territories, limber pines and bristlecones elbow their way up through the undergrowth, muscling it out with aspens and confronted at streamside with thigh-thick water birches. As the years and the miles pass by, we see more and more beavers, reclaiming territory for themselves and for all the species that depend on their engineering virtuosity. And we see more and more signs of elk, until the carpet of elk scat in the meadow becomes troubling. How many is too many? Is there an important ecological difference between meadows overgrazed by elk and meadows overgrazed by domestic stock?

Once in a while, the walk up the canyon spooks a familiar black bear sow, one cub jet and the other rust, every other year, as if she knew what colors pleased her. If you happen to leave the trail and brave the oak brush, ant-and-acorn-charged bear scat will tell you that there is only one creature more omnivorous than we are. And always, if you pay attention to territories, there are the droppings of coyotes and the formidable scrapes of mountain lions, advertising the aromatic news that the elk and deer populations are thriving.

What's missing? There are no wolves, and there are no grizzly bears. Abigail Shellabarger tells how her sons trapped a grizzly a few miles south, in Rito Alto Canyon, in 1895. In 1887, Theodore Cockerell's hunting companions blazed away at grizzlies and wolves maybe a mile higher over De Anza's shoulder, in Horseshoe Bend.

Dropping our packs at the trail junction, we take a day to walk up De Anza's backside, toward the saddle that leads on the south to Horseshoe Bend and on the north to the Banjo Lake crossover and then Electric Peak. The trail steepens and switches back, passing through dry aspen clones as ancient, stunted, and twisted as the knots of clichés about old growth in the Sangres. Three Step Pass is cruelly named.

Horsethief Basin has an air of remoteness that says "too steep!" Climbing out, we blunder into one of the finest stands of old growth anywhere in the Sangres. This is not the cathedral-like old growth of the Pacific Northwest; this is bristlecone, the crooked timber of the Sangres. And this stand is rivaled, perhaps, only by the vast bristlecone wealth on a similar slope and aspect above Rito Alto Canyon.

How old is old? I'd like to get to the core of the matter. But my fourteen-inch steel increment borer balks at the bulk of these twisted titans, widespread and lonely, dotting the switchbacks and casting cones, pollen, and seeds all over—as if to say that here, too, sex and territory remain the ancient message. Up near the timberline, here in the krummholz—here is the super old growth of the Sangres, not in the insect-infested, fire-prone forests below. Would a thousand years be enough? How about two? Are we talking forests or trees? In the Sangres, you learn to question such questions. Is it the trees we value or the tales of climatic variability told by their growth rings?

Knock on wood. These stately bristlecones play as resonantly and vibrantly as an eighty-year-old Pablo Casals at the cello. Looking up-valley from here, we can see, at about 11,500 feet, where calamitous forest fires and bug infestations burned and ate their way through everything from creek to crag—everything, that is, but the widespread bristlecones.

Once we near the saddle, the altitude pounces on our backs, heavier than any lion. Unusual for the Sangres, it is a close, warm, breezeless summer day, wan, dull, and glaring, with a dripping fog, low-hung and thick, that covers all the sky. We set our foreheads earthward, as if set in opposition against the enemy. Too breathless to talk, each pensively sinks into his private thoughts. As we ascend at a loose distance each from each, I chance to lead. At my feet, the ground appears to brighten, and with a step or two it seems brighter still.

We have reached the saddle, and beneath the clouds our vista sweeps away across the Wet Mountain valley, across the Arkansas River valley, and all the way to Pikes Peak. As this vision closes, we shelter under house-sized boulders, where ambient electricity stands our hair straight on end. The thunderheads first ascend and then bottom out above Electric Peak, above Gibbs, above De Anza. Then they wheel about and bear down on us, huddled in the saddle, riding out the storm. When this tempest passes, soaking us with terror and elation, San Luis or Our Lady of the Grottos blesses us with a double rainbow over the Wet Mountain valley.

Scared stiff, we hobble off that ridge as soon as sunshine allows. Back down in the canyon, we continue on past the Middle Fork, all too ripe with elk, and on up Cotton Creek. What appear to be mine tailings marring the entrance to Henderson Gulch turn out on closer inspection to be a small, orphanlike volcanic cone. Red cinders abound. So do avalanche chutes, beheaded trees, and logs piled up like a child's game of pickup sticks.

As we ascend toward the lake, a series of punishing sections in the trail tells us where each glacier gave up its ghost. When we finally reach Cotton Lake, its setting seems too beautiful for the hard use it receives. Too many camping parties treat the lakeshore and campsites as if they were the first and last to occupy the site. Boy Scouts, old enough to know better, amuse themselves by rolling boulders from the heights down into the lake, endangering fishermen and destroying the peace of the scene. When I question their adult leaders, they tell me that this is a free country, that this is their right. They rolled boulders into Cotton Lake when they were boys. When the Scouts finally depart for the trailhead, taking their adolescent war-of-all-against-all elsewhere, we have the lake to ourselves.

Next dawn, as the morning shift of lake beavers reports for work, we cross their dam near the rock glacier as we head for the pass leading into the Rito Alto drainage. On our way, we want to spend some time on the cliffs overlooking the lake, good places to roll rocks—or Boy Scouts—into the lake. Or to sit quietly and scan the depths of Lion Gulch. As we traverse last night's engineering triumphs, we can see where the beavers slapped willow sticks and mud into place. And there, in the soft, brown mud: the paw print of a lion.

PART TWO

Old Traditions and New Ideas

It can be argued that the public lands of the West were founded on a combination of scientific progressivism and salvation by heroes. Gifford Pinchot and Theodore Roosevelt perhaps did more than any other leaders to set the destiny of the West in motion in the twentieth century, and both of them were at once scientific progressives and perpetrators of heroic acts. The legacy they left—chiefly in the form of public lands and national parks and monuments—is unparalleled in any nation on earth. These resources clearly lie at the heart of the West. But recently, the paradigm of scientific progressivism has come under attack. Many commentators have pointed out how various special interests have perverted the original intentions of scientifically based natural resource conservation. Several of those commentators present original essays here in part II, and several others argue against them.

In "The True-Mann's West," John Baden focuses on the forces that shaped much of the economy of the West. He points out that from the mid-nineteenth to the mid-twentieth century, with the best of intentions and through the creation of institutions that made sense in their day, people, businesses, and government in the West inadvertently unleashed a set of economic incentives that no longer make sense and that now violate the public's values. Nevertheless, these incentives remain fixed in place because of the ways in which they reward a small but powerful elite. He uses two Wyoming families as lenses to focus on the changing public values of the nation and the West. The Manns, a family of subsistence-level ranchers from Newcastle, Wyoming, and the Trues, a leading petroleum family from Casper, represent the working paradigm of the Old West, a paradigm based on extraction of resources from the land. This old vision of public good in the West is under attack from all sides, but as Baden points out, the region will be much poorer if the honest values of people like the Manns and the Trues are somehow crushed beneath an overload of "enlightened" bureaucracy.

In "Saving the Marketplace from the Market," Mark Sagoff summarizes the critique that the "new resource economists" level at mainstream environmental economics and at public policies based on 1970s notions of ecology in which we presume a "balance of nature." He then turns to a discussion of the differences between the marketplace (meaning the commerce of all manner of exchange, including ideas, goods and services, barter and voluntarism) and the market (meaning the global economy of anonymous transactions). Recognizing "the dead hand of the federal bureaucracy" as one manifestation of the market in the West, and corporatism as another, Sagoff contends that the market will inevitably overtop the marketplace in every instance unless exceptional efforts are made to protect the things people most value about place.

In 1953, Wallace Stegner all but canonized John Wesley Powell, an early western explorer and the second director of the U.S. Geological Survey, in his great biography *Beyond the Hundredth Meridian.* Range ecologist Karl Hess Jr. revisits the environmental record of the esteemed major and arrives at a very different conclusion about the Powell legacy. In "John Wesley Powell and the Unmaking of the West," Hess argues that the American West, both mythologically and historically, has always looked to heroes or saviors to redeem it from its tendencies toward exploitation, and its first and greatest hero was John Wesley Powell. But heroics have been bad for the West, says Hess, for the heroes have almost always come from afar and have possessed little affinity or even respect for the region's community and citizenry. Worse, federal heroics have managed to insulate westerners from real political responsibility. Hess suggests that it is now time for a West of everyday people to assume responsibility for their own destiny—economic, political, and cultural.

The inadvertent creation of the West's public lands was the happiest accident in American history, argues Montana writer Donald Snow in his essay, "Empire or Homelands." Although these lands have often been abused by a citizenry and government wedded to the notion of unbridled development, they have always embodied the greatest hopes of communitarian and utopian thinkers. Whereas many libertarians and conservatives deride the federal lands as "political lands," it is precisely their political nature that makes these lands and resources critically important to the American experiment in democracy. The logic of the market will never fully express the human values that attach to the open, public lands of the West, for the ultimate market logic is privatization, the only outcome in which political interference can be avoided or minimized. This author argues that in the management of the West's public lands, political "interference" is to be not avoided but encouraged, under a new regime of land management that would force westerners to come to grips with real political responsibility. His essay suggests a new approach to federal lands management—an experiment in a decentralist vision to be tried out in a few carefully selected laboratories.

"Is 'Libertarian Environmentalist' an Oxymoron?" That's the question asked by Robert H. Nelson, an economist whose years as a policy analyst for the Department of the Interior spanned the period of perhaps the greatest political upheaval in the West. Nelson explores the abundant philosophical common ground between environmentalism and libertarianism and suggests that environmentalists have been lulled into a tacit acceptance of regulatory and coercive approaches. Such approaches, he points out, end up serving the organizational needs of governmental agencies and the nonprofit groups that lobbied for their creation but often have negative outcomes in the natural environment. In an especially intriguing twist, Nelson posits a strong affinity between libertarianism and deep ecology, arguing that both philosophies tend toward radical decentralization.

We close the book with an indirect attack on some of the ideas presented in the previous essays. In "Ideology, Wishful Thinking, and Pragmatic Reform," economist Thomas Michael Power questions the limits of free-market environmentalism as a benign guide into the Next West. Power argues that free-market approaches to improving environmental quality can be well used only after political and values-based decisions clarify society's expectations of what must be achieved in any given land use or resource issue. The market is a tool, not a value in itself, yet its most ardent proponents speak and act as if nearly any outcome dictated by a market approach will be preferable to outcomes based on well-articulated public goals. Power argues that clear public goals can indeed be articulated and then, through the legislative dialectic, hammered into reasonable prescriptive mandates from the state.

CHAPTER SIX

The True-Mann's West

Endangered and Forsaken?

JOHN A. BADEN

His friend at the hardware store told me that to catch Tedd Mann, I'd have to arrive early. So just before 6:00 A.M., I pulled into his driveway. Although nearly thirty years have passed, my recollection of that morning is still fresh and clear.

"If you ain't a Democrat or a salesman, come in and grab a cup of coffee."

The invitation came from a tall, weathered man who had stepped onto his porch and into the morning frost. He was wearing a light Levi's jacket and carrying a rifle—the first, and last, model 95 Winchester I'd seen in use, a .30–.40 Krag. For most people it would be a wall hanger, but for Tedd it was a tool. Without looking, he reached up and grabbed a bullwhip from a nail on the porch wall. He was off to work, and if I wanted to talk to him, I'd have to grab a mug of cowboy coffee and tag along.

In his fifties and a bit deaf, Tedd had a small ranch on the South Dakota–Wyoming border. He was one of the most generally competent people I've ever met. Tedd could set up a shingle mill, braid a loop in a wire rope, play the fiddle, hot-wire a pickup without shorting out the dash, call a square dance, fill a grease gun from a barrel and not make a mess, shrink a steel rim to fit a wooden wagon wheel, and explain why his Catholic neighbor on a nearby ranch voted Republican in national elections. He'd launched three kids into the world, where they would produce more than they'd take. He could probably roll a cigarette with one hand in the dark, on a horse, in the rain.

When I met him, back in the mid-1960s, I was studying the economics of Hutterite communes. I had been living and working with the Hutterites on and off for nearly two years. Of the dozens I had met and come to know, I liked several a great deal, and I still remember them with affection and respect. But I am allergic to "chosen people." At the corpuscular level, I'm wired libertarian. People who have received revelations granting them a sanctified monopoly on the great truths of life grate on my most deeply held conceptions of civil society. I needed a safe haven.

Tedd and his wife, Gertrude, provided it by offering me their old bunkhouse. There was no rent—I was just to help out. With their boys gone, they'd enjoy the company. And, especially between stints among the pious Hutterites, so would I.

Theirs was a storybook ranch. To get there, driving between Custer, South Dakota, and Newcastle, Wyoming, you turned south on a gravel road going up a canyon. At about ten miles, the canyon opened up like a keyhole, revealing the Manns' house, the barn and shed, the blacksmith's shop on the right, and "my" log bunkhouse, near the corral on the left. A spring lay just beyond; water pressure on the ranch was a gift of gravity. Although it was the mid-1960s, the Manns had just gotten electricity. They had no telephone.

Tedd knew that country as did few others. He was born in it, grew up in it, hunted in it, grew hay and grain and ran stock on it, and guided hunters through it. Talent rich but money poor, he also hired on as a freelance stock boss at the neighboring L.A.K., the biggest ranch in Tedd's part of the world.

The L.A.K. belonged to Dave True, a Casper oilman who had grown up in Cutbank, Montana, earned an engineering degree from Montana State University, and gone on to a career as a highly successful drilling contractor. Dave was probably as fine a businessman as one could find, and he was clearly cut a lot like Tedd. In my eyes, they were two great men of the West, each anchoring the end of his own quality continuum. They were linked by place, but they had disparate interests in the L.A.K. The trouble was that Dave True did not live anywhere near the ranch he owned, and he never knew Tedd Mann; that distance came to be the source of a well-rubbed sore spot.

For years, Tedd had been hired on as a freelance leader each September when the wranglers of the L.A.K. went up into the forest to drive the cows down to winter pasture. But it wasn't Dave True who hired Tedd and dealt with him year after year. If he had, Dave would have seen that Tedd was dependable, honorable, smart, and competent—exactly the man he'd want as lead man when it came time to gather the cattle from the hills—and that Tedd deserved compensation beyond what was normal for the L.A.K.

At least since the late 1940s, there's been a saying that goes like this: The way to make a small fortune in ranching is to start with a large one. So if you're a successful oilman in Casper with a large ranch half a day away, you're likely to pick a manager with an accountant's, not a cowboy's, mind. The stock manager who hired Tedd was a ledger man, not a cow man, and of course there was recurring conflict between the two. A lot of it centered on the issue of worth.

At the L.A.K., hired labor could not be paid more than thirty dollars a day. For a top hay hand, irrigator, or member of a fencing crew, those wages were sufficient. But in Tedd's case, for the fall drive of cattle from the hills, he was surely worth much, much more. He was cow-smart, he knew the country, and the men knew him well and trusted his skills and judgment. He'd always find the cows and lead them and the men safely out.

But the stock manager didn't have the latitude to pay Tedd what he was worth. Every autumn, the ledger man told the stock man, "This is a business, and rules are rules, and I'm not Mr. True, and unless he says different, a hand can't be paid more than thirty dollars. You run the men and the cows, but I run the books."

The rules forbade fair payment, yet somehow over the years the cow man and the ledger man worked out a deal and got the system to balance. Here's how it worked.

To make Tedd's wages equal his worth when leading the cattle drive, the stock manager arranged for Tedd to be a contract fencer. The manager would identify a piece of fence to be built by an outside contractor. Tedd would be awarded the contract at a rate sufficient to compensate for his underpayment on the cattle drive. It was a circuitous route to justice, but they always managed to get there.

Watching how that deal got figured each autumn was among my first acquaintances with the older ways of doing business in the West. Tedd Mann, the little guy, and the L.A.K., the big boss ranch, worked out a tacit agreement based on mutual need and respect. They bent the rules but never broke them. And they never gave in to bitterness surrounding Tedd's real worth. Like a lot of things in the real West, it was a peculiar arrangement, but it worked.

For my part, I enjoyed working with Tedd. Other than talking of stomach pain when drinking straight whiskey and griping about politicians who promised much but seldom delivered and always took in more than they gave back, he had few complaints. Tedd's doctor thought the stomach problem was an ulcer, but Tedd believed it was cancer; a neighbor had experienced similar symptoms the year before.

Tedd and Gertrude, who gave me refuge from the chosen people, were an important part of the West I loved. I think of them often and miss them a lot. A Next West without them, and people like them, will be much impoverished. These people constituted a key indicator species as important to the West's integrity as a region as those listed in the Endangered Species Act. And now, people like the Manns are endangered. How that came to be so is a story of perhaps tragic inevitability.

The Original Western Vision

For more than a century, from at least 1846 until the late 1960s, a single vision dominated humankind's relationship with the western lands: the exploitation of natural resources.[1] Cultural values, economics, and political institutions legitimated and encouraged the pursuit of resource extraction. The Manns and the Trues were at home in that environment. They would be less so today.

Demographic, economic, and technological changes have fundamentally altered the face of the West. Yet although resource extraction is no longer central to the values or economic pursuits of most of the West's present residents, political institutions continue to subsidize and encourage an extractive way of life. This creates a tension between the growing desire for environmental quality and the persistent political inertia that preserves old patterns of exploitation. To a large extent, governmental institutions and policies are at odds with the emerging culture and economy of the West.

Reform is possible, but it requires that we understand why a harmony between western values and resource extraction once existed, why it has disappeared, and how we can foster a new coherence among values, politics, and ways of life. Can Tedd Mann's core values persist and be respected? Can Dave True's entrepreneurial talents complement heightened environmental sensitivity? Or must the skills and lifeways represented by people like Mann and True be erased in order for the West to somehow reinherit itself?

I will explore these and other questions from a political economy perspective—that is, by considering how major social institutions channel our choices, providing incentives for some kinds of actions and discouraging others.

The core of my argument is simple. Institutions generate information and incentives. Old institutions often generate poor or outdated information and an endless stream of perverse incentives. Thus, new institutions are required to reharmonize the economy with our values.

The Beginning and End of Sanctified Exploitation

To understand the origin and nature of many contemporary environmental problems, it is important to understand why people, businesses, and government acted as they did from the middle of the nineteenth century through the 1960s. What incentives encouraged the development of an extractive culture and economy, and how did cultural-economic pressures lead to political institutions that reinforced and deepened a reliance on extraction? I argue that a harmony did in fact exist and that it existed because of the resource endowment of the West and predictable cultural, economic, and political responses to that endowment.

Secretary of the Interior Bruce Babbitt, formerly governor of Arizona and president of the League of Conservation Voters, seems to agree, for he observed the following:

> Traditionally, the American West has been something of a third-world economy based on resource extraction. We earned a living by sawing timber, grazing cattle, and mining the earth. . . . And in those days our political system reflected the realities of the resource economy. When so many jobs depended on the sawmills, there wasn't much of a constituency for forest wilderness. In fact, most people were hostile to the very idea.[2]

Similarly, Wallace Stegner, one of the West's foremost historical and environmental writers, reminded us:

> There are plenty of people in the West—millions, probably . . . who approach western land, water, grass, timber, mineral resources, and scenery as grave robbers might approach the tomb of a pharaoh. . . . Too often . . . western states have been prosperous at the expense of their fragile environment and their civilization has too often mined and degraded their natural scene while drawing most of its quality from it.[3]

These observations illustrate one of the most important facts in the history of western political economy: resource extraction and development dominated the West's politics and economy for a very long time.

Extractive lifestyles became entrenched in the West in two ways. First, cultural values and low population densities dictated that to make a living, almost everyone had to farm, log, or mine or service those who did.

Moreover, economic and technological constraints helped keep the traditional economy of the West intact. High transportation costs, manufacturing processes that were wasteful of natural resources, weak economies of scale, and relatively low labor productivity and per capita incomes all tended to constrain the region's economy. Scarce water and long distances to major markets kept communities small and scattered. Although economic self-sufficiency and individualistic credos of self-reliance were revered, communitarian values were often practiced.

Second, the geologic, demographic, and economic realities that entrenched resource extraction as the driver in the region's development also created the impetus behind public policies encouraging extraction-based economic growth. The irony of this situation has been noted by western law scholar Charles F. Wilkinson:

> A great many natural resource laws have their genesis in the mid- or late-19th century, a time when westerners held extreme laissez-faire attitudes toward public resources such as water, wildlife, timber, minerals and rangeland.[4]

Behind a credo of rugged individualism, westerners demanded and received governmental subsidies to help subdue nature and stabilize economic life. Miners were lured to the West by the promise of minerals made easily accessible by the General Mining Law of 1872. Specifically designed to encourage western economic growth, this law made mining one of the most attractive uses of public lands.[5] It reads:

> Except as otherwise provided, all valuable mineral deposits in land belonging to the United States, both surveyed and unsurveyed, shall be free and open to exploration and purchase, and the lands in which they are found, to occupation and purchase, by citizens of the United States.[6]

Similarly, the Desert Land Act of 1877 offered 640 acres of arid lands to homesteaders; the Reclamation Act of 1902 encouraged farming by authorizing and subsidizing federal irrigation projects in the West; and the Stock Raising Homestead Act of 1916 authorized 640-acre ranch homesteads on all public lands.

The Reclamation Act offered particularly egregious development subsidies. It led to the creation of the Bureau of Reclamation, which constructed massive irrigation projects subsidized by costly water cheaply delivered, all to facilitate settlement of western lands. Politics segregated price from cost, with western politicians claiming credit for the high-priced spread. Likewise, the Bureau of Land Management and its predecessors, the Government

Land Office and the Grazing Service, promoted the welfare of established ranches by keeping itinerant herders out and grazing fees far below market levels. For decades, grazing fees remained locked at five cents per animal, far below even the cut-rate fees charged to ranchers on Forest Service lands.[7]

Understandably, such policies created constituencies committed to the continuation and expansion of government support. The Grazing Service, for example, was controlled by stockmen who consistently thwarted efforts to raise grazing fees.[8] Many western logging communities became dependent on subsidized timber cuts in national forests. Western legislators such as Senator James McClure of Idaho and Congressman Wayne Aspinall of Colorado consistently fought for federal policies guaranteed to keep grazing fees and timber costs low and to raise farm commodity prices above market rates.

Ironically, many of these politicians claimed to be conservatives in favor of free-market capitalism. Nevertheless, they responded predictably to voters who applied pressure to keep the subsidies flowing. Proextraction laws and agencies nurtured constituencies that relied on these programs for their livelihoods, creating a culture dependent on political privilege beneath a public veneer of rugged self-reliance. But politics is a poor substitute for market allocation; political "war" is the logical outcome as the various multiple users scramble for their shares, each claiming the moral high ground.

The symbiotic relationships between government programs and their farming, logging, ranching, and mining constituencies have a simple, but extremely important, consequence: they tend to hold in place a kind of antique economy anchored by the federal land base in the West. But clearly, these policies no longer serve the interests of most westerners. Again, here's Wilkinson:

> In field after field, the controlling legal rules, usually coupled with extravagant subsidies, simply do not square with the economic trends, scientific knowledge, and social values in the modern West. . . . These outmoded ideas pervade land and resource decision making in the West, far more so than in almost any other area of American public policy. This is the dead hand of the law at its most stultifying.[9]

Such relics and their defenders constitute what Wilkinson calls the "lords of yesterday"—tenacious political groups, institutions, and policies that refuse to die even though demographic, economic, and technological changes have eroded the original justifications for their existence.

These results should not surprise us, for they are not unique to environmental public policy. Public agencies are always hard to eliminate or remake, and laws are difficult to rescind when bureaucrats, businesses, or private citizens become dependent on them. Concentrated, motivated interest groups formed to preserve specific political benefits have significant advantages in struggles against more diffuse and disorganized groups, such as unorganized citizens of the West with a general interest in environmental quality. Moreover, institutional inertia retards or actually prevents laws, policies, and political institutions from changing along with a society's values and economy.[10]

Only when interest group pressures and institutional inertia are overcome and the various lords of yesterday are reformed or beaten will the most serious environmental abuses of the West end. But in the process, what will become of the Tedd Manns and Dave Trues? Will there be a place for them in the Next West?

A New West

The original cultural and economic values of the West grew from a particular interaction of natural endowments, technology, and knowledge about human interaction with nature. But cultural and economic conditions changed, and a new culture began to develop rapidly in the 1960s. This was concurrent with my time on Tedd's ranch.

Across time and across cultures, concern for environmental quality is fostered by rising incomes and better knowledge of how humans stress natural systems. In the West, the stage is now set for an economy in which environmental quality is extremely important. Entrepreneurs, businesses, and people with income independent of location are drawn increasingly to the West, to the extent that the West's environmental quality is both dependent on and the source of its future prosperity. Neither is possible without the other.[11]

With this in mind, let's consider factors contributing to a growing expression and indulgence of environmental affinity during the past century. First, scientific knowledge has increased. Greater knowledge of the natural world has taught us how human actions affect the environment and shown us some of the consequences. We know more about the adverse health effects of pollution, the destructive consequences of elk overpopulation in Yellowstone National Park, and the devastating impact of soil erosion on agricultural productivity, streams, and wildlife. New knowledge has sparked impassioned debate about the extent and causes of environmental problems.

Second, popular awareness of issues and problems grew tremendously in the 1960s and 1970s, and that awareness often resulted in environmental hysteria. The public's awakening to ecological problems was driven in part by publications such as Rachel Carson's *Silent Spring*[12] and the Club of Rome's *The Limits to Growth*[13] and by environmental catastrophes such as the toxic waste debacle at Love Canal. Environmental education widened as new scientific insights were brought to public awareness. However, we should not exaggerate the quality of popular understanding. Innumeracy, overestimation of small risks, and neglect of technological benefits seem to dominate popular culture. As in other areas of public policy, people seem to be well aware but ill informed.

Third, we have obvious and compelling evidence of humanity's growing impact on the environment. Until the twentieth century, with few exceptions, resources of the West seemed inexhaustible. Nature appeared to have the advantage. Today, the perception is that the tables have turned and nature is everywhere besieged by civilization. Desertification, aquifer depletion, destruction of salmon runs, and rampant pollution of all kinds have contributed to the perception that modern humanity everywhere destroys the environment. Although this impact is at times exaggerated, growing populations are unquestionably placing ever greater demands on nature, providing further reason for environmental concern.

But the existence of environmental problems and the fact that people enjoy pleasant vistas and wild places do not imply a lack of interest in other goods. This is especially true of the poor and materially insecure. In the past, we willingly gave up environmental quality to foster economic growth, often not even noticing the resulting harm to nature. To some extent, these same trade-offs still exist. An investment in environmental quality implies that it offers higher payoffs than more traditional forms of economic development. This varies by class, and it is disingenuous to pretend this link away. Environmentalism is an elite movement.

Trade-offs between economic activity and environmental protection have changed throughout the West. These changes are the essence of the New West, and they explain why behavior changes even when attitudes remain constant. There certainly have been loggers, farmers, and ranchers such as Tedd Mann who loved (and still love) the land. Many knew their livelihood was intimately connected to the continued health of the land. Nevertheless, their economic well-being depended on extracting or reshaping natural resources. For them, pristine nature and economic extraction were in conflict.

All this leads to our fourth factor. Compared with those living in earlier periods, more people in the contemporary West are relatively well educated and wealthy. Technological advances and growth in education and personal wealth correlate strongly with higher demand for outdoor recreation. As people become wealthier, their inclination for biking, boating, camping, cross-country skiing, fly-fishing, hiking, and similar pursuits increases. Their enjoyment depends in part on the quality of the natural environment. Heavily logged or clear-cut forests, polluted waters, and scarce wildlife greatly diminish the outdoor experience. Thus, recreational interests provide further impetus for environmental protection and wise stewardship.

Although outdoor recreation has an impact, it generally helps maintain environmental quality for another reason: it causes far less damage to the environment than strip-mining or clear-cutting. Motorized outdoor recreation and ski runs may have substantial impacts, but they are far less severe than those of the open pit mines near Butte, Montana, or the thousands of square miles of clear-cuts readily seen all across the Pacific Northwest.

Environmental protection and environmentally oriented recreation are far more important in people's lives than they were a century ago. The three dimensions of environmental concern weave together: people enjoy participating in the natural world; they now possess the knowledge to be more effective stewards; and the opportunity cost of using that knowledge is now relatively low.

These changes help explain how the West's cultural and economic future is inextricably linked to environmental quality. The West fulfills environmental longings better than most places; it is scenic and relatively unspoiled, and it possesses a revered tradition of active, outdoor lifestyles. Visitors, new residents, and new businesses are attracted by recreational opportunities, high quality of life, and ecologically friendly forms of economic development. "Greenness" has become more valuable than resource extraction.

In addition, the cost of living in remote places has declined dramatically. Falling costs of communication and transportation have strengthened the compatibility of economic activity and environmental protection and enhancement. Thirty years ago, Bozeman, Montana, and similar places were isolated from markets, culture, and urbanites. Today, Bozeman enjoys the advantages of twenty jet flights per day, Federal Express service, cheap telecommunications, satellite dish reception, grocery stores with huge selections—and a stream of interesting visitors.

The Changing Economics of Space

The emergence of environmental values makes the West attractive at a time when its extractive sectors offer steadily fewer economic opportunities. Many companies, such as the Boeing Company, Microsoft Corporation, and

Immunex Corporation in the Pacific Northwest, are drawn to or supported by a region's high-quality labor pool, which itself is attracted by the region's quality of life.

Political and business leaders recognize this relationship. Seattle's mayor, Norm Rice, observes, "If you destroy [Seattle's] physical beauty, you destroy the magnet that attracts people here."[14] And Boeing's chief executive officer, Frank Schrontz, says that Boeing remains in Seattle partly because of "the wealth of talent not keen on abandoning the mountains for [Wichita or Kansas City]."[15] The same reasoning holds for smaller western communities such as Boise, Idaho; Bozeman, Montana; and Bend, Oregon.

The emergence of new communication and transportation technologies heightens the effect of environmental values on traditional extractive activities. In some areas of the West, these technologies have completely eliminated dependence on extractive industries. They have made it possible for environmentally sensitive workers to move into beautiful but relatively remote western cities and towns. By allowing environmental quality to coexist with economic prosperity, these technologies are fundamentally altering the nature of the West's political economy. Power is shifting from those who own and move "stuff" to those who manipulate symbols.

Cheap, reliable transportation and communications have fueled the growth of highly specialized "footloose" manufacturing and service firms. Many are knowledge-intensive concerns relying on the skills of their workers to create or improve products or to move information, be it airline reservations, credit card data, or money management expertise. Others make highly specialized goods with high value-to-weight ratios. Products that are lightweight and easy to ship, unlike cars or steel, are increasingly made in remote areas. In Bozeman, Montana, alone, we find such firms as ILX Lightwave Corporation, manufacturer of electro-optics; Lattice Materials, manufacturer of silicon and germanium wafers; and TMA Technologies, manufacturer of industrial measurement equipment. Even firms with hard-to-move products can use advanced communications to coordinate facilities in widely scattered locations. Production and storage facilities can be placed near major transportation arteries while accounting, advertising, and management take place thousands of miles away. Freed from geographic constraints, firms can locate in places attractive to their environmentally conscious workers.

Increased mobility has also fostered a stunning rise in the number of retirees living in the West. They too are footloose, and they are eager to retire to places where the quality of life is high. With them come sources of so-called unearned income—pensions, retirement benefits, rents and royalties, and

Social Security payments. Such income from sources other than salaries and wages now accounts for 40 to 50 percent of the personal income in some of the region's communities.[16]

The shifting statistics on national forest uses offer further evidence of these tectonic changes across the West. For example, recreation accounted for 83 percent of the forest-based employment in the Greater Yellowstone area in 1987 and accounts for even more today. (The Greater Yellowstone includes mostly national forest lands in the three states immediately surrounding Yellowstone National Park: Montana, Idaho, and Wyoming.) Similarly, recreation provides 47 percent of forest-related jobs in the Lewis and Clark National Forest in west-central Montana, nowhere near a national park. Together, recreation- and community-oriented firms serving the new immigrants join footloose firms in providing the bulk of many communities' employment.

The switch from extraction to an economy driven by environmental quality is good for most people, but it does create losers as jobs and livelihoods disappear for some native westerners, particularly in smaller communities. Efforts to preserve and enhance environmental amenities will accelerate these trends.

All across the West, extractive industries constitute a low and falling percentage of total jobs and income. Volatility, minimal job creation due to increased automation, and few prospects for future growth cripple the outlook in all extractive sectors. In recent years, Montana has seen the closure of major copper smelters in Anaconda and Great Falls, 2,000 fewer jobs in the wood products industry, major debt and credit problems for farmers, and falling demand for coal and oil products. Since 1989, Idaho has suffered severe shrinkage in its metal-mining sector. Oregon and Washington lost 48,000 wood products jobs during the 1980s—largely independent of the controversy over protection of the northern spotted owl.

The impact of these losses can be devastating for individuals, families, and sometimes entire communities. Losses often fall disproportionately on workers, such as copper industry employees in Butte, Montana, and loggers in Forks, Washington, who had enjoyed several generations of relatively stable, high-paying, and rewarding employment. Years of economic stability and specialized training are often lost. Many have few other marketable skills, for most of their experience is specific to extracting resources from the land.

Many of the communities suffering the greatest losses belong to the traditional political constituencies of the USDA Forest Service, the Bureau of Land Management, and other governmental agencies. As a consequence, political repercussions follow. There is a predictable, often zealous effort to protect the power of the lords of yesterday and to insulate extractive lifestyles from market changes. As Secretary of the Interior Bruce Babbitt can well attest, the West's most deeply embedded interest groups can mobilize politically to prevent changes in institutions or laws that threaten them. Consider, for example, the nascent "wise use" movement, an ideological enemy of modern environmentalism. Wise use leaders are determined to slow, halt, and ultimately reverse environmental protection measures established in the past generation. Wise users argue that environmental laws and regulations are too costly, are inimical to private property rights, and are destructive of traditional lifestyles and livelihoods.

The wise use movement arose largely in response to regulations that constrain development. Its members oppose restrictions on grazing, hunting, mining, oil exploration, and off-road vehicle recreation. Their rhetoric exalts private property ownership and the free market, but in practice they seek to maintain established subsidies and deny legitimacy to "green" values and interests.

The West is a region built on subsidies and giveaways and costs pretended away. It is not a "nanny" state but rather a corrupt avuncular one. The rich Uncle Sam runs Ponzi schemes and sells adulterated products with false labels and rigged accounting. The beneficiaries receive cheap grazing rights, water, predator control, recreation, timber, and an endless stream of disaster payments. Those who tell truths regarding such issues are derided by all sides.

Wise use is not a fringe movement. Groups such as the Alliance for America, the National Inholders Association, and the Multiple Use Land Alliance boast over 10,000 members and a combined mailing list of 1.4 million names. [17] Emotions among their adherents run high. In one incident, a convoy organized to carry logs to a closed Montana mill was "26 miles long and people stood on the side of the road and waved American flags and cried." [18]

The emergence of a New West, propelled by new values and technology, is inhibited by those allied to the old. The threatened are not just loggers, miners, and graziers; they are also many average citizens of the West who have long profited from destructive but popular environmental policies. Their influence is augmented by the power of governmental agencies that safeguard traditional values and occupations at the expense of the new. Taken together, these lords of yesterday pose a formidable obstacle to a new western consensus. It is both prudent and sensitive to consider the impact of environmental policies on traditional economic activities.

And so we come to the heart of reform. Beyond the short run, the West will reap real benefits by restructuring the political institutions and laws that continue to encourage destructive extractive practices of the past. But in the process, people like Tedd Mann are likely to lose. If we lose them—and they truly are endangered as middle-class keepers of values—we'll have an impoverished West. This is the catch that so many environmentalists pretend away. It is disingenuous to describe the wise use movement merely as an outside force, a political creation of public affairs departments of big companies and their complements, for behind the acerbic rhetoric of wise use there are faces and lives like those of Tedd Mann and Dave True.

Institutions and Incentives in the West Today: The Lords of Yesterday

The critically important role political institutions play in environmental policy is often misunderstood. Damaging policies are seldom due to an absence of good information or good people. The principal problem of environmental stewardship, be it public or private, is that institutions create incentives for financially wasteful and environmentally destructive behavior. Additionally, our present economic arrangement does not capture all benefits of environmental quality or all costs of environmental harm. Thus, it *systematically undervalues* both costs and benefits.

If we change the incentives of public employees and private citizens and give them a stake in better management, we will see a decline in many environmental problems. Political institutions will once again be aligned with the practices and occupations that drive the West but will be in harmony with the newly green culture and economy.

How do incentives encourage destructive policies? First, many bureaucratic incentives promote extraction, typically because the budgets of federal land and water agencies are tied to the extraction of resources. The more they produce from the lands they manage, the larger their base of support.

Second, special interests have been created and nurtured by past bureaucratic policies. Dependent on federal largess, these interests vigilantly safeguard the continuation of their "welfare" benefits.

Third, well-intended, historically useful, but outdated legal principles remain in force, often because they are integral to holding certain property rights in place. Perhaps the best example is the doctrine of prior appropriation, the principal law governing the use of the West's scarce water. This antique doctrine safeguards a system of water rights; in some western states, the law's effect has been to inhibit all competing rights so that, for instance, water used for irrigation could not be transferred to other, less ecologically damaging uses. Embedded property rights are very difficult to displace.

Fourth, a lack of adequate information about how people value the environment often leads to shortsighted opposition to reforms that can improve environmental quality—even among dedicated environmentalists. For many years, major environmental groups such as The Wilderness Society and the Sierra Club opposed recreation fees on most public lands. Thus, the value of recreation was discounted and its potential influence on the budgets of land management agencies was mostly lost.

Finally, distorted incentives among bureaucrats and the extractive sectors they regulate are the norm. With massive public ignorance of how these incentives and relationships function, a new understanding of possible environmental–economic relationships has not emerged. Western opinion leaders have offered plenty of critiques but few realistic reforms.

The point about bureaucratic incentives is critically important. Following are some examples of how these incentives typically foster poor environmental practices.

PERVERSE FORESTRY

The Forest Service possesses powerful budgetary incentives that favor logging and road building over other national forest activities. One result is that the Forest Service owns eight and a half times as many miles of roads as are contained in the entire U.S. interstate highway system. Why? Because cutting trees, even at a loss, expands and justifies the agency's budget, and when the Forest Service sells timber, it customarily builds a road so that the buyer can access it (and then justifies the road building as a legitimate cost of forest management).

Nothing pads the Forest Service's budget like timber sales. And nothing motivates the agency more than its budget. In 1989, Forest Service Chief F. Dale Robertson admitted as much when he declared, "It's the budget that energizes the Forest Service." If there are changes in the way the agency is funded, there will be changes in the way national forests are managed.

The most important influences on the Forest Service's budget are the Knutson-Vandenburg Act of 1930 and the National Forest Management Act of 1976. Together, these allow the Forest Service to keep a percentage of the funds it receives from timber sales to "pursue reforestation, thinning, wildlife habitat improvement, and other activities." Perhaps a third of these funds become benefits for agency employees such as "salaries, rents, and travel [expenses]." The promise of "K-V" funds gives Forest Service bureaucrats a strong personal interest in selling even low-quality, remote, and economically unviable timber. Designed to maximize agency budgets, Forest Service policies encourage wasteful timber sales that cause significant ecological damage. Unless incentives are credited that allow the agency to benefit from promoting other values, these paradoxes will persist. To end the Forest Service's focus on building logging roads in national forests, the budgetary incentives encouraging roading and logging must be reduced or eliminated. Repealing the Knutson-Vandenberg Act would be a move in that direction.

A NATIONAL PARK MANAGEMENT PROBLEM

Distorted bureaucratic incentives are also the primary cause of the National Park Service's frequent mismanagement of the parks. Two substantial and well-documented threats to Yellowstone and Rocky Mountain National Parks appear to be tied to the agency's unique political pressures and institutional biases. Public resistance to the culling of elk herds and public anger over fire damage to park landscapes impose significant costs on park managers who carry out scientifically justifiable wildlife and fire management policies. The control of fires, in particular, is far from an exact science; mistakes and accidents are inevitable. Even a generally successful policy produces some failures, and the public (and Congress) tends to fixate on failures.

The short time horizons of park managers and their administrative and congressional overseers ensure that the long-term consequences of elk overpopulation and fire suppression are given less weight in policy decisions than are the public relations costs of culling and controlled burning. The public fallout from failures is high and immediate, whereas the consequences of ignoring the problem are safely in the future and easy to discount. Thus, ecologically beneficial policies are ignored or minimized.

THE FEDERAL GRAZING MUDDLE

The Bureau of Land Management's grazing fee subsidies have similar effects. With fees far below market rates and use restricted to domestic stocks, commercially unviable ranching and ecologically destructive overgrazing are inevitable. Taxpayers spend millions of dollars annually ($78 million in 1992) subsidizing grazing damage to public lands. Since the Bureau of Land Management (BLM) bears neither the financial nor the ecological costs of subsidies and overgrazing, it has little incentive to change its policies. The destructive effects of bureaucratic indifference are reinforced by ranchers who lobby their congressional representatives to keep the BLM on its present course. Presidential efforts to raise fees have been repeatedly thwarted by ranching interests and their allies. Would-be reformers within the BLM are at risk from political pressures. Jim Baca, former director of the BLM, was removed from his position by the Clinton administration for his advocacy of grazing and mining law reform on public rangeland. Baca's positions were vehemently opposed by many ranchers and miners who benefit from existing subsidies. Special interests created by political policies are much more difficult to eliminate than to establish. They play a major role in perpetuating ruinous and outdated political policies.

Institutional arrangements create further problems in the management of federal rangeland. The BLM sharply restricts the uses of it: essentially, people who have rights to federal rangeland can graze only domestic livestock. They cannot allow the land to lie fallow for more than a year and cannot let wildlife, rather than domesticated livestock, consume their allotment of grass and forbs. Moreover, since the use of these lands is a privilege rather than a legally protected right, ranchers cannot legally transfer their privileges to others who may want to use the land for something besides livestock. In essence, the BLM biases land use toward raising of domestic stock. Even when organizations such as The Nature Conservancy acquire grazing permits and attempt to retire land for ecological reasons, they are stripped of their privileges, which are then reallocated to those who will graze livestock.

WATER, WATER EVERYWHERE . . . NOW CAN WE RETHINK?

Special interest and budgetary pressures are also central to the operations of the Bureau of Reclamation. Farmers, bankers, and machinery and agricultural supply dealers support the agency's dam and canal building and subsequent sale of water to farmers at prices below delivery costs. These projects continue to be built even though the economically and geographically viable locations for dams were long ago exhausted; and in spite of evidence that they harm many species of fish and valuable riparian areas. Most of these dams are economically and environmentally wasteful, yet they continue to be supported for three reasons, all related to the incentives people are offered and the institutions or rules under which they operate.

First, farmers, especially those with water-intensive crops such as the rice farmers of California's Central Valley, want to preserve their access to cheap water. Price is often less than cost, and the beneficiaries want to keep it that way. Second, the Bureau of Reclamation needs dams to preserve its budget and thus its employees' salaries and power. Third, congressional representatives continue to propose and fund many of these projects as a visible way to bring pork home to their constituents—a way to keep the home district happy with jobs and cheap water or hydropower.

The Bureau of Reclamation further exacerbates water problems in the arid West by making it difficult for its "customers" to resell water to other users. For instance, farmers who use Bureau water usually cannot resell their surplus to municipal users. Primary users such as farmers are thus encouraged to use their entire allotment or to waste the portion they do not. If farmers were able to resell their water, they would have stronger incentives to conserve, thus increasing the efficiency of water use. Conservation incentives might also promote more sustainable irrigation practices such as drip irrigation, increasing the productive life span of valuable agricultural land. Moreover, conservation would leave greater reserves of water available to fish and other wildlife.

Outdated legal arrangements created by the doctrine of prior appropriation (a state, not a federal, legal construction) also create ecological and economic problems in western water policy. Prior appropriation grants people with the earliest water claims the primary right to use that water. Problems occur because people can lose their water rights unless they put their allotment to "beneficial use," a term traditionally meant to cover only extractive, diversionary, or commercial uses of water. Thus, legal claims to water historically have not included leaving water in rivers, streams, and lakes to protect ecological values. It is not uncommon for western rivers and streams—even valuable trout meccas such as Montana's famed Big Hole River—to be run completely dry during the heavy irrigation months of summer. The doctrine of prior appropriation virtually guarantees that this happens repeatedly.

Recent—post-1970—attempts to rectify this debacle have not fully resolved the dilemma presented by western water law, for even when states have granted rights for in-stream flows, they have often blocked provisions that would allow environmentalists to transfer "senior" water rights (the oldest, most viable rights) to new uses such as fish and wildlife protection. Granting in-stream flow rights but forcing them to remain "junior" has meant that in many cases, in-stream flows are never serviced during dry years. In the coy parlance of western water policy, in-stream flows are often "paper rights" that do not guarantee "wet water" during the dry years, when they are most needed to protect the ecological viability of rivers and streams. Once again, the settled interests of the West preserve the status quo while appearing to make grand concessions to the New West.

REFORM WILL COME HARD, IF AT ALL

Until the lords of yesterday—particularly the "iron triangle" of commodity interests, bureaucrats, and politicians—are overcome, they will continue to stifle the new culture and economics of the West. Reform, though difficult and complex, is not impossible. But if ignored, the assets that make the West attractive and valuable will continue to erode, assaulting deeply felt values, economic viability, and environmental quality.

And Then What?

Thus far I have dwelt on the West's many problems caused by rapacity and perverse policies and incentives. The region is well known for these, but it also possesses a robust tradition of resistance to environmental harm. Some of that resistance has been expressed in fine writing and environmental philosophy that attaches to the western landscape.

Unfortunately, among the West's articulate defenders there are many who seem fond of repeating the tired refrain that we North Americans should renounce materialism, live in voluntary simplicity, and adopt a culture and outlook similar to that of Native Americans and adherents of some Eastern religions.

This arcadian fantasy has been with us since Thoreau. Although its epicenter may have moved from Massachusetts to Montana, its followers have consistently confused their hopes with their expectations. Hopes for a greener environment have been linked with unrealistic expectations for environmentally friendly actions that are not closely bound to individual and institutional self-interest. However, there is encouraging evidence that some intellectual leaders of the West have at last begun to learn.

Kris L. Hardin, professor of anthropology at the University of Pennsylvania and a summer resident of Livingston, Montana, relates how, after returning from an extended visit to Africa, she was initially overwhelmed by the wastefulness of American life.[19] But over time, self-interested choices compelled her to adopt these "wasteful" ways. Even the well-intentioned are usually unable to escape the gravitational imperatives of self-interest. Her story illustrates the norm, not the exception.

Many others, writers included, still seem ignorant of how institutional incentives can channel and distort individual action. They rely on a green Platonic despot, an eco-Cincinnatus or a Bruce Babbitt, to use state power to set things right. An increasingly pressing question is how many will escape this mental bondage and articulate a coherent and realistic new vision for the West.

Institutional reforms can realign the incentives and information available to decision makers in business and government agencies with emerging environmental goals. Indeed, there is a great potential for the West's strongest economic, cultural, and political interests to support environmental protection. But the relationship between economic growth and individual self-interest is much more complex than often portrayed by either environmentalists or their critics. The success of efforts to "green" the West will be heavily influenced by how well the region's leading scientists and opinion leaders understand economic and political institutions. Many of them have traditionally been co-opted by federal agencies and private interests.

In considering this, let's return to the L.A.K.

Meanwhile, Back at the Ranch

People who knew Dave True would understand why it's so much easier to deal with winners than with whiners. Dave was a smart, quiet, generous, and gracious leader. He was respected and admired by associates, and I would be most surprised if he were not loved by family and friends.

I would not be surprised if Tedd Mann were equally smart and, at a time when it mattered, worked equally hard. But he was playing in a different game. Tedd ran a modest but proud family ranch. He knew much about its history and the animals on it; he introduced wild turkeys to it, lived lightly on it, took little, knew much. Financially, he was always on the edge. There were a lot of things he didn't get to do and, no doubt, some things he did that he wished he hadn't.

Although I certainly don't know what the Next West will be, I am sure it will be much impoverished if it's shy of people like my friends Tedd and Dave. The lifeways and livelihoods these two men pursued and, perhaps, perfected may be fading into eclipse, but I sincerely hope that their fundamental ethics and values, and their profound grip on hard reality, will not. Perhaps watching the moves of Dave and Tedd can offer us some clues as we search for new ways to harmonize personal liberty and environmental quality in the West.

Each man in his own way was a steward, and each accepted full responsibility for his actions and decisions. Both men were engaged in moving what I like to think of as the furniture of the world—real stuff like oil and cattle and all that goes with them: steel pipelines, thumper trucks and derricks, stock racks and grain sacks, and old, squeaky leather. Each man secured his claim on the land through a network of rights and privileges, and, I believe, each took those very seriously. Both men trusted society to hold those rights and privileges in place, for without them there is no certainty, and without certainty, the sense of responsibility can easily begin to ebb, grain by grain.

It's important to understand the difference between stewardship that grows from personal risk and gain and stewardship that is conferred by statutory mandate. It's equally important to understand the risks inherent in a bureaucratized West—one in which key decisions are made not by the people whose very lives will reflect the consequences but by those whose actions are always insulated, who live in a world of institutionalized irresponsibility.

The economy of the West is moving inexorably away from its old dependence on natural resource extraction, and a lot of that movement will have good environmental results. But we must take pains to be sure that the emerging economy does not arrive wrapped in bureaucratic insulation. One way to do this is to extend property rights carefully into the public land domain while cutting back those incentives and hidden subsidies that wreak environmental destruction.

For example, we could work to change grazing privileges into secure and transferable rights. These rights to use federal land could be bought and sold as clear property rights to forage. To prevent environmentally destructive uses, the sale of grazing rights might incorporate deed restrictions limiting how they could be used. If such rights were created, ranchers could use the lands more imaginatively as they sought to maximize their individual interests. They could retire and rest overgrazed land without fear of losing their rights. Environmental and wildlife organizations such as the Rocky Mountain Elk Foundation and the North American Wild Sheep Foundation could buy rights and reserve the land for wildlife habitat.

In addition, across the West we could "marketize" water rights through a leasing system (similar to one enacted in Montana in 1995) that protects valuable senior rights, leaving those rights in the hands of agricultural families but allowing the families to lease water to conservation groups during extremely dry years for the purpose of protecting rivers and streams.

Moreover, we could greatly expand experiments with nonprofit public land trusts—citizen boards empowered with decision-making authority pertaining to specific tracts of public land. These would be run by boards of directors from a variety of environmental, academic, and business backgrounds. People with the rich local knowledge of a Tedd Mann would be vital members of such trusts. Citizen boards would have to be financially independent of the federal government, insulated as much as possible from transitory political pressures.

In considering the future, we should recognize that in today's West those who deal with real stuff, the concrete furniture of the world, and those who broker symbols rarely engage one another in any positive and meaningful way. This lack of genuine communion is perhaps our greatest shortcoming as we struggle to create a new future for the West. Dave True and Tedd Mann and many others like them represent, among other virtues, generalized competence blended with high integrity, deep experience with the land, and good humor. I would like to help pass on a West where these values still count in a world that gives greater rewards to experts in symbol manipulation. Bridges between people like Dave and Tedd and those who interpret our evolving culture would be valuable. Indeed, a few well-constructed bridges of this kind might be worth far more than a haystack heap of all our recent policy proposals combined.

NOTES

1. See generally Bernard De Voto, *Across the Wide Missouri* (Boston: Houghton Mifflin, 1992); Wallace Stegner, *Where the Bluebird Sings to the Lemonade Springs: Living and Writing in the West* (New York: Random House, 1992); and Charles F. Wilkinson, *Crossing the Next Meridian: Land, Water, and the Future of the West* (Washington, D.C.: Island Press, 1992).

2. Charles F. Wilkinson, *The Eagle Bird: Mapping a New West* (New York: Pantheon Books, 1992), ix.

3. Stegner, *Where the Bluebird Sings,* xvii, xv.

4. Wilkinson, *The Eagle Bird,* 136.

5. George C. Coggins and Charles F. Wilkinson, *Federal Public Land and Resources Law* (Mineola, N.Y.: Foundation Press, 1981), 334.

6. Congressional Quarterly, *The Battle for Natural Resources* (Washington, D.C.: Congressional Quarterly, 1983), 175.

7. Wilkinson, *Crossing the Next Meridian,* 93.

8. Congressional Quarterly, *The Battle for Natural Resources,* 66.

9. Wilkinson, *Crossing the Next Meridian,* xiii.

10. See generally M. Olson, *The Rise and Decline of Nations* (New Haven, Conn.: Yale University Press, 1982).

11. Thomas Michael Power, "Avoiding the Passive/Helpless Approach to Economic Development," *Forest Watch* 10, no. 4 (1989): 16–18.

12. Rachel Carson, *Silent Spring* (New York: Fawcett Books, 1962).

13. Donella H. Meadows et al., *The Limits to Growth: A Report on the Club of Rome's Project on the Predicament of Mankind* (New York: Universe Books, 1972).

14. B. Saporito "Best Cities for Business," *Fortune* 126, no. 10 (1992): 43.

15. Ibid.

16. Montana Department of Commerce, 1992.

17. C. P. Alexander, "Gunning for the Greens," *Time* 139, no. 5 (1992): 50–54.

18. M. Dolan, "Bush Woos West by Trying to Ease Land Restrictions," *Los Angeles Times*, 4 August 1992.
19. Kris L. Hardin, "Symbols," in *Sacred Trusts: Essays on Stewardship and Responsibility*, ed. Michael Katakis (San Francisco: Mercury House, 1993), 21–29.

CHAPTER SEVEN

Saving the Marketplace from the Market

One View of the New Resource Economics

MARK SAGOFF

What most impressed French statesman and social philosopher Alexis de Tocqueville during his 1835 visit to America was the extent to which Americans put aside their private interests to participate in achieving the common good. He observed that every public concern bred a voluntary association. "Americans of all ages, all stations of life, and all types of dispositions, are forever forming associations," de Tocqueville reported.[1] And Americans debated every issue publicly. "Even the women," he added, "often go to the public meetings and forget household cares while they listen to political speeches."[2]

De Tocqueville understood the arguments with which Federalists such as John Randolph, James Madison, and Alexander Hamilton had convinced the nation to accept the United States Constitution and thus a strong national government. At the same time, he also respected the arguments of the Anti-Federalists. In that spirit, he praised the way townships—local governmental entities—promoted civic virtue in the hearts and minds of citizens: "[M]unicipal institutions constitute the strength of free nations.

Town-meetings are to liberty what primary schools are to science; they bring it within the people's reach, they teach men how to use and how to enjoy it."³ Local jurisdictional governments and voluntary associations—for example, church groups and fire brigades—impressed de Tocqueville as the idiosyncratic and successful strategy by which Americans solved everyday problems of living, problems that typically required face-to-face contact and cooperation.

The spirit of voluntarism that characterized the American polity in the nineteenth century is still found today, although, as de Tocqueville feared, the growing strength and authority of the national government has come to dwarf and to some extent displace the activities of smaller jurisdictions and voluntary associations. De Tocqueville described the tension between two great systems of governance, one centered in federal agencies and the other in local jurisdictions and citizen associations. The great feat of democracy, he believed, is to divide power and responsibility among individuals, local and state jurisdictions, and the national government.

The Lure of "Devolution"

The role of local governments and associations in solving environmental problems has captured the attention of resource economists, nature writers, geographers, anthropologists, and others who believe that local groups, associations, and jurisdictions are better situated than the federal government to solve most problems related to land use, resource allocation, pollution, and the like.⁴ These writers apply to environmental matters many of the principles of decentralization and "devolution" of power to local authority invoked by other social commentators to reform federal welfare, housing, education, and other bureaucracies. "By devolution," write Terry Anderson and Peter Hill of the Political Economy Research Center (PERC), "we mean returning standard-setting and policy-making to lower levels of individuals. Devolution will advance federalism, the term traditionally used to describe powers distributed among the state governments rather than the federal government in Washington, D.C."⁵

Economists associated with groups such as PERC and the Foundation for Research on Economics and the Environment (FREE), who sometimes identify themselves as "new resource economists,"⁶ have framed theoretical arguments and described historical examples to show how federal control over lands in the West tends to frustrate the aspirations not only of user groups but also of environmentalists and others dedicated to preserving the beauty and history of particular places. These resource economists generally share the belief that much of the federal government's authority over public lands should be reassigned to states and other local jurisdictions. As one FREE researcher summarizes, by "integrating communities into environmental policy, [we may] not only strengthen certain weaknesses in strictly economic approaches [but also] overcome . . . bureaucratic inertia."[7]

These economists and environmentalists argue that distant bureaucracies seldom can be held accountable for the consequences of the policies they pursue. They point to unfunded mandates as examples of how Washington announces the good news—for example, that a watershed will become perfectly clean—while leaving the local jurisdiction to deal with the bad news— namely, the cost.[8] Critics of federal land management describe instances in which federal authorities have prevented loggers, farmers, and other property owners from using their land in profitable ways that cause no harm of a sort cognizable in tort.[9] Federal bureaucracies, these analysts contend, respond not to the concerns of small landowners but to political forces brought to bear in Washington. Accordingly, management of western lands reflects the efforts of lobbyists in the nation's capital rather than the values of these citizens most concerned with and tied to those lands.

These critics of federal control have also mounted an important critique of land management imperatives that are based on abstract principles drawn from the science du jour, whether it is the latest advances in "contingent valuation" of environmental goods associated with conventional environmental economics or the succession of mathematical breakthroughs and paradigm shifts that characterize community and systems ecology. New resource economists deplore as specious and self-serving "scientific" arguments such as these—whether founded in welfare economics or in systems ecology—used to lend credibility or legitimacy to decisions that are plainly motivated by political interests.

New resource economists repeat a warning first sounded by Patrick D. Moynihan in 1965 concerning what he called "the professionalization of reform."[10] According to Moynihan, social progress requires a stirring of the public conscience and a shared sense of collective morality and responsibility at the local level. This public moral commitment may dissipate as the provision of social services becomes entrusted more and more to professionals who appeal to science as the reason why they should have their way. The same analysis applies to environmental problem solving. Communities may best deal with environmental issues by enlisting the commitments of individuals and local associations to preserve the natural characteristics that create the spirit or sense of place where they live. Such moral commitments sometimes cannot survive the onslaught of technical expertise that eventually absorbs available resources in an effort to get the ecological or economic analysis right.

On the following pages, I will discuss and defend the criticisms new resource economists mount against the idea they associate with the progressive era: "that benevolent, unbiased scientists should manage resources. This philosophy is termed scientific management and represents the sylvan analogue to the quest for a Platonic despot."[11] The authors I shall cite add that scientific managers at such agencies as the USDA Forest Service, the National Park Service, and the Bureau of Land Management "assume that the problem of finding optimal resource allocations is scientific and technical, unaffected by subjective valuations and the political process. . . . With the institutionalization of this ideology, a caste of resource management despots was born in the United States."[12] New resource economists criticize both mainstream environmental economics and system and community ecology for being handmaidens of economic interests and political positions rather than independent sciences. "Despite claims to the contrary, bureaucratic scientists cannot escape subjectivity and politicization, and their science degenerates into the pursuit of special interests of their own and others."[13]

A Critique of Mainstream Environmental Economics

As a critical project, the new resource economics seeks to debunk much of what passes for environmental science. The essence of the mainstream scientific approach is the contention that since third-party effects, or "externalities," are pervasive and ubiquitous—markets often fail to reflect in prices paid for goods and services the full costs of producing, consuming, and disposing of them—scientific managers can be trusted to allocate resources more efficiently than would be done through free or consensual exchange. Fred L. Smith, Jr. of the Competitiveness Enterprise Institute has written: "In a world of pervasive externalities—that is, a world where all economic decisions have environmental effects—this analysis demands that all economic decisions be politically managed."[14]

Of course, it is true that there is hardly a transaction, however intimate or private, for which an inventive economist cannot plausibly find myriad external effects. E. K. Hunt, a radical critic of mainstream economics, emphasizes this point:

> Since the vast majority of productive and consumptive acts are social, . . .
> it follows that they will involve externalities. Our table manners in a

restaurant, the general appearance of our house, our yard or our person, our personal hygiene, the route we pick for a joy ride, the time of day we mow our lawn, or nearly any one of a thousand ordinary daily acts, all affect, to some degree, the pleasures or happiness of others. The fact is . . . externalities are totally pervasive.[15]

In *Free Market Environmentalism*, Terry Anderson and Donald Leal attack mainstream environmental economics, particularly the assertion that because of the pervasiveness of externalities and other impediments (such as high transaction costs), free markets fail systematically and pervasively to allocate resources to the highest would-be bidders. The mainstream approach, they point out, "has been premised on the assumption that markets are responsible for resource misallocation and environmental degradation."[16] Mainstream economists then call on the government to correct these market failures by setting prices in ways that will reflect the "true" worth of those resources. Mainstream economists conclude, as they must from these premises, that expert managers (presumably themselves) rather than free markets ultimately ought to be in charge of allocating environmental goods and services.

Anderson and Leal conclude correctly that mainstream resource economics advocates a kind of collectivism: the view that society has a common goal—namely, efficiency in the allocation of resources,—of which these scientists are the appropriate guardians. Anderson and Leal summarize their criticism as follows:

> To counter market failures, centralized planning is seen as a way of aggregating information about social costs and social benefits in order to maximize the value of natural resources. Decisions based on this aggregated information are to be made by disinterested resource managers whose goal is to maximize social welfare.[17]

Anderson, Leal, and Smith rightly believe that mainstream resource economists, by finding market failure everywhere, build a case for a centralized economy. At Resources for the Future, for example, mainstream economists Allen Kneese and Blair Bower noted as early as 1972 this consequence of the neoclassical, or Pigouvian, paradigm. Free markets, they argued, "developed on the presumption that virtually everything of value is suitable for private ownership with little or no 'spillover' to other persons, households, and firms." They added: "Of course, it was realized that sometimes adjustments had to be made for 'market failure,' but these were implicitly, if not explicitly, regarded as minor with respect to the overall allocation."[18]

The principal idea behind the approach mainstream economists advocate lies in the conviction that markets are so riddled with flaws and failures that they rarely if ever allocate natural resources to the uses people most prefer as measured by their willingness to pay. Kneese and Bower, who pioneered the externality approach, wrote that by the 1960s it had become clear "that the pure private property concept applies satisfactorily to a progressively narrowing range of natural resources and economic activities." Market failure was pervasive. If environmental resources were to be allocated efficiently, the government must allocate them. "Private property and market exchange," they concluded, "have little applicability to their allocation, development, and conservation."[19]

New resource economists offer several reasons, four of which are most important, for questioning the aspiration of mainstream economists to get the prices of natural resources "right" by scientific surveys and other "objective" investigations. First, these critics of the mainstream approach argue that free markets encourage individuals to take responsibility for their own choices rather than to seek favors from or lay blame on an all-powerful government. As soon as the government, in the name of correcting market failures, seeks to establish the "correct" value of resources, individuals will spend their time and energy in trying to influence public officials rather than in bargaining with one another. Second, markets function marvelously well in gathering information not available to any public official or agency. In the 1940s, political economist Friedrich Hayek argued that the principal advantage of a market is not the organization of self-interest but the organization of knowledge. Markets thus address "the constitutional limits of man's knowledge and interests, the fact that he cannot know more than a tiny part of the whole society."[20]

Political economists in the tradition of Hayek doubt that centralized planners or scientific managers can either master enough information or detach themselves sufficiently from their own interests and prejudices to allocate resources better than individuals themselves will through voluntary systems of exchange. Hayek notes that the practice of experts to refer to the wants or preferences of individuals either

as "data" or as "given" (or even by the pleonasm of "given data") often leads economists to assume that this knowledge exists not merely in dispersed form but that the whole of it might be available to some single mind. This conceals the character of competition as a discovery procedure.[21]

Third, critics of the mainstream position observe that an environmental economist would have no trouble at all identifying thousands of externalities and other instances of market failure that "show" that any project at all is economically inefficient—that the benefits do not equal the costs, or that the reverse is true. A project might be "inefficient," for example, because it would affront the aesthetic, moral, or cultural beliefs of environmentalists, who therefore may be assumed to be willing to pay to prevent it. Thus, mainstream economists magically convert into data for cost-benefit balancing all the political and moral views opposing that centralized approach to policy making.

Fourth, economists themselves incur costs in undertaking cost-benefit analyses and employing other techniques to determine how much individuals will pay for public goods in hypothetical markets. These costs mount as economists are hired as expert witnesses in litigation over dueling cost-benefit analyses. For example, the cost of determining the value of even a single oil-soaked otter may be unlimited as long as "deep pockets" are willing to pay for contending estimates. Since there is no ideal market against which one can test predictions about what would occur in the absence of market failures, disagreements over the "correct" price of any resource are unresolvable in principle.

During the 1960s and 1970s, environmentalists found that the externality argument gave them instant legitimacy within the established legal and scientific culture. Accordingly, environmentalists redescribed their deontological—that is, ethical and cultural—values, ideals, and commitments in terms of spillovers, welfare, and willingness to pay. Those who were deeply and legitimately motivated by spiritual or moral tenets opposed to a utilitarian ethic found themselves locked in the language of contemporary utility theory. Fred Smith, Jr. notes wryly that the impetus for the "market failure" approach to regulation was entirely self-serving. It came primarily "from economists desperately eager to play a more significant role in environmental policy and environmental groups seeking to gain the support of conservatives."[22]

A Critique of Ecology as Law

In his recent book *In a Dark Wood*, Alston Chase describes what he calls the "tyranny of ecology."[23] He discusses in particular the effect of the Endangered Species Act (ESA), which, he argues, embraced the view associated with ecologists such as G. E. Hutchinson and Eugene Odum that groups of

137

organisms in nature form "systems" or "communities" defined by feedback loops that promote their self-regulation and persistence. The ESA, Chase writes, "made Hutchinson's model, nurtured by government and popularized by [environmental activist Barry] Commoner, the law of the land."[24]

Chase argues that mainstream ecological scientists of this century built their theory on equilibria concepts, including the ancient notion of the balance of nature, "not because the evidence supported it but because their mathematics demanded it."[25] Once nature was perceived to exhibit a balanced order rather than a random patchiness—once the ideal of stability replaced the reality of flux—"the ecosystem idea would have implications far transcending science."[26] It would provide a rationale for extending through law the power of professional managers over public and, to a lesser extent, private land in the West, for they could claim to understand the ecological science, of which local users may be ignorant.

Critics of the application of "balance of nature" ecology to environmental law have pointed to a range of reasons for doubting that there is much real science to be applied. First, the concept of the ecosystem is so inchoate and indeterminate that it is little more than a will-o'-the-wisp. Karl Hess, Jr., in his influential book *Visions Upon the Land*, observes that ecosystems, "however defined, are still fuzzy concepts, lacking discrete boundaries that might otherwise allow separation of smaller from larger units."[27] Hess describes the demise of the picture of ecosystems as organized communities and the ascent of "an altogether different world—a natural world characterized more by indeterminacy and disturbance than by climax and predictability."[28]

Since the early 1980s, ecologists have repeatedly debunked the view associated with Frederic Clements, G. E. Hutchinson, and E. P. Odum that groups of organisms in nature form systems or communities defined by feedback loops that strongly promote their self-regulation and persistence. Critics of this view object that no one has shown that competition or any other factor significantly influences the structuring of communities; hence, "null models" of random interaction are as predictive as any.[29] Others contend that the ways in which species interact provide a comparatively poor basis for classifying organisms.[30] Ecologist E. D. McCoy and philosopher K. S. Sreder-Frechette conclude, "No one had established that whatever community 'structure' might be thought to exist is stable in the way a self-regulating feedback system should be." As a result, these commentators write, "ecologists called into question foundational community concepts, particularly in the field of ecosystems ecology."[31]

Despite the persistence of popular belief in the "balance of nature," ecologists over the past two decades have all but abandoned equilibria assumptions. "Wherever we seek to find constancy, we discover change," Daniel Botkin observes in a book written as an epitaph for equilibria theories. We find "that nature undisturbed is not constant in form, structure, or proportion, but changes at every scale of time and place."[32] This Heraclitean view of nature—asserting that one cannot visit the same ecosystem twice—may be the only approach that can be justified without a leap of faith. Environmental historian Donald Worster summarizes, "Nature, many have begun to believe, is *fundamentally* erratic, discontinuous, and unpredictable. It is full of seemingly random events that elude models of how things are supposed to work."[33] He concludes: "Nature should be regarded as a landscape of patches, big and little, patches of all textures and colors, a patchwork quilt of living things, changing continually through time and space, responding to an unceasing barrage of perturbations. The stitches in the quilt never hold for long."[34]

Critics offer a second reason to doubt appeals to ecology as a basis for governmental control of land use. If the term ecosystem or community is to be predicated on any collection of objects over time, there must be a way of telling when this collection is the same community or ecosystem first observed and when it has evolved or changed into a different one. After all, ecosystems do not simply disappear; they turn into other ecosystems. Accordingly, we must have concepts—that is, a classificatory scheme—that enables us to determine when a collection of creatures and conditions remains the same ecosystem (even though its qualities change) and when it has been replaced by another ecosystem of a different kind (because disrupting forces were too great).

This is an important conceptual condition for doing ecology because without it, crucial notions such as resilience and stability would have no meaning. If we cannot sort ecosystems and communities into natural kinds, we have no basis for interpreting the same phenomena in the same ways. Indeed, any observation could be used both to confirm and to disconfirm the same hypothesis, depending on whether one chooses to say that the ecosystem soldiers on under the particular stress or that it has collapsed and been replaced by a different ecosystem.

Third, critics note that since ecosystems are always in flux—they change greatly due to natural causes over periods of time—there is no historical point at which we can say that a biological community is in the "original" condition to which it should be restored. Since ecosystems have been altered dramatically everywhere human beings are found, what do we use as a baseline? Where in the flux of a biological community do we take a snapshot and say, "Here it is in equilibrium"? All we really observe is change; it is impossible to set out a baseline condition when the ecosystem was most truly itself, in which condition it should be maintained or to which it should be restored.

Finally, a fourth argument may persuade us not to take the ecosystem or community concept seriously as a basis for policy making. Suppose for a moment that ecologists in the tradition of Clements, Hutchinson, and Odum are correct in believing that ecosystems and communities exist as equilibria or as otherwise strongly ordered and intelligible arrangements of flora, fauna, and other components. We must then ask how this order or structure came to be. How is it caused? Although random mutation and natural selection explain the evolution of organisms that breed true, systems that do not reproduce—artifacts such as pianos or clocks come to mind as examples—must be explained in terms of an external cause, such as a piano maker or a watch maker. We lack a theory to explain how heredity can operate at the level of ecosystems. Without reference to a Creator, no cause can be offered to account for the order—the stability, resilience, integrity, structure, unity, balance, and so on—ecosystems and biotic communities are said to possess. But how else do they achieve such cohesiveness?

As Kenneth B. Cumming, chairman of the biology department at the Institute for Creation Research, has written, God's work is evident in "the hierarchical design of living systems especially in organization, cycles, and homeostasis. . . . These properties support the creationist perspective and conflict with evolution, which requires randomness, non-directional progression, and liberal opportunity for change."[35] The dilemma is obvious: we may wish to assert that there is design in ecosystems, but we may not want to commit to the notion of a divine designer.

The Role of the Human Community

Although new resource economists mount a powerful attack on the weaknesses inherent in policies based on ecosystem theory and on mainstream environmental economics, their views are not all negative. If the new resource economics has a principal constructive thesis, it is this: "To minimize the costs of monitoring federal agencies, authority should devolve to the lowest level of government that also allows for the control of pollution or other spillover effects."[36] Two further principles are also central. First, solutions to environmental problems should often be sought by establishing property rights in the relevant resources so that those who own those resources will both value and care for them. Second, we should recognize "the potential for voluntary nonmarket groups to meet a significant portion of the national demand for environmental protection."[37]

In emphasizing the difference between distant and local authority, new resource economists distinguish between what one might call the market and the marketplace. Virtually all economists who study the function of markets emphasize the global reach of abstract trading networks reflected, for example, in the vagaries of computer-driven commodities and stock exchanges. The marketplace, in contrast, includes all voluntary or uncoerced problem-solving activity, often involving the exchange of time, goodwill, effort, or money, that takes place or could in principle take place on a face-to-face basis among people whose relationships are more enduring than the transactions that occur between them.

Geographers may separate the market from the marketplace by invoking a distinction they have made familiar between space and place. The market is global, abstract, and impersonal; it exists in what geographers refer to as space, as visualized, for example, in the trading networks over which computers exchange securities or speculate on future prices of commodities. Global markets exist in cyberspace; capital flows with the speed of light. Economies of scale require that everyone everywhere want and buy the same things; brands such as Nike and Reebok are sold everywhere in place of local offerings. One commentator describes global market forces as market forces that "mesmerize the world with fast music, fast computers, and fast food— with MTV, Macintosh, and McDonald's, pressing nations into one commercially homogeneous global network: one McWorld tied together by technology, ecology, communications, and commerce."[38]

The marketplace, in contrast, always has ties to a particular location: it differs from "One Big Market" (as economic historian Karl Polanyi described it)[39] in that the individuals involved are not anonymous to one another. Local resources often bring individuals together into communities— logging communities, farming communities, resort communities, university communities—in which they can cooperate as well as compete. These communities seek to remain economically viable even when faraway competitors underprice them in the context of global markets. And they seek to maintain some control over and responsibility for their environment when distant authorities, corporate or governmental, would wrest control from them. Such communities might hope to substitute the logic of the marketplace for that of the market; they might try to find in what is unique to their culture, geography, or environment a basis for their cultural identity and economic survival. Wherever these groups develop and flourish, they can and do protect local landscapes. Home owners who form associations to preserve common land, ranchers who protect wildlife on their ranges, hunters and anglers who protect the quality of game and streams (organizations such as Ducks Unlimited and Trout Unlimited come to mind), farmers who enter into voluntary covenants and easements to set aside their landscapes from development, and many other owners and users of natural resources have repeatedly shown themselves willing to enter into voluntary associations and agreements to protect those resources as public rather than as private goods, even at some cost to themselves. Those who are close to nature and natural resources take pride in the character of the places they inhabit; they care as communities, not just as individuals, about the quality of those places and the integrity of the natural resources in them.

To examine the possibilities for and impediments to local environmental initiatives, the new resource economics calls attention to the capacity of communities to solve problems through the marketplace—that is, through voluntary local cooperative activities. Karl Hess, Jr. for example, recalls Charles Murray's conception of the "vital 'tendrils of community'—families, neighborhoods, churches, and voluntary associations—[which] were being steadily displaced by intrusive laws and distant governments."[40] Hess describes the creative force of local and voluntary environmentalism, based on "the politics of decentralism—the raucous debates of a New England town meeting as well as the voluntary negotiations between landowners and concerned neighbors wishing to make the land healthier and more fruitful for both people and wildlife."[41]

Hess advocates a political rather than a scientific approach to identifying and solving environmental problems. (Of course, a scientific approach is itself political, since scientific debates so often shadow political ones.) To be sure, technical know-how is useful once political questions are settled, which is to say, once the community knows what it wants to achieve. The progressive faith in professionalism and expertise, in contrast, assumes that science itself can be normative—that it can determine the goals of society, such as restoring market or ecological equilibria. For these progressive sciences, there is a "perfect" market or a "balanced" ecosystem somewhere to be achieved or sustained. This approach empowers scientific managers with the "optimistic assumption that people and nature [are] malleable building blocks readily shaped and formed by engineers."[42] Hess and other writers criticize the technocratic approach of federal land management agencies precisely because it resists political give-and-take: these agencies create a smoke screen of expertise to shield themselves from political review and reform.

The constructive project of the new resource economics lies in designing local political or other management bodies that can supervise resource use in a way that is responsive to the concerns of those who use, know, and care about those resources. This is not the same thing as leaving the disposition of the land to market forces alone. On the contrary, responsibility for the quality of natural environments, new resource economists contend, should vest first with those who have made the commitment of living in or near them. This argues for decentralized and responsive political and social authority, as distinct from a laissez-faire market in which everything—parks, forests, ranches, whatever—is offered for sale to the highest bidder.

The New Resource Economics as an Institutional Economics

In his last book, *Where the Bluebird Sings to the Lemonade Springs*, Wallace Stegner joined a century-old populist tradition in condemning the predatory corporations—particularly mining companies—that exploit the landscape of the West. But he saved his greatest ire for that other target of populism, the federal government. Stegner correctly traced many—possibly most—of the environmental woes of the West to governmental decisions and projects such as "highways, and the federally financed dams, and the write-offs against flood control, and the irrigation water delivered at a few dollars an acre-foot." Stegner wrote: "Your presence as absentee landlord offends us, Uncle," and he cited "grazing fees and coal and oil lease fees and timber sale prices . . . so low they amount to a fat subsidy."[43] Like many western authors, Stegner noted that political forces can be as destructive as market forces when exerted from afar.

Many westerners are sensitive to the power of federal bureaucracy, since it controls vast amounts of land in the West. Local residents condemn, for example, the way the federal government appeals to the lowest common denominator to attract the greatest number of visitors to Yellowstone and other national parks. This well-founded criticism of the government may concede, however, that the Walt Disney Company might market Yellowstone much as the federal government has done. Indeed, Bambi provides a model that characterizes the way any distant authority—whether governmental or corporate—might market and therefore manage wildlife. Local people who know the forests, the savannas, the prairies, and the plains will be brushed aside in favor of the science du jour or the current fashion in retailing nature to transient consumers.

The new resource economics argues that current policies for managing the resources of the arid West are not working. Political economists of this school therefore remind us of the original problem envisioned by the founders of this nation. For them, the challenge was to build institutions that would facilitate the ability of individuals to join together and make choices while ensuring that they would be held responsible for the outcomes of these choices. One of the most effective ways to do this, assert analysts in the tradition of Thomas Jefferson, would be to make local landowners responsible for the decisions that affect their lands. This is exactly the reverse of the situation today, which amounts to a hegemony of absentee landlords presiding over various fiefdoms—for example, the Forest Service, the Bureau of Land Management, the Park Service, and so on. There are plenty of absentee landlords on private lands as well.

The new resource economics seeks to show how individuals and groups in the West can make responsible decisions for western resources rather than abdicating that responsibility to absentee landowners. As a constructive discipline, the new resource economics may be seen as a kind of institutional economics. It analyzes the systems of incentives that determine behavior and proposes voluntary arrangements more likely to manage resources effectively and to maintain the integrity of the environment.

Many of the specific suggestions offered by new resource economists are well worth trying. John Baden and Richard Stroup, for example, have proposed that "land presently included in the wilderness system be put into the hands of qualified environmental groups such as the Sierra Club, the Audubon Society and the Wilderness Society."[44] The point of such suggestions is not to turn public places into private property, although under the Baden–Stroup proposal, environmental groups would own wilderness areas in fee simple. The point is to make a representative body accountable for the consequences of its decisions so that interested individuals and groups can present arguments on the merits to their peers rather than be turned away because they lack the necessary professional credentials or scientific expertise.

The new resource economist confronts an interesting dilemma when market forces rather than political ones threaten the "sense of place" of the West. Some skeptics have suggested that if the best private land (or public land, for that matter) went up for auction, local buyers would not be able to outbid Hollywood celebrities, famous athletes, dude ranch operators, and religious cults, who would then buy up the land. The best land in Montana, for example, may simply be worth more to those wishing to train adepts in New Age metaphysics than to those who raise cattle. (The Church Universal and Triumphant already owns tens of thousands of acres neighboring Yellowstone National Park.) Yet the way one might resist these market forces—by appealing to ecological science to define natural communities in need of protection—is precisely what new resource economists condemn. That sort of appeal simply replaces one New Age metaphysics with another.

This is a perplexing dilemma. On the one hand, the new resource economist could simply endorse whatever outcome a market actually reaches. In that event, the economist should view with equanimity the felling of ancient forests to ship raw logs to Japan, the ownership of Yellowstone by the Walt Disney Company or the transfer of the water in their favorite streams and rivers to suburban lawns in Las Vegas and Phoenix. One must remember that people in the cities and on the coasts or in the newly industrialized Asian nations may pay top dollar for western lands and forests.

On the other hand, new resource economists could join with mainstream environmental economists in playing the "find the market failure" game—a game anyone can win. On that basis, no matter how much celebrities or churches or theme park operators with ready money might bid for an area, one could always construct a politically correct cost-benefit analysis to show that right-thinking environmentalists, but for transaction costs or free-rider problems, would outbid them. The upshot would be a substitution of centralized planning for the functioning of free markets. Economic efficiency, in other words, exists in the eye of the beholder. By appealing to allocative efficiency, new resource economists would invite in by the back door the cost-benefit scientific management they kicked out through the front door.

Plainly, both horns of the dilemma are unattractive to new resource economists. Leave land use to the free market and you may see the Church Universal and Triumphant, along with a few movie stars, buy up Montana. As long as the cults and the celebs have a lot more money than ranchers, that is the outcome one must expect. Perhaps Disney will operate dude ranches, thereby trading on local history by making the area a sort of theme park. Since they favor decentralized control and local management, however, new resource economists must view ownership of the ancient forests by either Disney or Uncle Sam as a Hobson's choice—a "free" choice where there is in reality no alternative.

In order to wrest resources from the dead hand of federal bureaucracy yet avoid consigning the West to global market forces that are likely to obliterate its history and character, new resource economists propose a number of strategies, all of which adhere to a single principle. The principle is that of making the managers of resources responsible and accountable for the ways those resources are managed. Consider, once again, the management of

Yellowstone and other national parks. At present, bureaucrats manage the parks in order to gain advancement within their bureaucracies—which may mean maximizing tourist visits, applying the latest management science, or following the ecological fashion of the day. Bureaucratic aggrandizement and sound resource management are not the same thing. That is why a resource such as Yellowstone National Park should not be managed by a bureaucratic agency based in Washington.

A better proposal might be to make the parks autonomous institutions—the Smithsonian Institution would be a model—directed by boards of trustees. The trustees, who would represent environmental and other constituencies with local commitments and ties to the particular park or forest, would have to work out policy on a consensual basis. Since each park or forest would be constituted under a different set of trustees, the boards could learn from one another and even compete to do the best job of management. The parks could function as laboratories of both democracy and ecology. And if the trustees lived near the resource, they would be intimately related to and responsible for the results of their actions.

Some of the new resource economists—Richard Stroup is an example—have gone so far as to suggest that national lands such as forests and parks be privatized in fee simple to consortia of trustee-owners drawn from mainstream environmental groups. The idea would be to make these groups responsible to the resource rather than to their own political and economic agendas. Then they would have to consider the costs and benefits of the proposals they adopt—rather than, for example, simply how these proposals might affect their ability to raise funds. Incentives count. And there is nothing like responsibility or accountability—such as people bear for the property they own in the context of strong ties with their neighbors—to concentrate the mind on the advantages and disadvantages of various actions.

In general, the instinct of the new resource economics is to move away from the emphasis mainstream economics places on market failure and instead to examine the successes of the marketplace and explore creative uses of market incentives. This new discipline seeks to understand and improve the incentive structures local communities, associations, and landowner groups confront in managing the resources of the West. The vision of the new resource economics is to reinvigorate the marketplace that existed when de Tocqueville visited America—the marketplace of ideas, of property, of local control of resources. The kinds of information taken into consideration by the local marketplace, its patterns of responsibility, and the forms of accountability it puts into practice are essential to the sound management of resources, especially in the American West.

NOTES

1. Alexis de Tocqueville, *Democracy in America*, ed. J. P. Mayer, trans. George Lawrence (New York: Anchor Books, 1969), 513.
2. Ibid., 243.
3. Ibid., 76.
4. Major studies of this kind include Robert T. Deacon and M. Bruce Johnson, eds., *Forestlands: Public and Private* (Cambridge, Mass.: Ballinger, 1985); Scott Lehmann, *Privatizing Public Lands* (New York: Oxford University Press, 1995); Terry L. Anderson, *Water Crisis: Ending the Policy Drought* (Washington, D.C.: Cato Institute, 1983); Terry L. Anderson, ed., *Water Rights: Scarce Resource Allocation, Bureaucracy, and the Environment* (San Francisco: Political Economy Research Center, 1983); Terry L. Anderson and Peter J. Hill, eds., *The Political Economy of the American West* (Lanham, Md.: Rowman & Littlefield, 1994); and Gary D. Libecap, *Locking Up the Range: Federal Land Controls and Grazing* (Cambridge, Mass.: Ballinger, 1981).
5. Terry L. Anderson and Peter J. Hill, "Environmental Federalism: Thinking Smaller," *PERC Policy Series* PS-8 (December 1966). (Published by the Political Economy Research Center, 502 South 19th Avenue, Suite 211, Bozeman, MT 59718.)
6. See, for example, John Baden and Andrew Dana, "Toward an Ideological Synthesis in Public Land Policy: The New Resource Economics," pp. 1–20 in Philip O. Foss, ed., *Federal Lands Policy* (New York: Greenwood Press, 1987).
7. Gus diZerega, "Communities and the Environment," *FREE Perspectives* 8, no. 3 (summer 1997). (Published by the Foundation for Research on Economics and the Environment, 945 Technology Boulevard, Suite 101F, Bozeman, MT 59715.)
8. See, for example, Richard L. Stroup, "Superfund: The Shortcut That Failed," *PERC Policy Series* PS-5 (1996).
9. See, for example, Hertha L. Hund, "Property Rights Legislation in the States: A Review," *PERC Policy Series* PS-1 (1995).
10. Patrick D. Moynihan, "The Professionalization of Reform," *The Public Interest* 1, no. 1 (1995).
11. Baden and Dana, "Toward an Ideological Synthesis in Public Land Policy," 2.
12. Ibid., 6
13. Ibid., 8

14. Fred L. Smith, Jr., "The Market and Nature," *The Freemen* 43, no. 9 (September 1993): 350–357; quotation at 352. Smith adds: "The world has recognized the massive mistake entailed in economic central planning in the former Soviet Union; yet the 'market failure' paradigm argues that we embark on an even more ambitious effort of ecological central planning."

15. E. K. Hunt, "A Radical Critique of Welfare Economics," pp. 232–249 in Ed Nell, ed., *Growth, Profits, and Property* (New York: Cambridge University Press, 1980); quotation at 245-246.

16. Terry L. Anderson and Donald R. Leal, *Free Market Environmentalism* (San Francisco, Calif.: Pacific Research Institute for Public Policy, 1990), 9.

17. Ibid.

18. Allen V. Kneese and Blair T. Bower, eds., *Environmental Quality Analysis: Theory and Method in the Social Sciences* (Baltimore: Johns Hopkins University Press and Resources for the Future, 1972), 3–4.

19. Ibid.

20. F. A. Hayek, *Individualism and the Economic Order* (London: Routledge & Kegan Paul, 1949), 14.

21. F. A. Hayek, *The Fatal Conceit*, Vol. 1 (Chicago: University of Chicago Press, 1988), 8–9.

22. Fred L. Smith, Jr., "A Free-Market Environmental Program," *Cato Journal* 11, no. 3 (winter 1992): 457–475, quotation at 468n.

23. Alston Chase, *In a Dark Wood: The Fight over Forests and the Tyranny of Ecology* (Boston: Houghton Mifflin, 1995).

24. Ibid., 101.

25. Ibid.

26. Ibid., 112.

27. Karl Hess, Jr., *Visions Upon the Land: Man and Nature on the Western Range* (Washington, D.C.: Island Press, 1992), 40.

28. Ibid., 218.

29. E. F. Conner and D. Simberloff, "Species Number and Composition Similarity of the Galapagos Flora and Avifauna," *Ecological Monographs* 48 (1978): 219–248.

30. J. Vandermeer, *Elementary Mathematical Ecology* (New York: Wiley, 1981).

31. E. D. McCoy and K. S. Shreder-Frechette, "The Community Concept in Community Ecology," *Perspectives on Science* 2, no. 4 (1994): 445–475; quotation at 462, citing A. J. Underwood, "What Is Community." pp. 351–367 in D. M. Raup and D. Jablonsky, eds., *Patterns and Processes in the History of Life* (New York: Wiley, 1986).

32. Daniel Botkin, *Discordant Harmonies* (New York: Oxford University Press, 1990), p. 62.

33. Donald Worster, "The Ecology of Order and Chaos," *Environmental History and Review* 14, nos. 1–2 (spring–summer 1990): 1–18; quotation at 13.

34. Ibid., 10.

35. Kenneth B. Cumming, "Design in Ecology," *Impact*, no. 131 (1984). (Published by the Institute for Creation Research.)

36. Anderson and Hill, "Environmental Federalism," 9.

37. Ibid., 22.

38. Benjamin R. Barber, "Jihad vs. McWorld," *The Atlantic Monthly* (March 1992): 53.

39. Karl Polanyi, *The Great Transformation* (Chicago: University of Chicago Press, 1944), 178.

40. Hess, *Visions Upon the Land*, 245.

41. Ibid., 247.

42. Ibid., 101.

43. Wallace Stegner, *Where the Bluebird Sings to the Lemonade Springs* (New York: Wings Books, 1992), 66.

44. John Baden and Richard Stroup, "Saving the Wilderness," *Reason* (July 1981): 35.

CHAPTER EIGHT

John Wesley Powell and the Unmaking of the West

KARL HESS, JR.

Environmental historians have a fondness for the American West, for it is there that the squandering of America's wealth of natural resources is so conspicuous and, by modern standards, so shameful. It is there that the causes of overgrazed ranges, clear-cut forests, wildlife losses, regimented rivers, and lakes of toxic sludge are as crystal clear as the azure western sky. There, the sages of the West, from their easy chairs, from their lofty perches above the one-hundredth meridian, and from the besieged gates of the lords of yesterday, decry the sins of private greed, waste, and abuse that were and are, they claim, the unmaking of the West.

Who can deny the environmental record of unbridled individualism or question the gallantry of a federal few who have fought to save the West from capitalist exploitation? And make no mistake: there has been exploitation. Grass has been extracted from arid prairies at rates that outstripped the historical harvests of tens of millions of migrating bison. Forests have been cut at rates that exceeded the natural periodicity of fire and regeneration. Rivers, wild and choked with salmon, have been blocked, stair-stepped, and channeled to make way for a new breed of animals: cultivators and stockmen. And mountains that had taken ages to thrust upward, and then ages more to be sculpted by wind, water, and ice, have been deconstructed to their basic elements of rubble.

In fact, much of the West has been deconstructed. A generation of daring and insightful historians has dismantled the edifice of myth—the cultural belief that this home-on-the-range of the winsome cowboy somehow steered clear of the ills endemic to the rest of America and stayed true, instead, to its ethos of individualism and its birthright of frontier democracy. But there is a problem here, or, more accurately, a hesitancy. Slash and burn as they might, western historians have shown a stubborn reluctance to dismantle the one icon that is most responsible for the West's environmental undoing: the western hero.

By western heroes, I do not mean the fictional agents passed down to us through the ages or the manufactured legends that occasionally grace the cinematic screen—though their ethos shares much in common with what I have in mind. Rather, the heroes I refer to—the ones who deconstructed vast areas of the West to stubble, stumps, and stagnant pools—were flesh and blood, mostly male, living yet much larger than life. They are the ones who won the West of "wise use," the scribes who, in a historical spin of irony, are now celebrated as the seers and prophets of a kinder and gentler native home of hope. They are John Wesley Powell, the man himself; his progenitors; and the atoms of his spirit that have found fertile soil beyond the hundredth meridian.

A Fertile Soil for Heroes

There are good reasons why the West and the western mind are home to heroes. For starters, the West has the space. Its towering mountains, rolling prairies, and gaping canyons are monumental stages well fitted to the larger-than-life heroic figures whose visions match the grandeur of the land. The West has contrasts. Desert abuts forest, arctic cold melts to searing heat, and Mount Whitney tumbles to the depths of Death Valley. These and other polar opposites parallel and oddly reinforce the synergy between heroic good and villainous evil. The West is also primal. The unbridled forces of nature—cataclysmic fires, volcanic explosions, shattering earthquakes, and relentless erosion from wind and water—position life precariously between resistance and oblivion. Stoicism and heroism meld in the shadow of a less than benign nature.

Heroes also measure up to a western range of profound moral implications. The West has, from the nation's inception, been a moral landscape, a vast stretch of terrain set apart from the original thirteen states and territories and celebrated as the nation's repository of republican virtue and its best hope for perpetuating liberty and democracy. J. Hector St. John Crèvecoeur, from his estate on the Hudson River, looked to the western province of North America "as the asylum of freedom."[1] Thomas Jefferson, from his home at Monticello, envisioned sufficient land in the West "to employ an infinite number of people in [its] cultivation" and, in the process, to nurture a virtuous citizenry.[2]

The West as landscape of hope, asylum, and freedom materialized in law with the passage of the 1862 Homestead Act. It became the formal fountainhead for Jeffersonian democracy, the political platform for protecting cherished American values, and the vehicle to carry forth the spirit of American nationalism. With 160 acres reserved to every individual and family capable of braving the journey west and staking a homestead claim, the 1862 act turned morality into a precondition for western settlement. It elevated the American West from a mere sparkle in an agrarian's eye to the land of equality and opportunity; indeed, western lands became America's moral outposts.

Graced with soaring expectations, the West became the nation's bellwether. Policy makers, agrarian reformers, and western promoters followed the advance of settlement to assess democracy's progress, and whenever it became clear to them that obstacles blocked the destiny of Jefferson's yeoman farmer, they mounted the bully pulpit. They vilified Indians for standing in the way of expansion into the heart of the nation's moral landscape. They alchemized wild nature into an object of danger, preparing the way for demonization of the wolf, the cougar, and the grizzly bear. While doing this, they saved the full fury of their wrath for the western stockman, the kingpin of the cattle kingdom and the greatest threat to a land of virtuous farmers.

Walter Prescott Webb wrote that agrarian opinion of the time considered the livestock grower "a trespasser on the public domain."[3] Congressman Tom Patterson of Colorado worried that the western plains "would be filled with baronial estates."[4] The *Laramie Sentinel* prophesied peace on the range only when Cain, "the tiller of the soil," dealt the fatal blow to Abel, "the stock grower."[5] The secretary of the interior proclaimed in 1902 that there was no greater foe to the public weal "than the class that seeks to occupy the public lands for grazing purposes."[6] And figures such as Gifford Pinchot, who insisted that "the single object of the public land system . . . is the making and maintenance of prosperous homes,"[7] and Bernard De Voto, who lambasted the "cattle kingdom" for its greed, power, culture, and maiming of nature,[8] heightened and extended the moral debate.

The epochal struggle between an undemocratic cattle barony and a democratic agrarian vanguard highlighted a persistent and sweeping national theme, one that positioned the West as catalyst of American civilization. In his 1893 essay titled "The Significance of the Frontier in American History," Frederick Jackson Turner redefined the moral landscape of the West. It was no longer, as Jefferson and his agrarian supporters had contended, a passive stage on which crucial American institutions and culture could be extended and upheld. Instead, the West was the forge of democracy and egalitarianism and the fertile soil of American identity. By the turn of his pen, Turner raised the moral stakes, elevating the American West from a populist farmland to a national shrine of freedom.

Today, Turner's thesis is under assault. New western historians dismiss the transforming role of the West by correctly reminding Americans that western history is replete with repression, injustice, inequality, and violent conquest—traits that contradict and undermine Turner's celebratory view and make the West not unlike the rest of the nation. Yet the very indignation of the new western historians to the region's moral shortcomings suggests that even they are captive to its moral landscape. Their strident attacks on Turner's thesis and their obsession with the failings and trespasses of the region and its people speak to their own expectations and hopes for the West. Try as they might to discredit its moral landscape, their commitment to making the present West a place befitting its past mythology merely attests to the region's hypnotic hold.

As a moral landscape, the West has also become a battleground for forces of good and evil outside the realm of human equity and justice. From the moment the first Anglo settlers set foot beyond the hundredth meridian—the invisible line separating the humid East from the arid West—a sense of loss and violation has weighed heavy in the hearts of the region's most staunch admirers and defenders. The Eden that was once the West was disappearing before their eyes.

That it might disappear altogether had been prophesied a half-century earlier by Alexis de Tocqueville. He noted that settlers were "insensible to the wonders of inanimate nature" and were content to stream "across these wilds, draining swamps, turning the course of rivers, peopling solitudes, and subduing nature."[9] And in the West, where public policy made the moral decision to dedicate the western range to the welfare of the nation's yeomanry, taming Eden and subduing nature became a matter of law. But as a matter of law, it created a persisting schism in the moral landscape of the American West.

Naturalists such as John Muir rebelled at the thought of the pristine grasslands succumbing to the "hoofed locusts" swarming over the high Sierra Nevada and the Cascade Range and "carrying desolation with them."[10] He lamented in fiery words "the invading horde of destroyers called settlers" and lashed out in apocalyptic hyperbole at the "pious destroyers [who] waged interminable forest wars . . . spreading ruthless devastation."[11] At the same time, ecological pioneers such as Frederic Clements bolstered the moralism of Muir with the scientific certainty "that the white man was not part of [the western range]: he came as disrupter, an alien, and exploiter."[12]

Today, wilderness advocates and preservationists carry Muir's torch, striking out in righteous anger at the ranchers, loggers, and miners who dare to upset the delicate balances of nature. In turn, "wise users" sink their roots in agrarian tradition and righteously demand that the West be preserved exclusively for westerners, a catch phrase that roughly translates into ranchers, loggers, and miners. Each side entrenches itself in its respective moral landscape, certain that its cause is good and just and that its opponent's cause is evil and unjust.

Ironically, for all their differences, the two sides are strikingly similar. Each adorns its argument in the garb of democracy and egalitarianism; each argues that preservation, in the first instance, and "wise use," in the second, is in the nation's best interest; and each makes the case conclusive that the West of towering mountains, rolling prairies, and gaping canyons is forever fated to be a moral landscape.

The West is, indeed, a land of extravagance and exaggeration where good and evil face off on the open range, where heroics are not just needed but also addictive, where heroes find fodder for their appetites, and where those appetites feed on grass, trees, and water for the sake of grandiose dreams and even more grandiose schemes. There, amidst the landscape of moral absolutism and among the hordes of the victimized, the western hero finds his niche. He is—for he is almost always a he—every person's Shane, a Paladin figure of uncommon insight, a passionate leader, and an emblazoned symbol whose lasting mark on the West is written in literary bravado yet indelibly signed in stubble, stumps, and stagnant pools.

Fodder for Heroes

Cowboys are the best of heroes in the fictional West, where the common denominator of good and bad is always the individual and where nature is only a setting in which to highlight and display feats of uncommon courage. But in the nonfictional West, cowboys eventually had to fall short. Simply put, the moral landscape of the real West outgrew them.

By the time the first herds of cattle were moving north over the Sedalia, Chisholm, and Goodnight-Loving Trails to shipping depots on the Union Pacific, Santa Fe, and Kansas–Missouri Pacific railroad lines, the role of hero had passed from the lone rider on the range to the hired guns of government. Like Edward Abbey's brave cowboy, the archetypal American hero had no place of refuge, outside fiction, in a post–Civil War age consumed by nationalism, industrialization, and an obsession with divvying up the range into 160-acre homestead plots. The antebellum world of self-contained individualism that had been Thoreau's and that had contained the seed of the winsome cowboy simply dissolved in the prairie wind, leaving as its final testament in the next century only the screeching brakes of an eighteen-wheeler and the death of a brave cowboy. The province of the individual, the heroism of the untutored cowboy, yielded by historical circumstance to the realm of government, to the reality of state capitalism, and to the structured and entrenched machinations of institutions and bureaucracies.

Heroism in the shadow of the Civil War and the 1862 Homestead Act was, nonetheless, heroism in the true western mode. The region, as it would eventually be portrayed in classic western films and B-grade movies, was the land of the free yet victimized and the home of the brave yet powerless—a place and a people desperate for protection from both themselves and the hostile forces that would deter them from their national destiny. A hero of uncommon mettle was called for to uphold the grand purpose of the West and to protect western settlers in their noble calling. Into this heroic role government acquiesced and entered willingly and with a vengeance.

Indian threats to the nation's yeomanry were efficiently and savagely handled by the U.S. Army. Territories once under the control of native Americans were cleansed of danger and then safely opened to white settlement. The military forts and soldiers that followed in the wake of victory, and even in some cases the reservations of conquered Indians, provided the nucleus of new markets to sustain marginal homesteads and struggling western governments. "In those rough times," writes Patricia Nelson Limerick, "Washington was in essence subsidizing a government which had few citizens, no income, and a highly questionable future."[13] Later, when predators such as wolves, cougars, and grizzlies supplanted Indians as the major threat to the safety and economic welfare of still-marginal homesteaders and still-struggling western governments, federal money and federal trappers expedited their removal and, in some areas, their extinction.

Heroism on the range, however, was not limited to buffering settlers from the natural dangers of native people and animals. Time and again, the cavalry was called in to thwart an even graver threat. Cattlemen, who had arrived on the scene well in advance of homesteaders and dirt farmers, had a lock on much of the arid West by the early 1880s. Their pastoral livelihood and, until the killing snows and droughts of 1885–1887, their sometimes extravagant standards of living demanded units of land hundreds and often thousands of times larger than the 160-acre homesteads parceled out by the General Land Office. Unable to acquire by legal means the massive amounts of land they needed to sustain their livestock, cattlemen resorted to extralegal devices and activities to keep homesteaders off their customary ranges.

They monopolized life-giving watering points by making both lawful and fraudulent homestead claims. Control of the water gave them control of the land. They cornered the market on usable rangeland by erecting barbed wire fences to restrict access to the open range. And where fences were not possible, they divvied up the open range by agreement with their neighbors, policing the informal divisions with both voluntary and state-sponsored associations of kindred cattlemen. By whatever means they could, cattlemen sought to do what was prohibited by federal law—to stake their claim to lands that were, by virtue of aridity and isolation, far more suited to the growing of animals than to the cultivation of wheat and corn.

Whether cattlemen were right or wrong in their estimation of the land and its capability—and there was good reason to believe they were right if John Wesley Powell's *Report on the Lands of the Arid Region of the United States* was at all believable—the fact remains that the people who made and enforced settlement policies had a different agenda in mind. Cattlemen were subverting the noble purpose for which the West was intended. A mere handful of greedy and violence-prone cattle barons were claiming for their own estates a landscape intended by providence for the American farmer and the mule-drawn plow. Naturally, righteous leaders did what was good and just, calling forth the power of the U.S. government and the U.S. cavalry to rescue once again a land and a people victimized by outsiders posing, unscrupulously, as legitimate members of the community.

Congress passed the Unlawful Enclosures Act of 1885 to stop cattlemen from fencing off the open range. President Grover Cleveland backed up the act by sending troops to enforce it and to make sure that other devices and activities, such as unlawful control of waters and illegal policing of rangelands by cattlemen's associations, no longer frustrated the intent of western settlement. Good guys in cavalry hats did what cowboy heroes could do only on the silver screen. They tore down fences, broke the backs of associations, and opened the western range to every American. Yet cattlemen were not alone in suffering the disruptions waged by a caring government. In time, the land itself was affected in ways that not even the most gallant of heroes could have foreseen.

Overgrazing became endemic. As one official of the Colorado Stock Growers' Association testified in 1884, overgrazing had been a problem "ever since Mr. Jefferson began to attract immigration to this country by proclaiming to the world [its great store of free land]." [14] Now overgrazing was an even greater problem as homesteaders turned in desperation and failure from farming to cattle raising and as sheepherders moved freely across an unbounded western range. Unable to protect their rangelands from overuse by the livestock of others, cattlemen, farmers, and sheepmen razed the grasslands of the West in the quintessential tragedy of the commons. In the words of Albert F. Potter, first director of the USDA Forest Service's Grazing Section:

> Flocks passed each other on the trails, one rushing in to secure what the other had just abandoned as worthless, feed was deliberately wasted to prevent its utilization by others, the ranges were occupied before the snow had left them. Transient sheepmen roamed the country robbing the resident stockmen of forage that was justly theirs. . . . [As a result] class was arrayed against class—the cowman against the sheepman, the big owner against the little one—and might ruled more often than right. [15]

In its heroic bid to save the moral landscape of the American West from enclosure, the federal government turned the region's physical landscape into sacrificial lands. It ordained overgrazing as the law of the lawless range, enshrining erosion and desolation in public policies that made ideological sense in Congress but nonsense on the parched, windblown basins and ranges of the West. And as it took its historic stand against wealthy stockmen, the government transferred millions of acres to the railroads: the Union Pacific, the Kansas Pacific, the Atchison Topeka and Santa Fe, the Southern Pacific, and the Northern Pacific. The railroads, no less a special interest than ranchers and no less a beneficiary of the nation's largess, were the economic lifelines between the yeomanry and the clamoring markets of the industrializing East. They were needed and wanted; cattlemen were not. It was as simple as that.

Heroes, of course, are rarely discouraged by failure, and in the case of public land policy, overgrazing merely served to spur government on to newer and higher levels of heroic endeavor. Organizations such as the Forest

Service and, later, the Bureau of Land Management were established to bring order and protection to the abused lands of the arid region, and in many ways they did. They closed the open range to unregulated grazing, and they ended more than a half-century of ill-conceived homesteading laws. They were, in the mind of Gifford Pinchot, founder of the Forest Service, the spawning ground of a new breed of selfless men and women, heroes and heroines dedicated to public service, trained in scientific management, and capable of identifying and pursuing the resource needs of the land and the people of the West. They would be, he believed, an elite corps of public servants, "the one great antidote for the ills of the Nation" that would bring forth "the Kingdom of God on earth." [16]

Pinchot was most certainly not alone in his hopes for the youthful Forest Service and its sibling-to-be, the Bureau of Land Management (BLM). Ivan Doig, in his novel *Dancing at the Rascal Fair,* describes a poignant encounter between a Montana ranching family and a newly arrived Forest Service ranger—a fictional meeting that undoubtedly took place in fact on hundreds of homesteads throughout the turn-of-the-century West. The father, sensing the import of the ranger's arrival, is unsettled by his son's expectation. "From the instant he reached down to shake your hand, you looked at Stanley Meixell as if the sun rose and set in him. And I was already telling myself that you had better be right about that."

The young boy was certain he was right; he knew a hero when he saw one. But the father was not so certain; he knew only his hopes and his fears:

> While the man Stanley Meixell rode away, I stood staring for a while at the mountains. National Forest. They did not look like a national anything, they still looked just like mountains. A barbed wire fence around them. It did not seem real that a fence could be put around mountains. But I would not bet against this Meixell when he said he was going to do a thing. A fence around the mountains not to control them but us. Did we need that? Most, no. But some, yes. The Double W cattle that were more and more. It bothered me to think it in the same mental breath with Wampus Cat Williamson, but even Rob's penchant for more sheep was a formula the land eventually would not be able to stand. And without the land healthy, what would those of us on it be? The man Meixell's argument stood solid as those mountains. But whether he himself did . . . . Not Proven. [17]

Heroes, like good arguments, withstand the test of time, if only because they are timeless. Yet flesh-and-blood men and women are unproven; they have feet of clay that either hold or crumble by the dictates of history, not the adulation of a starstruck child. In this case, the test of time has been less than generous to the federal agencies that came forth to rescue the West from itself—from the economic vices of indulgent stockmen, miners, and loggers and the simple yet vulnerable virtues of sturdy yeoman stock. After nearly a century of intervention by Pinchot's elite corps, the human and natural toll of government caring is today reflected in the angry faces of the region's people and in the scars that riddle and demean its landscape.

A long legacy of fire suppression has turned national parks into tinderboxes, diminished the biological diversity of southwestern wilderness areas, and left multiple-use landscapes shadows of their former selves. The bulk of the West's old-growth forests, and most sadly those entrusted to public protection, have been cut. The public forests that remain have, in the most conspicuous places, been neatly blocked into mountain-sized clear-cuts. Meanwhile, logging communities that once trusted their fate to federal practices of sustained yield are now struggling to survive, and unemployed loggers who once practiced their machismo on trees are now learning, as nurses, how to practice humanity on people.

Public grazing lands that were plucked from the chaos of the open range and entrusted to the scientific care of the Forest Service and the BLM are still overgrazed. And private grazing lands that are now the protectorates of the Natural Resource Conservation Service (formerly the Soil Conservation Service), the Consolidated Farm Services Agency (formerly the Agricultural Conservation and Stabilization Service), and university extension services are no better off. After fifty years of studying how crested wheatgrass weathers a cow's bite and how many cattle can be turned out in a pasture the size of Rhode Island, experts are dumbfounded. Rangeland conditions remain far poorer than they once were and far behind what expectations would have them be. One-third of the American West is degraded; tens of millions of acres, both public and private, are weed infested and either stalled or collapsing in ecological health.[18] Streams and riparian oases in the western desert are mostly trampled.[19] And all this has happened under the watchful eyes of government agencies and a cornucopia of federal subsidies assigned to and lavished upon all the stockmen of the American West.

For whatever reasons, Pinchot's corps of elite public servants have failed; their achievements have not matched their heroic expectations. Perhaps they went wrong by not listening closely enough to John Muir, whose prescription for protecting the West was "one soldier in the woods, armed with authority and a gun." After all, Muir noted, God protected trees from droughts and avalanches, but "He cannot save them from fools—only

Uncle Sam can do that."[20] But then again, soldiers in arms—the civilian variety, with Aldo Leopold briefly at their head—waged, to borrow Muir's words, interminable wildlife wars on the wolves of the Kaibab Plateau, spreading ruthless devastation.

Heroes of many hues have carried forth the legacies of Pinchot and Muir in the quarter-century since Earth Day, 1970. So far, this has not entailed soldiers hiding in the shadows of primeval forests, though it has meant that federal codes and regulations standing behind nearly every tree, grass plant, and wild creature in the West. It's not a solution that Jefferson would have celebrated as democratic, Thoreau would have embraced as a surrogate for wildness, or Abbey would have hailed as a proper sanctuary for harried twentieth-century man and woman. But it is the real West, the West of new law and order where codification, far from quelling the tempests of good and evil, has simply raised the moral stakes for those who would be heroes.

An Architect for Arid Lands

Well before Gifford Pinchot articulated the saving grace of progressive, scientific land management, and well before he envisioned the Forest Service as a heroic and selfless vehicle for safeguarding the natural economy of the West, another hero of uncommon mettle had already set his surveyor sights on "the Kingdom of God on earth." Major John Wesley Powell, Civil War veteran, explorer, and principal architect of the Geological Survey, was the first truly modern western hero: the first to navigate the waters of the Colorado, the first to clear the rapids of the Grand Canyon, and the first to envision a guiding and paternal role for government in the future of the West. He was also the first to bring the West under the scrutiny of science, the first to meld that science with trained, disciplined bureaucracy, and the first to claim that scientific bureaucracy could evade the pall of politics and hitch itself to the public interest.

Powell was a progressive before there was a progressive movement. He laid the cornerstone for the environmental welfare state in the edifice of the Geological Survey.[21] He set the pattern and precedent for a century of western natural resource politics and consumption, for his prophetic voice was the first to preach the "principles of wise use for the benefit of the whole nation."[22] He blended the ideas of engineering and evolution to argue that humans and nature could and should be molded to whatever decision expert reason and rational planning deemed right. From the cauldron of the Civil War, he gleaned why democracy should be shorn of its rough edges and how economic progress could be engineered and tailored to suit a more disciplined people in an unforgiving land. He left a legacy that survives in the mythology of the West—and in its stubble, stumps, and stagnant pools.

A New Yorker by birth, Powell was an advocate for the West, a man whose uncanny powers of observation and understanding enabled him to grasp what made the region unique: its aridity. Parting company with Republican policy makers and western boosters of the time, he went against the American grain in his landmark 1878. *Report on the Lands of the Arid Region of the United States.* As geologist in charge of the U.S. Geographical and Geological Survey of the Rocky Mountain Region, Powell portrayed a West of somber and harsh reality, a West that could not be settled and managed by habit and customs formed in the humid East.

His report turned the presumptions of homesteading on their head. Water, he insisted, not land, was the true wealth of the region; it was the yardstick by which to measure the land's productivity and the principle around which to design and conduct a rational policy of western settlement. Quarter-section homestead parcels were simply too small to support a family and its livestock on lands where irrigation water was either short or absent—a condition that in most areas of the West was the rule, not the exception. "Four square miles," he wrote, "may be considered as the minimum amount necessary for a pasturage farm, and a still greater amount is necessary for the larger part of the lands; that is, pasturage farms, to be of any practical value, must be of at least 2,560 acres, and in many districts they must be much larger."[23] Where irrigation waters were accessible and abundant, however, Powell took a much different stance: "No one person shall be entitled to more than eighty acres."[24]

Refiguring the size of homestead units was only the first step Powell took in his bold attempt to reconstruct the American West. Where he was most innovative, and where he departed most strikingly from mainstream policy, was in the way he envisioned settlement. Dryland pasturage farms, he believed, demanded too many resources from resource-poor pioneers to be successfully settled and efficiently managed as isolated homestead units. In the future, the best way to establish and improve pasturage farms would be by "the colony plan," a blueprint for settlement based on cooperation and common land use. Similar in spirit to the *ejidos*—the village public grazing commons of Spanish New Mexico—the plan called for groups of nine or more homesteaders to combine into pasturage districts and to manage their 2,560-acre homesteads as integrated communal property. Each member of every district, in turn, would be allowed a maximum of twenty acres for irrigation and intensive crop cultivation.

Irrigated farms would be treated similarly, although on a much smaller scale. Groups of nine or more settlers would join together, forming in this instance self-governing irrigation districts. Within each district, the settlers would divide their commonly held land into eighty-acre family plots with water rights assigned, assured, and permanently attached to each parcel of land. To ensure that every member of an irrigation district, or for that matter every member of a pasturage district, had equal access to irrigation waters, Powell proposed that the system of rectangular surveys that already criss-crossed much of the West be abandoned and that surveys based on topography be adopted in their stead. By making farm and pasturage boundaries correspond to the topographic lay of the land, the number of viable homesteads could be expanded by virtue of reasonable and equitable access to the essential element of water.

Powell's proposals were ultimately ignored by his contemporaries and abandoned to the silent coffins of academic history. A Civil War figure of uncommon valor, an explorer of heroic proportions, and a civil servant of courage and audacity, he faded into near obscurity for want of recognition and understanding. He did not, however, vanish altogether. In 1953, Wallace Stegner rediscovered the visionary Powell and resurrected his life and story in the powerful and moving biography, *Beyond the Hundredth Meridian: John Wesley Powell and the Second Opening of the West.*

A Hero for All the West

Overnight, John Wesley Powell, the forgotten man, became a hero for all of the West, a thinker who thought straighter than his contemporaries, and a prophet who was forced by cruel fate to "wait for the future to catch up with him."[25] He alone understood the enormousness of the West and the essential need for a benign and enlightened government to steer the region in the direction of cooperation, coordination, and planning. He alone appreciated, in the midst of a nineteenth-century privatization frenzy, the absolute need to keep the public lands public and to guard them from private entanglement. And he alone foresaw the crying need for massive reclamation projects in the West that would churn out in extraordinary quantities the energy and water—the very lifeblood—that Jefferson's noble yeomen would need to cultivate and green the parched landscape.

But there is more to *Beyond the Hundredth Meridian* than a conventional biography embellished at critical points with praise; there is a latitude of generous speculation that fatefully catapults Major Powell to the rank of farsighted western hero and that indelibly etches his name in western legend and mythology. If Powell had only lived to the present, we are told, or at least to 1953, the date of his biography, he would have eagerly joined the ranks of the small but raucous western environmental movement. He would have known when dams were too numerous, clear-cuts too large, and forest harvests too extreme. He would have sided, Stegner claims, with the Sierra Club in fighting the damming of Echo Park. He would have fought to manage the federal lands rationally; he would have celebrated the reservation of more than 100 million acres of forestland by the federal government; he would have basked in the human and environmental triumph and legacy of the Taylor Grazing Act of 1934; and he would have spoken out with Civil War righteousness to defeat "the private interests that he feared might monopolize land [and] water in the West."[26]

Stegner's Powell was and is the perfect hero for a West torn and preyed upon by unrelenting forces of evil. "I fought for the conservation of the public domain under Federal leadership," Stegner quotes Powell, "because the citizens were unable to cope with the situation under existing trends and circumstances."

> The job was too big and interwoven for even the states to handle with satisfactory coordination. On the western slope of Colorado and in nearby states I saw waste, competition, overuse, and abuse of valuable range lands and watersheds eating into the very heart of western economy. Farms and ranches everywhere in the range country were suffering. The basic economy of entire communities was threatened. There was terrific strife and bloodshed between the cattle and sheep men over the use of the range. Valuable irrigation projects stood in danger of ultimate deterioration. Erosion, yes even human erosion, had taken root.[27]

In the grand tradition of latter-day western heroes, Powell *knew* what the West needed, even if the West itself had only a vague idea of its needs. Powell *knew*, as Stegner reminds us with glowing admiration, that no one could guarantee the future of the West "except the American government," and that for all its infirmities, government in its wisdom was vastly superior to a self-governing West of unprincipled predators and decent yet hapless prey. Yes, Stegner knew Powell's mind as well as he knew his own. He knew, as he asserted Powell had known from the beginning, that even if "government contained quarreling and jealous bureaus, that was too bad;"

> if it sheltered grafters as it did so spectacularly during the time of Grant, too bad. If it was too far from the resources in question to make every decision right, too bad. Too bad. But the alternative was worse. The alterna-

tive was creeping deserts, flooded river valleys, dusty miles of unused and unusable land, feeble or partial or monopolistic utilization of the available land and water. The alternative was great power and great wealth to a few and for a brief time rather than competence and independence for the communities of small freeholders on which [Powell's] political economy unchangeably rested.[28]

Powell was indeed a hero to match the moral landscape of a prodigal West. He had all the core attributes of complexity, contradiction, and ambiguity. He was, in part, as Stegner so proudly acclaims, "a democrat to the marrow," an agrarian idealist committed to carrying forth the republican program of his exemplar, Thomas Jefferson. The immigrant yeomanry who filled the valleys of the intermountain West were, in Powell's judgment, intelligent, industrious, and enterprising. "On this round globe and in all the centuries of human history," he proclaimed,

> there has never before been seen such a people. Their love of liberty is unbounded, their obedience to law unparalleled, and their reverence for justice profound; every man is a freeman king with power to rule himself, and they may be trusted with their own interests.[29]

Powell was clear and emphatic. He would give no ground in his faith in the people's right, power, and ability to rule themselves: "I say to the Government: Hands off! Furnish the people with institutions of justice, and let them do the work [of irrigation and farming] for themselves."[30]

Powell's Jeffersonian instincts led him, quite naturally, to an agrarian vision worthy of his mentor: "The march of humanity cannot be stayed; fields must be made, and gardens planted in the little valleys among the mountains of the Western land, as they have been in the broader valleys and plains of the East."[31] It was an uniquely American vision, a slice of Jefferson's reverence for the republican ways of a cultivator's life and a hearty dose of the utopian communalism endemic to the Jacksonian era and its flurry of social experimentation at Brook Farm, New Harmony, and the Mormon state of Deseret.

Powell sought to complete what the sage of Monticello had only speculated on—to people the West from the hundredth meridian to the Pacific coast, and to do it by irrigating the bottomlands and preserving the uplands for pasturage, timber, and watershed. "Ultimately," he predicted,

> the whole region will be covered with a mosaic of ponds fringed with a rich vegetation; and crystal waters, and green fields, and blooming gardens

will be dotted over all the burning naked lands, and sand dunes, alkali stretches, and naked hills will be decked with beautiful tracts of verdure. . . . [After all] arid lands are not lands of famine, and the sunny sky is not a firmament of devastation. Conquered rivers are better servants than wild clouds.[32]

Precisely. *Conquered rivers* were the thread Powell would use to weave disparate valleys into a singular new West—an irrigated yeoman's paradise spread across 120 million acres,[33] built from a system of canals and holding dams "unparalleled in the history of the world,"[34] and given unconditionally to the vigilant control, protection, and use of "these people who are interested therein."[35]

Powell's democratic bent, however, bent only so far. He knew the limits of the people and understood the obligations of the state. He had seen the fruit of an age of atomistic individualism, and he had lost an arm combating its antebellum excesses. The Civil War had taught him that unordered democracy was chaos and an untutored citizenry was hapless against the forces of capital and emerging industrial organization. He knew that the agrarian paradise he sought was beyond the financial means and planning capabilities of the lone yeoman farmer; it required resources only government could provide.[36] He also knew that solitary farmers with small holdings could not sustain themselves as lone individuals in the harsh and arid West. Government, he asserted, would have to establish local self-government for them—and would have to do so by carving rational communities out of each hydrographic basin and by laying down the law of how government-impounded waters would be divided and used among settlers.[37]

Powell knew the untapped possibilities of centralized government and organized science. A product of both, he boldly offered his own eight-point blueprint for engineering and orderly democracy on the western range. What he envisioned was a partnership "between the general Government, the State Governments, and the local governments." It was an arrangement well suited to the kingdom of God on earth—an arrangement that, once completed by the various levels of government, "would allow the people to regulate their own affairs in their own way."[38] It would be a tempered democracy, one bounded by the rules of others, in which the larger concerns of the people—such as the blueprint for living on arid lands—would be left, from cradle to grave, to the government but the minutiae of daily life would be left to the people for open and raucous Jacksonian debate.

Paternalistic as the blueprint was, it is unlikely that Powell saw any inconsistency between it and his Jeffersonian ideals. A partisan of Lester Ward in the national debate over social Darwinism, Powell staunchly defended the progressive doctrine of "anthropic evolution." Humans, he argued, were the masters of their own destiny, fully capable of adapting the natural environment to their collective wants and needs. They, not inscrutable forces of nature, explained the stepwise progression in societal evolution from property—the ownership unit being the individual—to the corporation. "The social unit," Powell wrote, "will eventually be a business corporation, and there will be a hierarchy of corporations, the highest of which will embrace the rest and constitute the government."[39]

Agrarian democracy as envisioned by Powell had not betrayed its Jeffersonian roots; it had only evolved to a higher, more progressive stage of corporate organization in which pasturage and irrigation districts did not "constitute a part of government, but they [did] form a part of the state and must necessarily be considered in the plan of the state."[40] It was only natural, in a naturally hierarchical, evolving state, for the government to assume a more active role in the affairs of Jefferson's, and now Powell's, noble yeomanry. What option was there in a late-nineteenth-century world where the once-clear boundaries between state, government, and community were now obscured by global markets and industrial giants?

It was also natural that Powell would become the greatest western booster of all—the very symbol of the West that Wallace Stegner lamented in *Beyond the Hundredth Meridian,* in which he convincingly portrayed Powell as the foresightful, countervailing force. In part, he was right. There was a telling difference between the commercial boosterism of western speculators and the hard-nosed, public-serving boosterism of Powell. Where speculators thought small, Powell thought big. Where speculators sought privilege from the federal government for their own personal gain, Powell sought the full muscle of the state for the loftier goal of sculpting a West to the blueprint of his dream. And where speculators boosted the West even to the mindless endangerment of its resources, Powell boosted the West ever mindful of what he was doing to the region's resources.

John Wesley Powell thought, acted, and wrote like a hero; he strode the western range and populated the western mind like a giant. He was, writes James M. Aton, "the scientist/hero who enters the fabled canyon country to roll back the myths, to reveal the secrets of the rocks and thus unravel the mysteries of the earth's origins."[41] But he was also mortal; he did not survive to see the West that would, over the next century, be built from a facsimile of his blueprint on a foundation of government, science, and water.

He died too soon to see the implementation of Francis Newlands's Reclamation Act of 1902 (Newlands being a staunch supporter of Powell)[42] and the birth of its offspring, the Bureau of Reclamation. He was denied the sweet victory of watching concrete and steel monuments, that celebrated and sanctified federal supremacy over nature, span and tame the wild Missouri, Columbia, and Colorado Rivers. And even if, as Stegner claims, Powell would have battled the damming of Echo Park, I suspect he would have welcomed the flooding of Glen Canyon. He would have been proud, as was Stegner, of such heroic federal achievements as the Central Valley Project of California[43] and would have embraced as a dream come true the Central Arizona Project and the production of cheap hydroelectric power in the Pacific Northwest. They represented an embodiment of his vision: 120 million acres of "green fields, and blooming gardens . . . dotted over all the burning naked lands, and sand dunes, alkali stretches, and naked hills . . . decked with beautiful tracts of verdure."[44]

Reclamation was Powell's vision; he saw it as the path to western prosperity and the key to turning western deserts into gardens that would "blossom like the rose." When he addressed Montana's 1889 constitutional convention and predicted that one-third of the state could be irrigated, Powell spoke of a dammed Montana that exceeded by leaps of imagination the fondest dreams of western boosters and proponents of reclamation:

> It means that no drop of water falling within the area of the state shall flow beyond the boundaries of the state. It means that all the waters falling within the state will be utilized upon its lands for agriculture.[45]

Salinized soils, exiled wolves, struggling salmon, and dead and dying rivers aside, Powell had a persuasive and powerful vision of the greening of the West. He would have celebrated the heroic making of what Marc Reisner calls the "Cadillac Desert," a cornucopia of federally subsidized water and energy projects that would entice millions of Americans to fill places where once only buzzards dared.

Had Powell lived long enough, he would have seen his dryland pasturage districts resurrected as grazing districts under the authority of the 1934 Taylor Grazing Act. Furthermore, Stegner points out, had Powell's ideas been listened to fifty years earlier, the West "would not have had so hard a lesson to learn in 1934."[46] Indeed, by 1934 we might already have known how effective the Taylor grazing districts would be in protecting the land and providing for the welfare of the little guy. We would have known then what we know today: that overgrazing is still endemic on too many ranges, that riparian areas are despoiled in too many canyons, and that massive federal subsidy programs too often fatten the pockets of everyone except the neediest, almost always at the expense of the land and its wildlife. Above all, we would have seen Powell's self-governing pasturage districts move that much sooner in the democratic direction that both he and his chronicler felt proper and inevitable: toward a highly centralized and bureaucratically orchestrated democracy of public participation, a paternal democracy fortified against the people of the West by a Maginot Line of unyielding rules and regulations.

None of this should be surprising. After all, as Stegner reminds us, Powell "was always one to take the long view . . . a bureaucrat before the name got either familiar or unpopular." His farsighted vision simply prophesied what the West was fated to become. He was just the right mixture of bureaucrat and idealist to see beyond the hubris and self-deception of the West:

> Both the bureaucrat and the idealist knew that private interests, whether they dealt in cattle or sheep, oil, minerals, coal, timber, water, or land itself, could not be trusted or expected to take care of the land or conserve its resources for the use of future generations. They could be trusted or expected to protect neither the monetary nor the nonmonetary values of the land: even in his day Americans had the passenger pigeon and the buffalo, the plowed and eroded plains, the cutover forests of Michigan, to tell them where "nature and the common incidents of life" would lead us. Later years have added the Dust Bowl and the eroded watersheds to the evidence.[47]

Powell was indeed a visionary man, so visionary that it would be wrong to harp on the nagging deficiencies in his bold scheme for the arid region. The high expectations he held for the watering of the West surely compensate for the environmental problems an orgy of dam building has brought; the idealism behind his pasturage districts certainly makes up for the real-world shortcomings of overgrazed grazing districts. The good intentions he felt for "savage" Indians excuse his willingness to overthrow their "institutions, customs, philosophy, and religion"[48] and to relocate them from their homelands in order to save them from "want, loathsome disease, and the disasters consequent upon the incessant conflict with white men."[49] And the self-governing, democratic principles by which he wanted to reform the western range, and on which Stegner anchors his biography, are not in the least diminished by his agenda to make Washington, D.C., master of the West and its people. It's all a matter of context.

Powell's farsightedness regarding the future of western forests is also a matter of context. Stegner, in one of the few understatements of his biography, notes that "Major Powell was never primarily interested in the forests. . . . But he would approve the reservations [of forests] that by the middle of the twentieth century totaled 139,000,000 acres, plus another 21,000,000 in Alaska."[50] Stegner is too modest. Powell by his own account was *very* interested in western forests.

When camping one night deep in the mountainous territory of Colorado, Powell kindled a fire for warmth. He watched in amazement as the fire mounted and climbed a nearby trunk, "crawling out along the branches, igniting the rough bark, kindling the cones, and setting fire to the needles, until in a few minutes the great forest pine was all one pyramid of flame. . . . On it swept for miles and scores of miles, from day to day, until more timber was destroyed than has been used by the people of Colorado for the last ten years."[51]

This is the version of the story Powell shared with the public—a version that omits his subsequent and strong recommendation to Secretary of the Interior John Noble that "the best thing to do for the Rocky Mountain forests was to burn them down." Powell was dead serious. In the private confines of the Interior Department, he bragged to the secretary "with gusto how he himself had started a fire that swept over a thousand square miles."[52] As one of his associates at the Geological Survey later confided, "it is advisable to cut away as rapidly as possible all the forests [of the West], especially upon the mountains, where most of the rain falls, in order that as much of the precipitation as possible may be collected in the streams. . . . It may be added that the forests in the arid region are thus disappearing with commendable rapidity."[53]

Powell cared deeply for forests, at least insofar as they were depriving the West of sorely needed irrigation water. That's why he promoted overgrazing by sheep in the Sierra Nevada as "a useful way to keep forest growth down."[54] Later, when he grudgingly acknowledged the importance of standing forests, not to maximize watershed yield but to reduce the clogging of dams with sediment,[55] he insisted on using domestic livestock to destroy younger growth and to consume grass that would only deprive downstream cultivators of precious water.[56]

Yes, Powell cared for many things, and always in heroic fashion and always on the scale of millions of reclaimed, burnt or logged, and overgrazed acres. But what he didn't care for, and what he never really understood, was the arid West, its native life, and its sunburned, wind-carved landscapes. These were merely natural impediments to anthropic evolution, to the progressive eclipsing of savage nature and its replacement with things more productive, more progressive, and more civilized. Powell had no remarkable powers of insight or foresight; he was simply a captive of his time, a booster of and believer in the West for what it could become, not for what it was.

Powell was, in the end, a true and tried progressive agrarian: he was true to his eastern environment of abundant green, and he tried, with a modicum of success, to transform the arid West into a new and more productive eastern Arcadia. To Powell, the West was but a challenge and an obstacle to be overcome by the late-nineteenth-century rising stars of Herculean statism and scientism. Ideology, not a kinder and gentler West, was the fuel of his dreams, the object of his self-styled heroism.

The Last Western Hero

The John Wesley Powell who is groomed and polished in *Beyond the Hundredth Meridian* is a man of legend and myth today—a man with a brain that weighed in at an awe-inspiring 1,488 grams and is now stored among sacred memorabilia in the back corridors of the Smithsonian Institution.[57] He is the reconstructed Civil War hero who inspired Secretary of the Interior Stewart Udall in 1961 to enlist Stegner in the knighthood of John Kennedy's brief Camelot and later to name him to the National Parks Advisory Board.

Stegner's Powell is the inspirational creation that moved a youthful Bruce Babbitt to a born-again experience—"as though someone had thrown a rock through the window"[58]—and to a quasi-religious conversion from the scion of an Arizona ranching dynasty to the son of an environmentally progressive West.[59] He is the larger-than-life figure who energized Babbitt in his role as secretary of the interior to push for a National Biological Survey modeled along the lines of the Geological Survey and poised, in true heroic form, "to save the West."[60] He is the righteous thunder of Babbitt's new covenant "to protect the *whole* of creation" in every corner of a world now perched precariously "between the flood and the rainbow."[61]

It was Powell who inspired law scholar Charles Wilkinson's Stegnerian *Crossing the Next Meridian*[62]—a book that reaffirms Powell's vision of federally circumscribed local democracy even as it serves as the bible and agenda of Babbitt's Interior Department.[63] And it was Powell's inspiration that enabled Wilkinson to divide the Anglo West into three broad historical epochs: before Babbitt, during Babbitt, and after Babbitt.[64]

John Wesley Powell is, in the final tally, both the creation and the creator of the last western hero: Wallace Stegner. By spinning a myth of heroic proportions, Stegner became the very white-hatted visionary about whom he had written in such stirring and eloquent prose. He became to those who read and knew his works the voice of the Next West, a kinder, gentler West where visionary leaders are accorded the respect due them, where cooperation perseveres over competition, where the public's interest takes precedence over individual interest, where government and local community combine in a transforming symbiosis to build an economically sound and environmentally healthy region, and where the moral values of democracy and egalitarianism are enshrined on a sacred landscape. In this Next West, the stumbling, bumbling everyday people of the range will be enlightened if possible, and if not, then restrained from harming either themselves or the land.

Stegner evoked a West he desperately wanted to believe in, but his versions both of the West and of Powell are flawed and dishonest. Powell never was the social and environmental visionary imagined by Stegner; he was the spirit that dammed the West's great rivers, clear-cut its primeval forests, turned its rangelands into permanent fodder for cattle, and parlayed its heritage of Jeffersonian hands-on democracy into a nightmare of bureaucratic red tape and mounting regulation. Through his vision of Powell, Stegner wanted to affirm and sanctify the positive role of bureaucracy and centralized authority in a postdepression, postwar world; to make that case, he envisioned a benevolent government for the West. But none of it was ever true. Instead, the real Powell merely proved Stanley Meixell's argument: mountains could and would be fenced in, and government was precisely the instrument to do it. That the region's own citizenry learned to sharpen that instrument, to use it keenly to its own advantage, gives the lie to the West's image of itself as a victim of federal planning. Far from being victimized, the West demanded, and received, every conceivable blessing from the federal landlord yet cried consistently for more.

Playing the Victim Game

Everything the West has gotten, including more dollars and more regulations, it has earned on its own merit and at the hands of its own people from a more than willing federal government. Whenever a special program, a new project, or a tantalizing subsidy has been championed by our senators and congressmen, we have gone giddy with joy and expectation. Naturally, we would have preferred to have simply taken from the trough of federal beneficence, but we were never so naive as to assume that there wouldn't be a price. Not only did we get the all-powerful centralized government we demanded of Washington and paid for, but we also welcomed and embraced it with open arms.

Selling the soul of the West became easier and cheaper for all of us in subsequent years. We bought into the federal damming of the region's rivers without suffering an ounce of coercion. We were not victimized by the engineers at the Bureau of Reclamation who wanted to rechannel our lifeblood, by the politicians who wanted to trade our future for votes, or by the private construction companies that made out like bandits with everyone's tax dollars. We did it all to ourselves. When the Bureau of Reclamation announced its plan to dam Echo Park, who was on the front lines begging for federal votes and federal dollars? It was the proud and independent people of Vernal, Utah. They did what the rest of us did with glee and abandonment. We jumped at the chance to have someone else pay for our prosperity, realizing only after it was too late that the cost of that prosperity was the despoiling of our land and the loss of our dignity.

We persevered, though. We went on to build our Indian-proof homes and to water our fields, livestock, and mines from federally tamed water. But just when we thought we had adversity conquered, we learned to our dismay that forces much greater than rampaging natives and torrential rivers threatened our well-being. Catastrophic fires that were vital to the ecological heartbeat of the West now menaced our families, communities, and livelihoods with alarming frequency. Rather than using prudence in selecting where we lived and how we worked, we threw ourselves at the mercy of a youthful Forest Service that was able and more than willing to put out the flames that so terrified us. We garnered the necessary votes in Washington to finance the most expensive fire-fighting force known to humankind, and it cost us hardly anything except another pound of flesh and another sliver of our disappearing souls. It gave us good seasonal jobs. Later, when we understood it better, it also gave us decadent wildlands and a new reason to chafe at the bit of federal land management.

We next bemoaned the loss of our old-growth forests, the skeletal remains of which lay in disarray from Washington State to New Mexico, and complained righteously of a legacy of bad federal policies that had plundered our finest resources. We pointed out, quite correctly, in our own defense that prior to the post–World War II boom in national forest cuts, we had harvested western timber at more modest, sustainable rates, most often in select or small clear-cuts. But then the Forest Service stepped in and changed the rules of the game. It opened up our forests by building thousands of miles of roads and then used timber sales to attract the commercial giants who had the resources and the markets to strip entire mountain ranges of virgin trees. Yet who lobbied for the federal appropriations to expand forest cuts, who provided the labor and equipment to do the dirty work, and whose communities lived off the excesses of the federal tree-cutting machine for so many years?

The flood of federal dollars—that's the resource that built the West, not the precious liquid Powell built a reputation around promoting as the nucleus for a sustainable arid land. We've always known this, of course; it's been our dirty little secret. When our rangelands were beaten and battered by years of overgrazing, our solution wasn't to rest the land with fewer cattle and to graze it more conservatively in the future. That would have been too reasonable and, in view of federal funding, downright foolish. We played our hands well, adeptly hiding our intent with the noble language of rugged individualism and minimal government as we raked in hundreds of millions of tax dollars to sustain our increasingly nonsustainable ranching operations. In places like the BLM's Vale District in southeastern Oregon, the federal government spent more than $300,000 per rancher in the 1970s and early 1980s to restore overgrazed rangelands. Since then, Uncle Sam has been handing out checks averaging $12,000 per rancher per year to buy emergency feed to replace the forage that no longer grows on those same depleted rangelands. And thanks to freely flowing federal dollars, 1994 was a bumper-crop year. Every rancher in the Vale District received a check ranging from a low of $30,000 to a high of $50,000.[65]

Today, western "wise users" and People for the West! are angered at being "victims" of federal meddling. Governors and state legislators, smelling votes, now chime in on the rising chorus of dissatisfaction. Forget the fact that federal jobs keep western treasuries afloat. Pick any western state and examine the impact of federal dollars. Pick New Mexico, where Sandia Laboratories, Los Alamos, The National Aeronautics and Space Administration, the White Sands Missile Range, three air force bases (Cannon, Holloman, and Kirtland), and regional headquarters for the Forest Service, the Bureau of Land Management, the U.S. Fish and Wildlife Service, and the National Park Service fatten the economy. So what if hundreds of rural communities throughout the West would be nothing but ghost towns today were it not for the free flow of money from the Forest Service, the BLM, the United States Postal Service, and dozens of federally financed welfare programs? These are just details. Wise users, People for the West!, and politicians have their reasons to chew at the bit.

They are fed up with being told what to do, with having every inch of their West pampered and regulated as though they were spoiled children incapable of self-control. They rebel at federal conditions that constrain their sovereignty, and they are maddened by the arrogant displays of power exercised by federal employees. They call for state's rights and raise the symbolic banner of the victimized rancher whose land and livelihood are threatened by a crazy-quilt pattern of undeserved yet oppressive environmental laws and regulations. They're certainly right about oppressive, but they're dead wrong about undeserved.

A West without Heroes—or Victims

By the time the New West began to dawn, around Earth Day, 1970, the region had become a child of subsidy, and a spoiled child at that. It all seemed too good to be true, and we quickly learned that it was just that. Our independence, our integrity, our spirit, and even our souls had been sold and now were owned lock, stock, and barrel by a good Samaritan, Uncle Sam. Cherished Jeffersonian ideals embracing community, grassroots democracy, self-governance, and self-help had yielded, with barely a whimper, to national values favoring the broader public interest, pork barrel politics, bureaucratic management, and gratuitous subsidies. Our very identity had slipped through our fingers without our realizing what we had lost. The West had become everyone's land, the nation's quintessential playground where universal and pampered—*not local and accountable*—citizens could do as they wished without obligation or responsibility for the region's affairs.

Over the past two decades, dependence and irresponsibility have escalated in the West. A geometric progression in federal laws and regulations has ended any illusion of community, self-governance, or local self-help. Grassroots democracy, like the western range where we hoped and were promised it would take root, has been trammeled and sacrificed in the headlong rush to make the region the nation's handmaiden. The West has finally shed any pretense of being its own keeper (as if it ever was since Anglo settlement); its *raison d'être* no longer rests in the familiar places and forms of its forests, grasslands, wildlife, rivers, and immigrant people. It is merely a kept and consumed mistress, a thing of pleasure and delight valued and exploited as a national repository for parks, recreation, energy, minerals, water, wood fiber, and Big Macs. Even the positive developments in its land management, such as wilderness designations, reintroduction of the wolf, and land restoration, are the products of imposition rather than the evolutionary outcomes of local choice, local ethics, and local responsibility.

We are told, of course, that localism doesn't work or, more accurately, that it won't work without outside aid and oversight. We must trust people who are wiser than us—people who are free of the provincial biases that make us, the westerners, enemies of the land and of ourselves—to make certain that democracy in the West works by making sure that it cannot fail. After all, the West is a moral, not a living, landscape, and we who dwell by permission on its material plane are flawed and weak, subject to temptations only heroes can grasp and conquer. "Home on the range" is at best only a half-truth, a tantalizing metaphor belied by a trail of broken promises. We may live on the land, but we cannot make decisions for the land; we cannot be responsible for ourselves and our environment. Our responsibility, to the extent we have any at all, is to the nation and to the destiny it has chartered for us. We are not to worry about the human and wild communities that surround us and sustain our homes and happiness. Others will guard what is closest and dearest to us, for us and in our names.

But the people of the West have traveled too far and surrendered too much to yield any longer on self-determination, local democracy, and sound environment. Of course, stalwarts of federal wisdom will disagree in principle and fact. They will claim that social welfare and environmental well-being in the West are too much of a burden and too great of a legacy to be entrusted to the whims of local people and the eccentricities of grass-roots democracy. They will argue that the West has not been responsible for itself in the past and that the environmental record of localism is dismal at best.

They will be right, of course, though not for the reasons they imagine. The West has been irresponsible precisely because responsibility has never been its obligation. Localism has failed precisely because responsible self-rule is an anachronism in a fairy-tale world of freely flowing federal dollars. The West of yesterday is not an accurate gauge of the workings of responsible self-governance. It cannot indict what has never existed, and it cannot foretell what is yet to be.

Still, federal stalwarts will point to the telling record of the past as reason enough not to gamble with decentralization and local sovereignty. But when all is said and done, what option is there? If democracy cannot be trusted at the local level, how can we expect it to perform any more wisely when displaced by thousands of miles and dozens of inscrutable governmental agencies? Experience tells us that democracy on the scale of the American nation is too extended, too impersonal, and too dilute to answer the needs of human and natural communities.

The Next West, if it is to be a different West, must and will be a West without heroes or victims—an unspoiled West unadorned by the trappings of federal subsidies, federal projects, and grand schemes. It will be a West where a staunch and fervent land ethic is possible and expected, an ethic whose roots are firmly grounded in the pride of responsibility, the obligation of caring, and the brute fact of necessity. It will be a West where everyday men and women, individually and in concert with their neighbors, assume the duties and affairs that until now have been the exclusive domain of heroes and their governments. It will be a West for ranchers, miners, and loggers as well as health care workers, retirees, and modem-connected urban transplants. It will be a place where heroics are brought down to scale, where heroes and heroines are nothing more than you and your next-door neighbor, and where good and bad are the natural human traits of an unforgiven, but not a victimized, people.

The Next West, if it achieves these things, will be a more modest West. Necessity will demand that it live within its own means, not the exaggerated means of heroes and their governments. Subsidies will yield to local responsibility. When communities cry out for more water, their modest means will dictate what they can do. In place of heroic dams, they will probably have to settle for conservation and protection of what little water they already have. If they do that, they will have learned more about an arid land than John Wesley Powell ever gleaned from his watery trek down the Colorado.

In the Next West, the answer to this question will be key: how can substantive community come about and persist if its members are deprived of the freedom to act and to be wrong? And how can local cooperation, coordination, and consensus have any meaning or value if the most they entail is mere affirmation of decisions preordained by distant laws and regulations? These are the tough questions begged by the visions of Powell, Wilkinson, and Babbitt and left unanswered in the cold and silent grave of the last western hero.

NOTES

1. J. Hector St. John Crèvecoeur, *Letters from an American Farmer* (London, 1782), x.

2. Thomas Jefferson to John Jay, 23 August 1785, in Adrienne Koch and William Peden, eds., *The Life and Selected Writings of Thomas Jefferson* (New York: Modern Library, 1944), 377.

3. Walter Prescott Webb, *The Great Plains* (New York: Grosset & Dunlap, 1972), 424.

4. Henry Nash Smith, *Virgin Land: The American West as Symbol and Myth* (New York: Vintage Books, 1959), 232.

5. *Laramie Sentinel,* 8 January 1887, cited in David M. Emmons, *Garden in the Grasslands* (Lincoln: University of Nebraska Press, 1971), 191.

6. U. S. Department of the Interior, *Annual Report of the Secretary* (Washington, D.C.: Government Printing Office, 1902), 11.

7. Gifford Pinchot, *The Fight for Conservation* (Seattle: University of Washington Press, 1967), 11.

8. Bernard De Voto, "The West against Itself," *Harper's Magazine* 194, no. 1160 (January 1947): 3.

9. Alexis de Tocqueville, *Democracy in America*, vol. 2 (New York: Alfred A. Knopf, 1945), 74.

10. John Muir, *Our National Parks* (New York: AMS Press, 1970), 362.

11. Ibid., 336.

12. Donald Worster, *Nature's Economy: The Roots of Ecology* (New York: Anchor Press, 1979), 217.

13. Patricia Nelson Limerick, *The Legacy of Conquest: The Unbroken Past of the American West* (New York: W. W. Norton, 1987), 83.

14. Silas Bent, Colorado Stock Growers' Association, quoted in Emmons, *Garden in the Grasslands,* 190.

15. Karl Hess, Jr., *Visions upon the Land: Man and Nature on the Western Range* (Washington, D.C.: Island Press, 1992), 60.

16. Pinchot, *The Fight for Conservation,* 95–96.

17. Ivan Doig, *Dancing at the Rascal Fair* (New York: Harper & Row, 1987), 232–233.

18. Hess, *Visions upon the Land,* 16–17; Karl Hess, Jr. and Jerry L. Holechek, "The Policy Roots of Land Degradation in the Arid Region of the United States" pp. 123–146 in David A. Bouat and Charles F. Hutchinson, eds., *Desertification in Developed Countries* (Norwell, Mass.: Kluwer Academic Publishers, 1995); Linda Joyce, *An Analysis of the Range Forage Situation in the United States,* General Technical Report RM-180 (Fort Collins, Colo.: U.S. Department of the Interior, Forest Service, Rocky Mountain Forest and Range Experiment Station, 1991); U.S. General Accounting Office, *Rangeland Management: More Emphasis Needed on Declining and Overstocked Grazing Allotments,* Report B-204997 (Washington, D.C.: Government Printing Office, 1988); and George Wuerthner, "Subdivisions versus Agriculture," *Conservation Biology* 8, no. 3 (September 1994): 905–908.

19. U.S. General Accounting Office, *Public Rangelands: Some Riparian Areas Restored but Widespread Improvement Will Be Slow,* Report B-230548 (Washington, D.C.: Government Printing Office, 1988).

20. Muir, *Our National Parks,* 359.

21. William Culp Darrah, *Powell of the Colorado* (Princeton, N.J.: Princeton University Press, 1951), 272.

22. Wallace Stegner, *Beyond the Hundredth Meridian: John Wesley Powell and the Second Opening of the West* (New York: Penguin Books, 1992), 357.

23. John Wesley Powell, *Report on the Lands of the Arid Region of the United States* (Cambridge, Mass.: Harvard University Press, Belknap Press, 1962), 32.

24. Ibid., 43.

25. Stegner, *Beyond the Hundredth Meridian*, 367.

26. Ibid., 353–362.

27. Ibid., 355–356.

28. Ibid., 362.

29. John Wesley Powell, "Institutions for the Arid Lands," *The Century Magazine* 40, no. 1 (May 1890): 115.

30. Ibid., 113.

31. John Wesley Powell, quoted in Darrah, *Powell of the Colorado*, 204.

32. John Wesley Powell, "The Irrigable Lands of the Arid Region," *The Century Magazine* 38, no. 5 (March 1890): 770, 767.

33. John Wesley Powell, *Eleventh Annual Report of the United States Geological Survey to the Secretary of the Interior: 1889–1890* (Washington, D.C.: Government Printing Office, 1891), 204; Powell "The Irrigable Lands of the Arid Region," 768.

34. John Wesley Powell, "The Non-Irrigable Lands of the Arid Region," *The Century Magazine*, 39, no. 6 (April 1890): 921.

35. Powell, *Eleventh Annual Report of the United States Geological Survey*, 212.

36. *Report of the Public Lands Commission Relating to Public Lands in the Western Portion of the United States and to the Operation of Existing Land Laws* (Washington, D.C.: Government Printing Office, 1880), xxi, xxvii.

37. Powell, "Institutions for the Arid Lands," 111–115.

38. Ibid., 113–115.

39. John Wesley Powell, quoted in Darrah, *Powell of the Colorado*, 265.

40. Ibid., 265.

41. James M. Aton, *John Wesley Powell* (Boise, Idaho: Boise State University, 1994), 34.

42. Marc Reisner, *Cadillac Desert: The American West and Its Disappearing Water* (New York: Penguin Books, 1987), 116–117.

43. Stegner, *Beyond the Hundredth Meridian*, 358.

44. Reisner, *Cadillac Desert*, 116–117; Stegner, *Beyond the Hundredth Meridian*, 358; and Powell, "The Irrigable Lands of the Arid Region," 770.

45. Michael P. Malone and Richard B. Roeder, *Montana: History of Two Centuries* (Seattle: University of Washington Press, 1976), 180.

46. Stegner, *Beyond the Hundredth Meridian*, 356.

47. Ibid., 361–362.

48. John Wesley Powell, "Report on the Methods of Surveying the Public Domain," quoted in Darrah, *Powell of the Colorado*, 256.

49. Peter Miller, "John Wesley Powell: Vision for the West," *National Geographic*, April 1994, 105.

50. Stegner, *Beyond the Hundredth Meridian*, 354.

51. Powell, "The Non-Irrigable Lands of the Arid Region," 919.

52. Donald J. Pisani, "Forests and Reclamation, 1891–1911," *Forest & Conservation History* 37 (April 1993): 70.

53. Ibid.

54. Ibid., 69

55. Powell, "The Non-Irrigable Lands of the Arid Region," 920.

56. Powell, *Eleventh Annual Report of the United States Geological Survey,* 208.

57. John Wesley Powell, quoted in *National Geographic,* April 1994, 114.

58. Bruce Babbitt, quoted in *News Summary* (U.S. Department of the Interior), 10 May 1993, A88.

59. Unattributed, "Western Heroes," *New Yorker,* 10 May 1988.

60. Bruce Babbitt, letter to employees of the U.S. Department of the Interior, 1 April 1993.

61. Bruce Babbitt, transcript of speech, "Between the Flood and the Rainbow: Our Covenant to Protect the *Whole* of Creation," U.S. Department of the Interior, n.d.

62. Charles F. Wilkinson, *Crossing the Next Meridian: Land, Water, and the Future of the West* (Washington, D.C.: Island Press, 1992).

63. Charles F. Wilkinson, "A Tribute to the Man Who Imagined the West We Now Seek to Build," *High Country News,* 3 May 1993, 16.

64. Charles F. Wilkinson, quoted in "Exploitation to Conservation," *Oregonian,* 23 May 1993.

65. Karl Hess, Jr. and Jerry L. Holechek, "Grazing in the Morass," *San Diego Union-Tribune,* 20 November 1994, G-3.

CHAPTER NINE

Empire or Homelands?

A Revival of Jeffersonian Democracy
in the American West

DONALD SNOW

Least explicable of all is the consistent rush of environmentalists to defend the federal agencies whenever the [public lands] title issue is raised. Having spent two-thirds of the twentieth century pointing out . . . the flaws of federal management, those groups' embrace of federal agencies and their stout unwillingness to consider alternatives to federal management is nothing short of sad and ironic. It demonstrates the bankruptcy of our ideas on the subject of public resources.
                                                                    —*Sally K. Fairfax*[1]

At a recent symposium honoring the life and work of Alvin Josephy, I heard rancher and poet Drummond Hadley give an impassioned talk on "grass banks," the voluntary pooling of forage among ranching neighbors who agree to help one another out during tough times. Along the way, Hadley dropped a term that I picked up and have been using ever since. The whole purpose of grass banks, he said, had to be part of a larger, grander strategy—really a kind of cause. Grass banks are one tool to help us, in Hadley's words, preserve "an open lands future for the West." When I heard that phrase, I knew the poet had speared it again. Grass banks, though fascinating to many of us city folks, probably aren't something we can participate in directly, but we can surely share in the cause of an open lands future for the West.

"Open lands," a phrase that rings with both literal and metaphoric resonance, captures very well what the American West has always been: a place of wide open spaces and wide open opportunities for individuals and society, a place not completely hemmed in by the pressures of urbanism or modernity. A wild place, or at least a place with wild areas large enough to support such big-range creatures as the grizzly bear and the Rocky Mountain elk. A place of ecological opportunities left open, where evolution is free to continue. A place of open, public access for all, not merely for the lucky few who can afford land or memberships in pricey outdoor clubs. An open, land-based society with its own traditions of hospitality, generosity, even innocence. An open polity in which the individual voice can actually be heard and can, perhaps, make a difference in government.

Undeveloped lands, long, unimpeded vistas, sparse population, wildness, and access to the countryside—these have always been the hallmarks of the West, and they are all part of the hope contained in Hadley's phrase: the hope that somehow we can find the courage and the means to preserve them.

Throughout the twentieth century, conservation and environmentalism in the West have sought in large part to preserve that "open lands" character. During the past thirty years or so—the years marking the era of modern environmentalism—it has been those very efforts to maintain the West's open lands character that have distinguished western environmentalism from that practiced elsewhere. Throughout my twenty-year career as a Rocky Mountain environmentalist, I have always been aware that I speak a different language from that of my counterparts in Vermont or Kentucky or New York City. We all discuss the same cluster of problems—pollution, land use controversies, social injustice, the ills of technology—but in the part of the country where I come from, these issues are cast against a very different backdrop.

There is an oft-repeated mantra about the West that grows out of the simplest kind of demographic research and is frequently cited to give the lie to the West's claim to the rural. Eastern critics of the West's subsidy economy, for example, love to cite this fact of demography: "The American West is the region with the nation's highest proportion of people living in cities and towns." Undoubtedly the statement is true, but like a lot of statistics, it is terribly misleading, for it masks a simple but compelling fact also captured in Hadley's phrase. Regardless of where they live, people in the West commonly have strong personal relationships with the land, and those relationships are profoundly important to the citizenry. This is the one region of the country where almost everyone lives near an enormous block of accessible public land. Moreover, the West continues to be a region in which relationships with people who live on the land—farmers, ranchers, outfitters, and others—are integral to the lifeways of urban dwellers. Hundreds of thousands of us hunt, fish, hike, watch wildlife, or otherwise recreate on private land owned by others; and practically everybody here spends significant time on the public lands—tracts large enough that a strong hiker can walk for days and never cross a road. In this important sense, western lands have always remained more open than lands anywhere else.

But there is a darkness underneath all this, and that is why Hadley's phrase also constitutes a challenge and a cause. To many, the West seems to be in the process of "closing," a perception captured in another poet's phrase, "the last best place." The sense of closure, of "lastness," has perhaps been felt most acutely during the early 1990s as population pressures throughout the West have vastly expanded. It comes in large measure with the realization that the riparian lands—the valuable "oasis" lands of any arid or semiarid region—are being subdivided and developed at an alarming pace.

Urbanism is now footloose and can exist anywhere by virtue of advances in transportation, communications, and marketing (a fact neatly captured in *High Country News* editor Ed Marston's statement that "all of Western Colorado is now urban above 8,000 feet and rural below"). As urban living, with its technological umbilicus, spreads into the small-town reaches of the West, we encounter many unpleasant outcomes. Housing prices, for example, are driving native and longtime residents out of their own towns, not just in the Aspen-like resort communities but also in more everyday places, long immune to glitter—places like Bozeman, Montana; Grand Junction, Colorado; and Idaho Falls, Idaho. With all the new growth, roads and highways simply have to be expanded, and with that expansion come increased speed, increased traffic, and increased wildlife mortality. We watch in dismay as people with surplus capital continue to plant ostentatious houses—some call them "starter castles"—on the ridge tops of the Gallatin and Popo Agie valleys or smack on the banks of Montana's remote Smith River or Idaho's Palouse. Building the dream palace is a practice that has taken root in the Rockies and is probably here to stay, and in our mass hatred of anything resembling coercion in governance, we have rendered ourselves powerless to do much about it.

That the region's growth is now explosive has been underscored by dozens of press reports during the past decade. In 1992 and 1993, the growth rate for the eight-state Rocky Mountain region—containing eight of the ten fastest-growing states in the nation—ran to 2.6 percent per year, approaching that of Africa, the fastest-growing continent, with a rate of 2.9 percent. More than 350,000 people flooded into the rural and small-town reaches of the Rockies during 1993, accounting for nearly half of the total nonmetropolitan growth in the United States. During the past decade in Montana—a state that was begging for national attention (or just any attention) when I moved into it nineteen years ago—every county touching the Continental Divide grew by 10 percent. Figures on personal income during this period show that people are hardly coming to the Treasure State for its treasure. In 1992, according to the Montana Department of Commerce, 40 percent of all personal income in the state was unearned income derived from investments, pensions, retirement funds, entitlements, and other non–wage earner sources.

In my short time in Montana, I have never witnessed such concern over growth as the sort I am hearing today—not even in the 1970s, when the energy barons appeared ready to overrun the coalfields of Montana and the northern Great Plains. This time, there is a reckless, desperate feeling to the growth, and it seems to be making many Montanans very grim in their view of the future. But even in the face of the heedless growth now occurring in every Rocky Mountain state, there is a strong hope that we can indeed preserve an open lands future, for the West still possesses a treasure that no other region can claim: fully one-half of its land is in the public domain.

In this essay, I will explore a few of the emerging problems and opportunities along the way to a Next West, focusing on the fertile political ground that now exists between the urban and rural contingents of the fast-growing Rocky Mountain region. In the background, I hope, will ring the resonances of Drummond Hadley's beautiful phrase, "an open lands future for the West," for in my view, he has captured the essence of what the great western debate is all about.

It is clear that we will not preserve the open lands character of the West, and all the social and political implications it carries, by resorting to what economist Thomas Michael Power describes as "a focus through the rearview mirror." Trying to lock the West into its mythic past—even a recent economic past of mining, logging, and agriculture—will protect nothing and no one, except perhaps a small cadre of investors, corporations, and others dependent on subsidies. If we are to preserve the open character of this region, we are simply going to have to loosen our grip on the antique natural resource institutions that do little more than hold in place the old "iron triangle" of the federal government, big business, and local chamber of commerce boosters.

Nor will we save the West's wildness and openness by yielding to the all-American allure of privatization. The West's greatness lies precisely in the fact—really an accident of history—that half of its land base has remained public for the entire twentieth century despite massive, repeated attacks on the federal land agencies and on the very concept of public land ownership. Privatizing or "marketizing" public resources will only hasten the closing of the open lands West.[2] But if the alternative to privatization is simply to hang on to the status quo—in which federal land agencies and Congress blindly plod along, subsidizing environmentally destructive development on the public lands—we will also see a gross diminution of wildness in the West, for federal "solutions" to natural resource problems have been among the most destructive of all.

Instead, I believe, it is time to effect a renaissance of the local, which must necessarily involve a new level of trust in both the individual citizen and the imperatives of governing. On the following pages, I will suggest a revival of Jeffersonian democracy in the West, which would necessitate the decentralization of much management authority, the devolution of real power to the citizenry, and the creation of new institutions of responsibility to manage that power and to enable us to learn over time to use it effectively and well. I will begin by discussing the region's most obvious economic and demographic trends and then move swiftly into politics, that most tarnished of arts. The local setting is the best place to effect lasting and palpable change, and politics is the arena in which we can best hope to influence the changes already under way in the West.

Happy Days Are Here Again?

Evidence suggests that the public land states of the West stand at the beginning of a massive power shift—a shift away from centralized management of natural resources and toward community-level involvement in major land management decisions, beginning with the federal lands. The forces driving this shift are economic, demographic, and political, and they are fast becoming inexorable. I base my argument here on essentially two lines of observation.

First, the West's environmental history suggests that centralized management of natural resources—spawned by the progressive era conservationists of the turn of the century—has become both unaffordable and politically unsupportable and, moreover, fits poorly with the imperative to manage natural systems at an appropriate scale. The large federal land and water agencies, created to foster orderly development of the public land states, seem to have entered an era of permanent flux. There is much uncertainty about their mission and purpose in a developed West.

What the region now faces is essentially the end of the great federal experiment. Public management of land and water and all the subsidies and supports that have come with it created a kind of nationalized economy for the region. But Americans' mistrust of the federal government, and their growing refusal to allocate public monies to an endless cavalcade of federal "solutions" to every imaginable social and economic problem, will gradually translate into decreased federal authority in the West. Just as the region benefited disproportionately from federal largess—due to the massive public land base—it will now suffer disproportionately from the gradual shrinking of the federal presence unless it creates new institutions appropriate to the many tasks of resource management.

Second, a series of important changes have recently taken place in the arena of environmental dispute resolution. What began as a challenging new effort to help environmental disputants negotiate their way to agreeable solutions—in issues ranging from waste disposal and pollution control to the reintroduction of wolves, land use planning, and sustainable forestry to the creation of in-stream flows in depleted western rivers—has now become a series of experiments in new governance. Since about 1990, these efforts have arisen with such force and have become so widespread as to constitute, in my view, a new environmental movement. They are attempts not to erase or abdicate existing structures of government—as some have erroneously argued[3]—but to make them more responsive, more attuned to public needs (especially local needs), more *democratic*. The coalitions that come together in this work, regardless of their political orientation, end up decidedly pro-government but often anti–status quo. They want governance that works.

The forces driving these great shifts in the West are as fascinating as the shifts themselves. There is much talk about a New West economy of information and services, but in fact that economy has existed in this region for as long as it has everywhere else. The only new aspect of it is the public's sudden awareness of its existence. Westerners have long been told that their economy rests on the three pillars of minerals, logging, and agriculture and that all other economic activity is tied to these. But in fact, much of the region long ago became dominated economically by its cities, and in those cities, with few exceptions, the "big three" are not critical aspects of very many working lives. Economically, the West has been split into the rural areas, where those so-called basic industries are often dominant, and the urban areas, where they are not.

One of the most fascinating aspects of the region's split economy is that whereas the "new economy" of information and services is largely free-market oriented, the "old economy" continues to be heavily subsidized. Increasingly, the old economy is a sentimental economy whose existence will depend on the continuing goodwill of taxpayers. Worldwide, a similar shift is underway toward the openness and fluidity of markets and away from the politically charged allocations endemic to "planned" economies. The wind blows away from the subsidized West.

The demographic shift in the West is much more dramatic. It is beginning to appear as if the boom-bust population cycles in the Rocky Mountain states have crescendoed into one long, sustained boom—and this one probably represents a national demographic translocation. Unlike the booms of the recent past, this new growth is not tied to the development of any particular commodity, so it doesn't follow the contours of coal beds, or mineral deposits or the pincushion pattern of holes in the petroleum basins. Instead, it's a boom based on human yearning—the yearning for a better life in a better place. Today's "ore bodies" are the well-protected environmental amenities of the West—its wilderness areas, national parks, wild rivers, and gorgeous intermontane valleys and the comfortable, friendly towns nestled among those beauty spots. The "miners" are arriving in a rush as did the forty-niners, but instead of gold, they are mining their own lives, and their minds and fortunes are not fixed on the exploitation of natural resources. Over time, these newcomers will grow into a substantial political force, but they have to stick around long enough to become both knowledgeable and effective—a point that brings us around to politics.

The Battle between Decentralization and Dependence

The West is struggling with the issues of decentralization and it's no wonder: the West owns the longest, deepest history of political centrality in the United States, a history now well documented by a spate of recent revisionist books.[4] The region's destiny has always been tied tightly to decisions made in the boardrooms of New York, Minneapolis, and Chicago, but the strongest tie has always been to Washington, for the West's massive federal land base had made the central government into the most powerful political force in the region. Its power is unusual in the West, a fact much amplified by the region's sparse, scattered population and its long-standing tendency to rely on the fortunes of a few major industries to maintain jobs and a modest prosperity.

This combination of economic "thinness" and dependence on distant decision makers, many of them in government agencies, is perhaps the principal hallmark of the rural West, if not so much of the urban. Yet this relationship continues to be one of the hardest points to get across to newcomers or to those living outside the region who remain skeptical about how unique the Rocky Mountain region is in this respect. A few simple, seemingly unrelated facts should suffice to make the point.

In Idaho, the Department of Energy's Idaho National Engineering Laboratory (INEL) is the largest single-site employer in the state, with some 9,000 workers on the payroll and perhaps a similar number employed in jobs related directly to servicing this 900-square-mile tract of scattered nuclear technology. Through the 1980s, at least, INEL's budget rivaled that of the state government.

In Montana, decades ago the city of Butte had more than 100,000 residents (Montana's largest city today, Billings, has about 80,000), most of them tied economically to copper mines owned by a single corporation. Until the mid-1960s, the Anaconda Copper Company owned six of the state's seven daily newspapers.

The mining industry in contemporary Montana reports that average wages in a large metal mine—typically a gold, silver, or copper mine—exceed $50,000 per year. However, wages in the service sector associated largely with the state's new tourist economy—typically jobs in restaurants, motels, retail shops, repair facilities, and the like—average only $20,000 per year. Although these low-paying service jobs make up only a fraction of the service sector as a whole, such numbers are extremely compelling to many westerners, who believe that their economy has been "stolen" from them.

The USDA Forest Service, whose landholdings are primarily in the western states, reports that there are 234 "timber-dependent communities" across the West. These are communities in which at least 10 percent of local employment is in the timber industry and at least 50 percent of the timber supply comes from national forests.

Dozens of other, similar facts about each of the Rocky Mountain states could be recounted. The point is that westerners long ago grew peculiarly dependent on the wishes of a few distantly centered organizations and agencies that held out the promise of good-paying jobs as long as the region continued to accept its Faustian arrangement with big government and big business. Westerners still struggle mightily with this legacy of dependence. Nothing else more clearly explains the sudden and dramatic rise of the "wise use" movement in every western state and its shrill insistence that the federal government redouble the flow of commodities from the public domain.

But the legacy of dependence runs much deeper than the rhetoric of the "wise users." Virtually every state and every *rural* county in the West remains profoundly dependent on the flow of revenues from the public lands. According to congressionally established allocation formulas, state governments receive 50 percent of all oil-, gas-, and coal-leasing revenues from production on federal lands and another 25 percent of all national forest revenues.[5] These revenue-sharing formulas translate into major additions to the budgets of the high-producing states. Wyoming and New Mexico, for example, received more than $200 million and $130 million, respectively, in 1984 from oil, gas, and coal revenues.[6] (It is important to note that these revenues do not include the states' own taxes on "mineral severance," production, or property related to the production sites.)

Moreover, many counties across the West receive PILTs, or payments in lieu of taxes, from the federal government. Because federal lands cannot be taxed as property by lower levels of government, Congress in 1976 created the PILT program to help compensate local governments for lost revenues. PILTs can be as much as seventy-five cents per acre per year (adjusted to incorporate payments already made under other revenue-sharing formulas, such as timber receipts).[7] Western counties receive about two-thirds of the PILT payments distributed nationwide, and though the amount of money involved may seem minor to city dwellers accustomed to urban budgets soaring into the billions (total PILT payments during the mid-1980s averaged $100 million per year), these funds are sometimes the very lifeblood of remote western counties.[8]

The political implications of this dependence are enormous; indeed, in my view, they constitute the single most important fact of the political West. Except in highly unusual cases, this is simply not a region in which plans for resource development—indeed, for *any* development—are ever denied. When economies and budgets remain so thin—and they always have, especially in the rural reaches—there is simply too much at stake to walk away from any promise of prosperity, regardless of the impact of the development or the degree to which it may actually increase dependence on outside decisions. Yet the West's epic and long-standing dependence remains largely hidden from public view. Westerners are fond of projecting an image of strong self-reliance, of rugged tenacity in the face of the historically poor odds of surviving in the region, and surely a major part of maintaining that image is suppressing the real one. Indeed, one can just about rely on the degree of projected independence being directly proportional to the actual dependence. This helps explain "western anger," a term commonly used by journalists to describe the populist rage that seems to burst forth periodically in the West. Western anger is mostly a reflection of western impotence; to the extent that it is directed against governmental agents, it is a simple reflection of an inability to steer local or personal destiny and the demonizing of those who appear that they can.

One unfortunate offshoot of a century of centralized resource management is that it has kept the West politically immature. The federal presence has insulated westerners from many of the key responsibilities of governance. As a result, many of the region's communities seem to have trouble with the notion of political responsibility; never having been asked to take full control of their own destinies, local boosters have substituted a form of political collusion for hard decision making. Westerners complain long and loud about "the Feds," but the fact remains that in counties composed of, say, 90 percent federal land, it's quite easy to avoid tough decisions. Under those circumstances, the real work is to reach deep into the pork barrel to keep the benefits flowing and the true costs of resource development hidden from public view. That the region has virtually institutionalized this practice is the dirty little secret of the West.

Enter the Naysayers

In recent years, however, the dependence and centrality of the rural West have come under vigorous attack. Environmentalists began this attack in the early 1970s, but for many years they were the lone negative voices of the West, decrying the abuse and mismanagement of natural resources. Since World War II, they pointed out, the national forests, once protected for their watershed values by uniformed agents in dimpled hats, had been plundered to feed the timber industry. Federal coal was being sold in unprecedented quantities, and various agencies of both federal and state government were winking at the egregious impacts of mining and power plant development and all the boomtown sprawl that went with them. Moreover, the Forest Service and the Bureau of Land Management (BLM) were constantly dragging their feet over wilderness designations, so any attempt to preserve what was left turned into a very tedious proposition.

Sometime in the mid-1980s, a small group of economists joined the naysayers. They began to point out the alarming extent to which subsidies propped up the West's resource economy, and a few of them—such as Terry

Anderson, Randal O'Toole, Richard Stroup, Ed Whitelaw, and Thomas Michael Power—convincingly suggested that sound environmental management and sound economics should go hand in hand and that acceptable environmental outcomes would not be obtained until the federal government stopped propping up destructive resource development with subsidies, both hidden and overt.

A third wave of criticism hit when a group of political economists— among them John A. Baden, Robert H. Nelson, and others—began to analyze the incentive structures of the federal land and water agencies. Their conclusions showed that the agencies were virtually mandated to "do the wrong thing" by a fatal combination of three factors. First, budget increases in many federal agencies were tied by statute to the maximization of development: the more development an agency could help foster, the larger its budget and the greater its prestige. Second, the game was rigged by statute: nearly every major resource policy governing the West was an antique, a holdover from the earliest years of the century, when promoting western development was regarded as an unqualified holy. Sharpshooting commodity group lobbyists saw to it—and still do today—that these policies remain in force. Third, many of the laws and policies governing the actions of federal land and water agencies directly conflict with one another. For example, the Multiple Use–Sustained Yield Act, governing much Forest Service activity, simply cannot exist in the same universe with the National Forest Management Act. In the midst of such conflicting signals, a bureaucracy's impulse seems to be to act in accordance with its prevailing organizational culture, which in the case of the land and water agencies is decidedly prodevelopment.

For a long time, the prodevelopment strategy and the many federal experiments it spawned throughout the region worked because they provided jobs, made quite a few fortunes, and allowed western communities to develop middle-class lifeways. But by the time the Reagan years rolled around, too many people were wise to the West. Reagan's habit of appointing corporate leaders (timber executive John Crowell to head the Forest Service) and martinet conservatives (James Watt as secretary of the interior, Robert Burford as head of the Bureau of Land Management, Anne Gorsuch Burford as head of the Environment Protection Agency) to key positions affecting the West only exacerbated the growing anguish over runaway resource development. In a particularly colorful burst of antisubsidy bravado aimed at the West, Senator Patrick Moynihan declared on the floor of the U.S. Senate, "The Great Barbecue is over!"

It may not have been over, exactly, but a lot of guests were leaving.

Let's Throw the Bums Out

In the face of the mounting scorn directed at the government's ungainly experiments with the West and its citizens (who often have been very willing subjects), there is a great temptation simply to abandon the art of politics in all matters pertaining to the great mass of public lands—lands that would have to figure prominently in any vision of an open lands future. Law scholar James Huffman is a particularly scornful critic of the dishonest shadow-boxing games westerners have long played with the politics of the public lands. "We call them *public* lands," I once heard him say in a seminar, "but in truth they are *political* lands. We ought to call them what they are."9 He has a point.

Resource politics, at least as practiced since the end of World War II, has served the West poorly, in no small measure because of the many masks worn by the region's politicians and their minions in the resource management agencies. There is probably no region of the country where the pork barrel reigns so supreme and where Democrats and Republicans elected to Congress are so indistinguishable in locally critical resource issues such as "getting out the cut" (to prop up yet another timber-dependent community), getting the next dam built (usually to benefit a handful of irrigators at national expense), getting the mine permitted (so that at least a few local workers can make real wages instead of burger-flipper scratch), or keeping the BLM off the backs of local graziers.

Especially irritating to many environmentalists is the mantra, still heard today (though increasingly in an embarrassed whisper), that the federal land and water agencies are performing "scientific management"—that their decisions are the dispassionate outcomes of rational, scientific investigations and therefore are above politics. In fact, anyone with two eyes and the vestige of a central nervous system can see the heavy hand of politics on virtually every major decision made by the land and water agencies and their counterparts in the state governments of the West. Now that the Great Barbecue is indeed winding down, the urge to gerrymander resource decisions through simple power politics has become desperate, and the results are often comically naked. A good recent example is a bill introduced by Senator Pete Domenici of New Mexico that would *mandate* the grazing of livestock on federal rangeland. Under this bill, ranchers would never have the option to manage, say, for wildlife if they believed that the presence of wild animals could increase their profits; nor could they sell or transfer their leases to organizations that wanted to manage the range to benefit wildlife. This is an excellent example of how ridiculous western resource issues have become. If a senator doesn't like the prevailing tendencies toward environmental amenities on the public lands, he or she just changes the rules, overthrowing ecology and any other inconvenient science in the process. The veil of scientific management has grown thin indeed.[10]

The libertarian urge to privatize the public domain is one recurring theme in efforts to depoliticize resource management. Privatization, it is argued, would replace political decision making with the more straightforward interplay of property rights. Instead of relying on distant (or not-so-distant) bureaucrats to act as environmental stewards, we could trust the marketplace, for private resource owners will always tend to act to protect their property, whereas bureaucrats will tend to act to protect their own rear ends. Moreover, the argument goes (in a twist I find especially intriguing), market processes are inherently more *democratic:* in acting out their desires through market transactions, people "vote" with their dollars. Thus there is less opportunity for Machiavellian manipulators to claim the high ground of "the public interest." The real public interest can be clearly measured—not guessed at—according to what people actually pay for. If you want wilderness, make its users pay the full costs for it; if you want to operate a pulp mill, make its owners pay the full costs of supplying it with timber. If we could somehow "purify" the markets for the West's resources, the libertarian view asserts, we would swiftly see that environmental amenities now carry real values that in most instances will exceed the values of extracting raw natural resources.

The privatization juggernaut may well clarify the public's evaluation of nature, and it might reduce our chronic heartburn over politics, but it would not necessarily guarantee or enhance the open lands future which Drummond Hadley dreams of. Indeed, privatization in the nature business is already occurring at breakneck speed, and the results are often appalling. In Montana, unlike the situation in the wiser state of Wyoming, "game farms" are permitted to operate on private lands even though the state claims ownership of all big game animals within its borders. There is mounting evidence that game farming has introduced alien and dangerous genes into the deer family's gene pool, especially that of the Rocky Mountain elk, an icon of the West.[11] In Colorado, Montana, and other western states, expensive guided hunts on private lands—many of them former cattle ranches—are becoming the wave of the future. Out-of-staters are willing to spend upward of $5,000 for a week of trophy elk hunting on the high ranges of private ranches. This would be nobody else's business except that as word spreads across the region, the lucrative "sport" of private hunting may slowly eclipse the older, more democratic practice of asking humbly for permission to hunt on private land and being granted it without a fee. Ditto for the practice of charging rod fees to fish in *public waterways* on private lands. Well-off anglers who look as if they just stepped out of a window display at Ralph Lauren perhaps can afford rod fees of fifty to seventy-five dollars per day, but the poor proles who actually live in the area must elbow one another aside at the crowded public access points along the West's fabled trout streams.

Stiff fees for hunting and fishing may be the leading edge of the nature business and, perhaps, the initial entry point for the privatization juggernaut, but these are mere portents of things to come. The West will not have an open lands future if access to premium experience is extended only to the rich. Nor will wilderness values necessarily be protected if the West is thrown open to a panoply of markets for nature's many goods. Most of the "rich" people I know spend their surplus on motorboats, jet skis, snowmobiles, and heli-ski adventures; indeed, there seems to be a direct relationship between the thirst to make money and the willingness to make noise and pollution. Moreover, there is simply no convincing evidence that property ownership, or market "voting," for that matter, automatically confers stewardship. If the history of the American West has taught us anything, it is that money corrupts and big money corrupts absolutely.

Far from shying away from politics simply because politics has served us badly, I am interested in learning how to perform politics better. There is no better place to begin afresh than with management of the West's public lands, those maddeningly troublesome political lands derided by James Huffman. Indeed, it is precisely their political nature that makes these lands and resources critically important to the American experiment in democracy. In the management of the West's public lands, political interference is not to be avoided but encouraged, under a new regime of land management that would force westerners to come to grips with real political responsibility relative to public lands management and community vitality.

I want to be part of a movement that struggles to find a politics appropriate to the stewardship of nature and community, and I believe that such a politics is to be found in a new approach to federal land management—an experiment in a truly decentralist vision to be undertaken in a few carefully selected laboratories.

The Birth of an Appropriate Politics

In my twenty years of environmental activism in the West, I have come to believe that "the risk of the local" is now the only plausible response to many of the region's pressing needs. If we do indeed want an open lands future, local activism and new forms of local responsibility will surely have to be key elements in creating it.

By taking the risk of the local, I mean simply entrusting local people with a major share of decision making about the lands proximate to their communities—both private and public lands. It is obviously a risk to do so because westerners have proved themselves quite amenable to dreaming up short-term solutions to almost every economic problem they have ever faced. It is risky indeed to trust people of a historically boomtown mentality with the future of anything. But that is what I am suggesting, for we have seen the alternative—remote-control land and water management, jury-rigged by the demands of national politicians—and it clearly does not work.

The most striking examples of people already engaged in the risk of the local lie in the many consensus groups now found in every western state.[12] Typically, these take the form of stakeholder coalitions composed of former adversaries. They come together, often out of frustration with politics-as-usual, to try to solve problems jointly that none of the parties could solve alone. Instead of relying on solutions put forward by a governmental arbiter or decision maker—a court, a governmental agency, a legislative body, or a specially empowered commission of some sort—consensus groups, often on their own authority, try to negotiate their way to agreements that will solve the problems at hand and withstand further challenge. Sometimes their agreements are formal (written out, signed, and so forth); sometimes they are not. Depending on their makeup, these groups may then submit their ad hoc agreements to some official, recognized body for ratification.

These groups take many other forms as well. Some grow to see their role as mostly advisory, working to help agencies fulfill new mandates. Others are chiefly informative or educational, helping the public understand the implications of resource use. Still others grapple with issues such as population growth and development, or local economic vitality, and may have little or no bearing on federal agencies and resource decisions. But they have the common characteristic that they are composites of the unalike; their strength (as well as their volatility) lies in their diversity.

Consensus groups seek to empower the disenfranchised, but the meaning of that troublesome word is often a little different in this context. It is typically the case that local people, no matter how powerful the organizations they represent, have at best only advisory responsibilities in matters of environmental decision making, especially as it relates to public resources. Consensus groups, when they work well, create powerful new coalitions that can bring people much closer to governmental decisions—sometimes placing the coalition itself in a position of decision-making authority.

They provide opportunities to solve problems through collaboration that none of the involved parties could have solved alone, through the force of a new critical mass. For frequently when these strange coalitions begin to jell, they overcome residual opposition through the politics of inclusion. They often maximize creativity through a form of synergy in which the results of collaboration exceed the sum of the parts. When they work, they prove that strange bedfellows make interesting kids.

There are dozens of examples of such efforts at work across the West. A few of the best known include the Applegate Partnership in Oregon, the Quincy Library Group in California, the Henrys Fork Watershed Association in Idaho, and the Blackfoot Challenge in Montana. Recently, various media sources have picked up on the "consensus fever" spreading across the West. National Public Radio has done a feature on the Seventh American Forest Congress, a massive national effort to use consensus processes in revising forest policies for both public and private forestlands. At least one major study of watershed councils has been published,[13] and a fine book on the use of collaborative processes applied to public and private rangelands has emerged.[14] *High Country News,* the West's influential environmental newspaper, dedicated a special issue to the emergence of consensus groups.[15]

It's easy to criticize these efforts for what they have not accomplished—and critics abound—but one must remember that consensus groups are still new, that they necessarily operate in an atmosphere supercharged with mistrust, cynicism, even hatred, and that a mountain of policy, law, and custom (most of it rotten to the core, but still hulking there) stands in front of them. The entire world screams that it can't be done, but in fact it *is* being done, and if the results are not yet dramatic, only the terminally naive should be surprised.

Yet consensus groups, popular as they now may be, are only a beginning in what could become a major realignment of power in western resource decision making. It appears to me that the consensus group concept is already beginning to mutate into a new notion altogether: the notion of community-based conservation.

I borrow that term from *The View from Airlie,* a booklet recently published by the Liz Claiborne and Art Ortenberg Foundation.[16] In 1993, the foundation sponsored a symposium in Virginia, in which leaders in international conservation came together to discuss the prospects for community-based conservation, or the deliberate processes by which communities become more intimately involved in the relationship between people and nature. In the wrap-up session of the conference, David Western of the Wildlife Conservation Society in Kenya observed that "the old approach [in conservation] was a heavy-handed, top-down, culturally insensitive set of procedures and attitudes. "We're on the verge of a sea-change in the way conservation is done," Western continued. "With this new approach, conservation will be 'embedded within' the human-modified landscape, rather than being separated from and imposed upon the landscape."[17]

Western's remarks were aimed at the learning that had recently taken place in the arena of international conservation, in which U.S. environmental groups had tried to impose American-style strategies for designating and managing nature preserves in developing countries. These often proved alien to cultures with no tradition of human-free landscapes (but long traditions of endemic poverty) and thus had to be modified to recognize people as part of a park's environs. With a little imagination, one can readily see that the broad distinction Western makes between the old and the new styles can apply to conservation practices anywhere.

As I think about the long-term potential for successful collaboration in the West, I would be inclined to modify the Airlie lexicon to include *community conservation,* a term sufficiently ambiguous, flexible, and brisk to accommodate many of the emerging processes now under debate. Community conservation implies three things: First, the deep involvement of local communities in the conservation and care of nearby natural resources for the benefit of people and nature together. Second, the conservation of community itself—of the attitudes, processes, duties, responsibilities, and relationships that go into forming and maintaining healthy communities, wherever they may be. And third, a sense of community involvement that is broader than local: a community of all who share a passion for accessible public lands. This final sense of the term *community conservation* is especially important, for it goes to the root of legitimate concerns about the management and care of public resources, treaty rights, and other institutions that are, and should remain, national and even international in scope and effect. I'll return to this last point in a moment.

For many in the West—including many environmentalists—community conservation represents a kind of homecoming, a way of bringing the implementation of sound environmental policy down to the ground and back into the lives of people who are directly affected by the outcomes. In my career as an environmentalist, I have long been concerned that far too much environmental work has tended to alienate the very people who can make good conservation happen—or who can block it through inaction, a never-ending search for loopholes, or just plain recalcitrance. So much environmental policy is coercive in its effects, and so few westerners—especially those living on the land—are apt to sit still for coercion. Community conservation of the kind I envision fosters on-the-ground responsibility by sharing both accountability and power.

Where public land management intersects with the economic health of local communities—a condition that applies to most of the rural, if not the urban West—the notion of sharing power (or, in today's popular language, "devolving power to more local levels") is understandably troubling to many. And here we come back to the difficult question of the extralocal, often expressed as the national interest in our public lands.

The chairman of the Sierra Club, Michael McCloskey, has pointed out that in some instances, local stakeholder groups working on public land issues represent a redistribution of power.[18] And he's worried about the implications: "This redistribution of power," he writes, "is designed to disempower our constituency, which is heavily urban. Few urbanites are represented as stakeholders in communities surrounding national forests. Few of the proposals for stakeholder involvement provide any way for distant stakeholders to be effectively represented."

Clearly, these are wise and legitimate concerns that demand discussion and debate as nascent efforts in community conservation continue to unfold. Many environmentalists remain concerned that any loss or significant reduction of federal management authority will inevitably lessen the possibility for long-range vision to guide the management and care of the West's priceless public lands.

But it's too easy simply to leap to the conclusion that either consensus groups or efforts in community conservation automatically translate into a triumph of shortsightedness. And it's easier still to assume that federal land managers (or any agents of centralized government) will look out for the public interest simply because legislative mandates or the courts tell them that they must. The old conservation paradigm described by David Western relies heavily on delegation of power and managerial responsibility to agencies of government; the new paradigm of community conservation seeks to formalize the recognition that agencies must be responsive to local interests in ways that reach well beyond time-honored tendencies to work in collusion with private business.

What many environmentalists seem to overlook when they reflexively attack the growing use of local consensus groups is that it was the work of environmentalists themselves that opened the door to these new experiments with accountability and power. Having demanded public involvement for more than twenty-five years, environmentalists are now seeing, in consensus groups and community conservation, some healthy outcomes of that demand. Moreover, devolution of power to local levels is a natural and expected outcome of the advocacy for responsive environmental management. Nature tends to decentralize.

Clearly, national interests—as well as *the national interest*—must be well represented in consensus groups that seek to influence public land decisions, no matter where those groups exist. Indeed, one limiting factor in using consensus groups to improve public lands management is the scarcity of potent, experienced environmental activists in some of the most rural reaches of the West. Without those voices at the table, local consensus groups can easily devolve into cheerleading squads whose main purpose is to help governmental agencies and/or corporate interests proceed even more efficiently with predetermined agendas to develop public lands in the name of local economic diversification or some other unquestionable holy.

A Call for a New Experiment

Despite a century of effort, residents of the West have never managed to democratize the public lands. Instead, westerners have mostly succeeded in shutting people out, fostering their collusion with big industry, or directing their input into the least productive channel—namely, the cold comfort of sniping at and naysaying the federal management agencies at every turn. Delegating land management authority to agencies filled with putative experts is hardly democratic, but because "public involvement criteria" have lately been written into federal land laws, westerners have been able to convince themselves that the faint base of "democracy" has somehow been covered.

Oddly enough, some environmentalists have been among those most deeply invested in the antidemocratic management regime exercised on the public lands. Any suggestions aimed at devolving power or land management authority to more local levels—even on a temporary, experimental basis—are met with howls of derision, especially from national environmental leaders. But these days, the federal emperors in the West are wearing hardly a stitch, and environmentalists who continue to defend the threadbare paradigm of remote-control land management are beginning to look like a court of fools. Perhaps it's time to try something bold.

In testimony before the House Committee on Natural Resources I called on the committee to engage in a radical experiment in community conservation. (The West, after all, is the land of such experiments.) I suggested that Congress authorize the creation of several citizen management councils to take over managerial authority of various well-defined units of federal land. I chose these more or less at random, simply to try to cover several kinds of lands and managerial problem sets. There would be, perhaps, a Bitterroot National Forest Council (I suggested nicknaming it the Bolle Council, in honor of the great University of Montana forester Arnold Bolle, whose 1970 study of the Bitterroot ended the practice of terraced clear-cuts in the national forests); a Glacier National Park Council; a Pawnee Grasslands Council; a Pyramid Lake Management Council; an Escalante Backcountry and Community Development Council; and an Idaho Council for the High Desert, nicknamed the Bruneau Canyon Group.

These councils, I suggested, would be not advisory but decisional. They would be granted—on a temporary, experimental basis—full managerial authority over the lands within their control. And they would have to be given great latitude to experiment with various fee structures for uses of the land, restrictions on roading and access, ecological restoration efforts, and so forth. Their mission would be to create demonstrably superior management of the resources under their governance according to a set of ecological and economic indicators established in advance. An Experimental Public Land Management Oversight Subcommittee would watch over and evaluate their work.

Instead of acting as advisors to federal management agencies, the councils would use agency personnel as advisors; but agency authority would be suspended. Special preference would be given to agency workers who had earlier distinguished themselves as whistle-blowers. They would be revered and honored for their penchant for truth-telling.

The experimental councils would be mixtures of local and national interests. Members would be carefully selected by the oversight subcommittee for their tendencies toward statesmanlike behavior. The point would be to avoid packing the councils with hidebound ideologues of any stripe. Two principal qualifications for service would be a demonstrable record of levelheadedness and a strong sense of humor.

And so forth. I got the idea across to the committee, but for some reason the members declined to draft it immediately into law. It is not an original idea, of course, and despite the committee's inaction, efforts much like what I proposed are now being mounted seriously in several places across the West. In fact, the idea is quite old and fairly well worn.

It is no more radical than the notion of self-governing Indian reservations on which local, native people assume managerial authority over trust-lands and natural resources. Indeed, many progressive tribal governments (which are often councils) are managing reservation resources in exactly the manner I envisioned before the committee. The Confederated Salish-Kootenai in Montana, for example, manage large tracts of their own timberlands, rivers, and streams and a tribally designated wilderness area. They recently entered into an agreement with the State of Montana to comanage sport fishing and upland game bird hunting on the reservation; even more recently, the tribes proposed that they assume management of the National Bison Range, which borders their lands to the south.

Community management of nearby resources is an idea that has migrated off the reservations and into some of the smallest communities of the West. Residents of San Luis, Colorado, for example, have an active proposal in the works to buy the Taylor Ranch, a 78,000-acre forest holding just east of town. The Taylor Ranch happens to comprise the watershed catchment for the local irrigation district, so protecting it is critically important to agriculture, which in turn is critically important to the culture and future of San Luis. The citizens there wish to take the State of Colorado as their land management partner (and co-owner) and devise a management plan for the entire holding. Such a plan would restore historical local uses of the Taylor Ranch, formerly a Spanish land grant used communally by the townspeople.

These are the kinds of ideas that will carry us into the Next West, and clearly they are fraught with uncertainty. But it is clear to me that if we are ever to ensure an open lands future for this region, the citizenry must become infinitely more involved in the management of land and resources.

Community conservation is hard work, but there's been no shortage of that in the West of the twentieth century. If westerners can build the great dams and open the world's largest ore bodies, if they can fill their canals with irrigation water and force the deserts to blossom like the rose, they can surely meet the civic challenges ahead.

Or can they?

NOTES

1. Sally K. Fairfax, "Thinking the Unthinkable: States as Public Land Managers," *Hastings West-Northwest Journal of Environmental Law and Policy* 3, no. 2 (winter 1996): 256. (Published by Hastings College of the Law, San Francisco.)

2. Privatizing and marketizing are two terms often used by so-called free-market environmentalists, who argue generally that many environmental problems can best be resolved through the use of markets and clearly defined property rights. But there is an important distinction between privatization and marketization—a distinction that probably arose from the failure of the Sagebrush Rebellion during the Reagan years. Aware that the notion of privatizing the public lands—selling them—was extremely unpopular, some libertarian environmentalists came up with the kinder, gentler notion of

"marketizing" the public lands and public land agencies: running the agencies more as private businesses and applying businesslike strategies of resource allocation to the public lands, without transferring ownership of those lands to private parties.

3. See George Cameron Coggin, "'Devolution' in Federal Land Law: Abdication by Any Other Name . . . ," *Hastings West-Northwest Journal of Environmental Law and Policy* 3, no. 2 (winter 1996).

4. See generally Charles F. Wilkinson, *Crossing the Next Meridian: Land, Water, and the Future of the West* (Washington, D.C.: Island Press, 1992); Marc Reisner, *Cadillac Desert: The American West and Its Disappearing Water* (New York: Viking Press, 1986); Donald Worster, *Rivers of Empire: Water, Aridity, and the Growth of the American West* (New York: Pantheon Books, 1985); Robert H. Nelson, *Public Lands and Private Rights: The Failure of Scientific Management* (Lanham, Md.: Rowman & Littlefield, 1995); and Richard White, *"It's Your Misfortune and None of My Own": A New History of the American West* (Norman: University of Oklahoma Press, 1991).

5. The best general discussion of sharing of revenue from federal natural resource development is found in Sally K. Fairfax and Carolyn E. Yale, *Federal Lands: A Guide to Planning, Management, and State Revenues* (Washington D.C.: Island Press, 1987).

6. Ibid., 64–65.

7. Ibid., 152.

8. Testimony of Commissioner Louise Liston, Garfield County, Utah, in U.S. Congress, House Committee on Natural Resources, *The Changing Needs of the West,* (Washington, D.C.: Government Printing Office, 1994).

9. For a more thorough treatment of James Huffman's views on the "political lands," see James Huffman, "The Inevitability of Private Rights in Public Lands," *University of Colorado Law Review* 65 (1991): 241.

10. For an excellent discussion of the failure of scientific management in western resource agencies, see Robert H. Nelson, *Public Lands and Private Rights* (Lanham, Md.: Rowman & Littlefield, 1995).

11. Connie Poten, "Altered States: Game Farms," *Northern Lights* (spring 1994). (Published by the Northern Lights Research & Education Institute; P.O. Box 8084, Missoula, MT, 59807.)

12. A more thorough description of "consensus groups" and how they operate can be found in *The Chronicle of Community,* a journal published three times a year by the Northern Lights Research & Education Institute.

13. Theresa Rice, *The Watershed Sourcebook* (Boulder: University of Colorado School of Law, 1995).

14. Daniel Dagget, *Beyond the Rangeland Conflict: Toward a West That Works* (Layton, Utah: Gibbs Smith, 1995).

15. *High Country News,* 13 May 1996. (Published by High Country Foundation, 119 Grand Avenue, Paonia, CO 81–428.)

16. *The View from Airlie: Community Based Conservation in Perspective* (1993) is available from the Liz Clailborne and Art Ortenberg Foundation, 650 Fifth Avenue, New York, 10019.

17. Ibid., 25.

18. *High Country News,* 13 May 1996.

CHAPTER TEN

Is "Libertarian Environmentalist" an Oxymoron?

The Crisis of Progressive Faith
and the Environmental and Libertarian
Search for a New Guiding Vision

ROBERT H. NELSON

More than any other region of the country, the West is a product of the American progressive movement of the late nineteenth and early twentieth centuries.[1] It was the progressives who abandoned the nineteenth-century policy of disposing of the public lands, resulting in almost 50 percent of the land in the West remaining today in federal hands. The federal government built the large dams and irrigation works of the West, dating from the founding of the Bureau of Reclamation in 1902. The tight federal control over routes and prices of railroads, pipelines, and airlines, particularly important to the West with its long distances, was administered—at least until their deregulation in the 1970s and 1980s—by the Interstate Commerce Commission and other progressive regulatory agencies. Western politics gives an especially important role to referenda, ballot initiatives, and other instruments of popular democracy, which is itself another product of progressivism. In the West, progressives found a land where their political philosophy held wide appeal and where on the frontier there were few obstacles to putting it into practice.

The great progressive faith in the future—in "progress"—came easily to westerners, many of whom had left home and family behind to build a new life. The new professional classes, the scientific aristocracy of progressivism, did not find old distinctions of class and rank standing in their way in the West. If the cause of progress meant abandoning the outmoded habits and practices of the past, the West offered a clean slate.

All this means that the demise of the progressive vision will have a particularly great impact on the West. And it is in the West, more than any other section of the United States, that the ideas to replace progressivism are taking shape today. Many of these ideas are associated with the environmental and libertarian movements, which both have stronger followings in the West than in other regions of the country. There is, as I will explore in this chapter, a much greater affinity between environmentalism and libertarianism—or at least between important segments of these movements—than most people realize. The implications of this affinity hold special relevance in the West and need to be explored as we struggle to envision a Next West beyond the New West of the progressive era.

The common ground begins with a hostility toward and a rejection of the basic tenets of progressivism. Leading advocates of both environmental and libertarian thought propose a sharp decentralization in the organizational arrangements for American society. A few even go so far as to propose secession from the United States, arguing that the nation-state as an institution is outmoded. Any major decentralization is likely to have the greatest effect on the western portion of the United States, the region farthest from Washington, D.C. The future of the West I envision is a future in which states and localities significantly loosen their bonds with the federal government and assume a greater autonomy to shape their own communities. For if progressivism was a political philosophy that brought an ever growing concentration of power at the federal level, the decline of progressivism is likely to operate in the reverse direction.

The Loss of Progressive Faith

In the twentieth century, thinking about American government was dominated by the progressive paradigm.[2] The basic premise of progressivism was that there must be a central coordinating intelligence for all of American society and that it must fall to the federal government to fill this role. Farmers left to the vagaries of the market, for example, face boom and bust, so government must act to stabilize agricultural supplies and prices. Owners of private forests will cut the timber too fast and will ignore social consequences outside the market, requiring that government oversee the management of the nation's forestlands. Moreover, the competitive marketplace creates many losers as well as winners; therefore, in a civilized society, government must provide a social welfare network to ensure a minimum living standard for every person.

All such efforts of government, the progressives believed, are to be administered with scientific efficiency. Indeed, the core philosophy of progressivism was the scientific management of society.[3] If science was transforming the physical conditions of human existence in the late nineteenth and early twentieth centuries, it could similarly transform social conditions, many people believed. Promoted by enthusiasts such as Frederick Taylor, the gospel of scientific management was spreading rapidly throughout the world of the American business corporation. Progressives argued that similar scientific methods must be applied to government as well. Noting that American industry was increasingly concentrated in a few large corporations of nationwide scope, early leaders of the progressive movement proposed that the federal government play the same kind of role in public affairs. Science is, after all, an enterprise in which one scientific truth is established for all places. The support of scientific research and then the dissemination of scientific laws and knowledge throughout the United States would be a task best undertaken by central authorities.

Although American government in the twentieth century was shaped by the progressive political philosophy, the progressive paradigm is now, as one critic recently wrote, "under skeptical reconsideration." Even though they offered "the story line for explaining America" and the development of its welfare state, progressive ideas are "more than a little frayed at the intellectual edges." Indeed, it is the crisis of progressive faith that is significantly responsible for "the current disarray and uncertainty in our politics."[4]

Many now doubt, for example, that the social and administrative sciences have achieved—or are even capable of achieving—a degree of knowledge sufficient to manage successfully the affairs of the nation. Even if scientific management of society is possible, the implications are troublesome in a democracy. Would scientific management also mean control of society by a scientific elite? Increasing numbers of people also doubt the very goal of the progressive scheme, the achievement of a high material standard of living through rapid economic progress everywhere on earth. Could the earth sustain an expected population of more than 10 billion people living at the same level of affluence as the citizens of the United States today—to say nothing of the much higher incomes expected in America in the future? Economic progress in the twentieth century has meant the loss of wilderness, the eradication of many species, and indeed, the wholesale alteration of the existing natural conditions over much of the earth.

The message of progressivism has been described by historians as the "gospel of efficiency." To the progressives, material progress had a higher purpose than a mere increase in consumption of goods and services. By eliminating poverty, it would also eliminate the main source of war, crime, and other past human misbehavior. Material advance was the correct route to moral and spiritual improvement in the world. In the end, the progressive faithful devoutly believed, economic progress would bring about a virtual heaven on earth.[5]

However, events of the twentieth century dashed many of these hopes. Two world wars, the Holocaust, Siberian prison camps, and other dismal occurences showed how technical efficiency all too often seemed to heighten the magnitude of the disaster. Contrary to the progressive assumption, it seemed that higher economic capacity could be a powerful force for evil as well as good.

An answer to our current problems of government thus is not a matter of better administration, a change in political practices, new court rulings, or any other mechanical or technical adjustment. It is a matter of finding a new political vision. In the twentieth century, Americans were brought together by a collective commitment to the achievement through material progress of the good life on earth for all. And this progress would be based on the ever wider application of science. This political religion, however, is no longer capable of providing a unifying faith to hold together the far-flung and diverse American community.

Rethinking Progressivism

Two movements of the late twentieth century have leaped to the intellectual forefront to challenge the old progressive ideology. Although at first blush these movements seem to have little in common—or even appear inimical to each other—a deeper investigation reveals many commonalities. The first (and older) movement, libertarianism, seeks to enhance the powers, responsibilities, and liberties of the individual, in part by reducing the powers granted to the state. The libertarian outlook, though commonly associated with the views of the Libertarian Party, is actually much broader than many think. It is an anticollectivist, proindividualist political philosophy with roots sunk deep in the economic and social liberalism of seventeenth-century Europe. It is clear that the influence of libertarian ideas (if not the libertarian party itself) has been growing rapidly in the United States, especially in the West.[6]

The many putative successes of progressivism in the twentieth-century United States have helped clarify one principal focus of libertarianism—a focus on the decentralization of political power. Libertarians seek, among other things, the dismantling of the welfare state in Washington. Moreover, most libertarian thinkers agree that the regulatory commissions, land management agencies, and other federal institutions created in the name of scientific management of society have failed their purposes. Libertarians claim that instead of a realization of the progressive ideal of a better and more just and equitable society, what has actually happened is the conversion of the far-ranging powers of government into a diverse set of instruments that are used for private purposes. The great intentions of progressive ideology invariably have been turned to perverse ends. Libertarians commonly argue that such perversion is to be expected in any political system that relies so heavily on centralized governmental control and the application of political processes to make most key decisions affecting society and the economy. Much mischief lies in the granting of far-reaching powers to progressive and supposedly benign agencies of government.

The second movement, environmentalism, is both more diverse and more successful politically than the libertarian movement. Within environmentalism, there are those who are, in effect, new progressives: they seek an improved scientific management of society that will take greater scientific account of the environment. Some of these scientific environmentalists are economists who consider that protecting the environment is simply a matter of doing economics better by factoring in all the social benefits (including nonmarket benefits) and taking proper account of private actions that have impacts not accurately reflected in market profits and losses (the "externalities" of economic jargon). The Clean Air Act of 1970 and the Clean Water Act of 1972 are leading examples of progressive environmentalism. These two laws created large new bureaucracies in Washington and extended federal power into many areas of American life.

Yet to dwell on these elements of environmentalism is to miss the full picture. The political meaning of the environmental movement is manifested perhaps most significantly in the "not in my backyard," or NIMBY, opposition that has spread throughout American life.[7] Environmentalists have led this powerful movement of grassroots opposition to power plants, apartment complexes, shopping centers, dams, mines, highways, and all kinds of development and facilities. In effect, the NIMBY movement represents a statement that the professional experts do not know best, that the federal government or any other central authority should not direct the lives of the citizenry, and that power in American society must be significantly decentralized. It is an expression of an understanding, however cloudy in the minds of many environmental activists, that those with claims to scientific authority should no longer have control of the direction of American society.

In the past, even when highways, power plants, and other obtrusive facilities had a negative impact on them personally, many citizens virtuously accepted these facilities as part of their civic duty in the name of progress. Today, they reject this obligation. The real message is that local groups no longer believe in the claims of progress—the argument that economic growth serves the cause of the whole nation (or even all humankind). The progressive cause no longer commands local deference and sacrifice among all citizens of goodwill.

However great the differences in formal reasoning to arrive at such conclusions, one must be mindful that they are remarkably compatible with significant elements of libertarian thinking. More commonalities may be revealed by examining the ideas of one prominent libertarian intellectual.

The Case of James Buchanan

As a founder and central figure of the "public choice" school of economics, James M. Buchanan is a leading advocate in America today for libertarian ideas. Although he has been outside the mainstream of the economics profession for many years, his writings on the workings of government and other subjects earned him a Nobel Prize in economics in 1986.

Buchanan points out that both in its practical results and in its intellectual foundations, the contemporary American welfare state is bankrupt. He calls for radical institutional rearrangements achievable only through basic revisions in the United States Constitution.[8] Progressive doctrines have imbued government, Buchanan asserts, with a pervasive "social engineering" mentality. In pursuing a vision of the scientific management of society, the welfare state has come to play the role of a "potentially benevolent despot." It is the role of scientists to "counsel this despot" on the best scientific instruments for the management of society. [9]

In the welfare state, according to the progressive prescription, the needs of the national community should be paramount. Speaking with the voice of authority for all the nation, a scientific priesthood is the deliverer of ultimate truths, and in the end, the commands of science must be obeyed. Buchanan's great mission, on the other hand, is to inspire a rebellion against this oppressive collectivism. Humanity must shift its fundamental allegiances "from the organizational entity as the unit to the individual-in-the-organization." If men and women will not stand up to the false claims of scientific authority, if they are so weak and craven as to fail to assert their individual freedom and dignity against the imperial claims of science, then "we do not deserve to survive."[10]

The contemporary economics profession is, for Buchanan, one of the chief offenders. The economists of our time assert that people should behave rationally to maximize their well-being ("utility" in economic jargon), a standard said to be achievable when individuals are guided by the investigations of economic science. Yet, as Buchanan laments, life for such individuals "could not be concerned with choice at all." In order that there may be choice, there must be a multiplicity of "imagined 'possibles.'" It is "internally contradictory" to speak of individual "choice making under [scientific] certainty."[11] Far from fostering the virtues of individual choice, the progressive teachings of the American welfare state would reduce the individual to an automaton who is to follow with unfailing loyalty the decrees of economics and other sciences. Just as Martin Luther once argued that the Roman Catholic Church had undermined the role of individual faith, Buchanan now calls for a new American reformation directed against a theocracy of science.[12]

Contemporary economists, Buchanan says, not only spread false teachings but have themselves fallen into evil ways. They have squandered the resources society has so generously provided them, wasting their time and effort on the "escapist puzzles of modern mathematics." Instead of intellectual advance, there has been retrogression. Buchanan writes that "most modern economists have no idea of what they are doing or even of what they are ideally supposed to be doing. . . . The king really has no clothes." Not only do economists deal only with "piddling trivialities," but also the "empirical work in economics" mostly confirms the obvious and is no more profound than "proving water runs downhill."[13] The economics profession, in short, is yet another of the many priesthoods of history to fall into a condition of cynicism, corruption, internal decay, and loss of purpose.

The acceptance of progressive ideas and the fate of the American welfare state are, for Buchanan, closely linked. Abandon one and the other is no longer tenable. Whereas few of his colleagues are willing to venture into such unchartered waters, Buchanan does not shrink from exploring the full consequences of this line of reasoning. A unified national community on the scale of the American state is simply not, in Buchanan's view, sustainable over the long run.

As the federal government has taken control of more and more areas of American life, the inevitable result has been that "the dependence of order on some extended range of moral responsibilities increases."[14] Although common values may exist at a local level, they are much less likely in a large nation with a huge diversity of beliefs, values, and backgrounds. A great crisis such as a world war may temporarily unify the nation, but in normal times national politics will tend to degenerate into the beggar-thy-neighbor subversion of broader purposes that has become so widespread in the United States today:

> What can a person be predicted to do when the external institutions force upon him a role in a community that extends beyond his moral-ethical limits? The tension shifts toward the self-interest pole of behavior; moral-ethical principles are necessarily sublimated. The shift is exaggerated when a person realizes that others in the extended community of arbitrary and basically amoral size will find themselves in positions comparable to his own. How can a person act politically in other than his own narrowly defined self-interest in an arbitrarily sized nation of more than 200 million?[15]

Buchanan thus calls for a radical decentralization of responsibility in the American welfare state—in essence, the abolition of the institutional products of twentieth-century American progressivism. In this context, he proposes, it is worth at least raising the possibility of the secession of some regions from the United States. Even if a movement for secession were not successful, at least "such a threat [might] force some devolution of central government power." Buchanan is searching for a "federal alternative to the enveloping Leviathan. . . . Who will join me in offering to make a small contribution to the Texas National Party? Or to the Nantucket Separatists?" In such a large nation as the United States, the very existence of "such things as 'national goals,' 'national priorities,' or 'universal objectives'" must be "absurd."[16] The breakup of the former Soviet Union thus may not be the isolated event most Americans have assumed but may prove to hold some lessons for another nation that has attempted to establish a community spanning an entire continent, the United States.

Not surprisingly, Buchanan finds few allies in the mainstream of the economics profession. Even among libertarians, he is unusual in his emphasis on the failure of the moral underpinnings—the theological deficiencies, one might say—of the progressive "gospel." Whereas some of his fellow libertarians recommend turning to the market as a technical mechanism that will efficiently solve the economic problems of society, Buchanan remains at least as interested in finding answers through a radical decentralization of political authority. Abolition of the administrative apparatus of the welfare state in Washington is, for Buchanan, a first step in breaking free from the great mischief spread by progressive ideas in the twentieth century.

The Message of Deep Ecology

As adherents of a political movement concerned with achieving practical and concrete goals, mainstream environmental leaders typically are anxious to avoid any seemingly extreme statements that might alienate public opinion and endanger current tactical aims. But other members of the environmental movement have made an opposite choice. They have sought to explore the far reaches of the implications of abandoning the progressive paradigm and are willing to carry an initial set of environmental premises to their full logical conclusion, wherever they may lead and however controversial that conclusion may be. This second group seeks to make explicit ideas that are only half formed or that may even be in conflict with the thinking of the first group. Yet it is in the writings of the iconoclasts of the environmental movement—the environmental Buchanans—that environmentalist's most distinctive contribution to contemporary social thought can be found.

Bill Devall and George Sessions give an overview of much of this thinking in their book *Deep Ecology*. They direct their fire above all at "the ultimate value judgment upon which [current] technological society rests—progress conceived as the further development and expansion of the artificial environment necessarily at the expense of the natural world." Rather than fostering progress, this development must be seen as promoting "unequivocal regress." Whereas Buchanan believes that the scientific ideal undermines moral responsibility and reduces life to the mere following of a scientific formula, Devall and Sessions write that in a technocratic society, people "come to be looked upon as a resource to be managed, in the best interests of the emerging urban-industrial society."[17] They assert that by following the precepts of "modern scientific management," people become "personnel," whose role in life is to be manipulated by scientific controllers in the interest of "more efficient production of commodities." The "experts" of the progressive paradigm are "in the business of managing people" according to their technocratic designs. The end result is a world in which men and women are alienated not only "from the rest of Nature but also . . . from themselves and each other."[18] This alienation from our true selves results not from original sin in the Garden of Eden but from the never-ending pursuit of material progress and economic efficiency.

Buchanan regards the welfare state's social engineering mentality as a main cause of the current overbearing quality of our government. Devall and Sessions perceive contemporary society as offering "bureaucratic hierarchies" that stifle the "individuality of persons" and create an environment that encourages people to behave and think "like machines." It is thus necessary to escape current "machine-based societies" in which scientific imperatives have taken over and dominate "the whole life of society." If the instrument of social domination for Devall and Sessions can be either the government or the "market," it may be necessary to abandon current understandings both of progress based on scientific government and of progress based on the workings of the market.[19]

Buchanan expresses a deep skepticism with respect to the current role of the social sciences. Devall and Sessions observe that social science is based on a view that "technological and social progress can continue without limit, making all social problems ultimately soluble" by the experts. However, in practice, the methods developed by social scientists often prove inadequate. Devall and Sessions note that in the field of natural resources, one finds "'abstract models' which . . . have little relevance to site specific situations." Misplaced confidence in the claims of social science often "lulls the manager into thinking he has the relevant variables under control," but the truth is that the world is "more complex than we now know and more complex than we possibly can know."[20]

Indeed, Devall and Sessions assert, "there is no reason to believe that scientific theories and models will ever capture the full intricacy of the natural ecosystem functioning." While Buchanan decries the false scientism of the progressive vision, Devall and Sessions argue that deep ecologists should "not be constrained by scientism, and by the definition of Nature as just a collection of bits of data to be manipulated by humans." It is imperative to recognize that "science and technology alone are a dangerous substitute for land wisdom." Buchanan decries the moral consequences of the view that humankind must follow the controlling prescriptions of economic and other sciences; deep ecologists argue that "scientists and technologists" do "not have objective, neutral answers." Although scientists do "not discuss ethical issues" in an explicit and honest fashion, deep ecologists warn, their outlook implicitly contains far-ranging and harmful moral implications.[21]

Devall and Sessions write that even though "resource economists look at wilderness," their outlook makes them incapable of really "seeing it." Even economists sympathetic to environmental causes regard designation of wilderness as an economic decision to maximize benefits over costs. The attempt to impose a utilitarian framework on a moral decision, however, inevitably must fail. It yields, as Buchanan sees in many other efforts of economists, irrelevant and misdirected economic analysis. While Buchanan decries the loss of human freedom implied in the utility-maximizing framework of economics, Devall and Sessions reject "the premise of instrumental rationality—the narrowly utilitarian view" of economics. This outlook must be rejected because it "fails to distinguish vital human needs from mere desires, egotistical arrogance and adventurism in technology."[22]

Buchanan suggests the need to revitalize the sense of community by means of a radical decentralization of American society—again, even going so far as to suggest that some regions might have to secede. Devall and Sessions note that a number of deep ecologists call for "the decentralization of society." For example, in the field of education it is necessary "to make the small community the primary environment for educational activity." One description of "an ecotopian vision" consists of a small and self-sustaining island in the South Pacific. An appropriate worldview emphasizes "small communal farms, monastic groups, and continuing attempts to scale down the size of institutions, organizations and industry." The goal should be a "decentralized, non-hierarchical, democratic society" of "small-scale community" that emphasizes "self-responsibility" and respect for "spiritual-religious mentors."[23] Buchanan, meanwhile, sees the large nation-state as lacking the "moral ethical cement" needed to hold itself together and sees smaller institutions as the hope for reasserting a sense of community identity and moral purpose.[24]

In Ernest Callenbach's novel *Ecotopia*, a utopian existence consists of a pastoral life in the Pacific Northwest, a region that has seceded from the United States, suspending both market and political relationships with the rest of America. It has done so in order to avoid any outside disruption or dislocation, whether market or government originated. The fundamental problem, and the reason for seceding, has been the deep offensiveness to the social values of Ecotopia of the "underlying national philosophy of America: ever-continuing progress, the fruits of industrialization for all, a rising gross national product"—that is to say, the premises of the progressive paradigm.[25]

The Obsolescence of the Nation-State

William A. Schambra a leading commentator on progessive thinking, comments that progressivism offered a vision of

> a genuine national community which could evoke from the American people a self-denying devotion to the public good, a community in which citizens would be linked tightly by bonds of compassion and neighborliness. Americans would be asked to transcend their traditional laissez-faire individualism (which had been aggravated by the forces of modern industrialism) in order to bond themselves as one to the "national idea."[26]

It was not only progressive ideology but also two world wars and then forty years of conflict with the Soviet Union that exerted a great unifying influence in American life. To a remarkable degree, as the progressives advocated, Americans did in fact commit their energies in the twentieth century to the development of a single community of one nation.

However, the end of the cold war has greatly altered military circumstances. The recent signing of the North American Free Trade Agreement and the formation of an economic union for North America mean that the boundaries of the United States are no longer as important economically as they once were. Two of the main practical reasons for forming a nation—military and economic—are much less relevant today to the circumstances of the United States.

The declining relevance of the nation-state is receiving growing attention in circles wider than those of James Buchanan and the deep ecologists. Norman Macrae is an economic journalist of libertarian persuasion who served for many years as a writer and editor for the *Economist* magazine. He offered in *The 2025 Report* a vision of what might be described as a libertarian utopia. Much as does Buchanan, Macrae sees the members of the nation-state as too diverse in outlook to be able to achieve a strong sense of community. He suggests instead a world of "genuine pluralism." It would have a few worldwide institutions that perform key global tasks but otherwise would encourage "free dispersal into small communities where everyone could do her or his own thing." Large nation-states would disappear and people would instead "set up their own forms of very local government—communes, monasteries, profit-making local governments run by private-enterprise performance contractors, beach clubs on desert isles. . . . whatever people wanted."[27]

Macrae thus offers a sort of modern feudalism. Each person finds his or her own fiefdom where one is free to pursue one's own style and preference in cultural, religious, and other matters. Unlike the feudalism of the medieval era, however, and departing as well from deep ecology in this respect, free trade would blossom in Macrae's vision of the future. Indeed, Macrae proposes, the spread of modern technology and the growth of economic interrelationships would bind the world together more closely than it ever has been. Ever-improving telecommunications technology would play an especially important role, transforming not only the ease of personal communication but also job markets, which would become highly decentralized:

> By the early years of the 21st century brain workers—which in rich countries already meant most workers—no longer needed to live near their work. They could live on the beach of Tahiti if they wanted to, and telecommute daily to computers and other colleagues in the New York or London or Hamburg or Timbuctoo-tax-haven office through which they worked.[28]

Macrae is looking into the future, but elements of his forecast can be found in developments in Europe over the past fifty years. After centuries of division, the European Economic Community is the most serious European effort at unification since the medieval Roman Catholic Church. Yet within this central framework, the European future may hold a diversity of cultures, lifestyles, languages, and ethical outlooks corresponding roughly to the boundaries of existing European nations. These diverse cultural communities could all be linked closely through the workings of a common economic marketplace.

It could be Europe, not the United States, that offers the model for the world social organization of the future. In the American system as it has developed since the progressive era, authoritative decrees of the nation-state are imposed over a vast area—larger in size than all of Europe—with substantial uniformity. America's individual states are bound together not only by the common economic rules of a single marketplace but also by many common cultural requirements extending into details of family life, sexual practice, housing arrangements, and personal lifestyle. In recent years, for example, the federal government has imposed decrees even in such local matters as speed limits on highways (recently repealed but unmistakable in origin nonetheless), hiring quotas, and the minimum age for drinking alcoholic beverages.

In 1981, Joel Garreau, a reporter for the *Washington Post*, published *The Nine Nations of North America*. His North American "nations" included Quebec, New England, The Foundry, Ecotopia (in the Pacific Northwest),

Mexamerica, Dixie, and the Bread Basket. Garreau wrote that "each has its capital and distinctive web of power and influence . . . . Each has a peculiar economy; each commands a certain emotional allegiance from its citizens." He suggested that "the more self-assured each of these Nine Nations becomes, the less willing it is to be dictated to by outsiders who show no interest in sharing—or even understanding—local values." Garreau described a diversity across North America that "emphasizes the real, enduring, and basic economic and social differences of each region, manifested in attitudes towards everything from nuclear power to unions to abortion."[29]

It is important to recognize that such regional differences have been under direct attack by progressive thinking. To American progressives, there are and always have been clear distinctions between science and religion, between fact and value, and between expertise and politics. In modern life, progressives believed, the trend of events was inexorably toward the dominance of science, fact, and expertise. As this trend marched forward, the world would inevitably converge toward one set of social beliefs and governing arrangements. Yet, as Garreau pointed out, this was not happening. Contrary to earlier expectations, the simple reality was that differences among peoples and regions were persisting and, in some cases, even growing.

Garreau's observations should come as no great surprise, for there is no particular reason to expect a general convergence of beliefs and institutions around the world. Indeed, in the minds of many people, perhaps most people, science is not separable from religion; nor is fact from value; nor is expertise from politics. Contrary to the progressive assumption, such convergences would require, in essence, a single world religion with a new World Catholic Church to maintain theological orthodoxy. Since this is highly unlikely, at least in the foreseeable future, it makes sense to plan for a future order of pluralism in religion and values. Even the United States may be too large geographically to sustain one community held closely together by the bond of common beliefs and values.

Yet such communities can be found at the level of smaller regions and localities. And if this is the case, the political locus of governing authority may have to shift to these regions and localities as well. If a more typical problem for government is deciding when sex education will be available in schools, as opposed to sending a man to the moon, the very legitimacy of the role of central government is undermined. Indeed, Garreau's description of the nine nations of North America may one day be more than a flight of his literary imagination.

Skeptical views concerning the future of current nation-states are found as well in the writings of prominent environmental thinkers. Barbara Ward and René Dubos, for example, explain in *Only One Earth* that

> concerns with global air pollution lie beyond the effective protection of individual governments. It is no use one nation checking its energy use to keep the ice caps in place if no other government joins in. . . . The global interdependence of man's airs and climates is such that local separate decisions, wisely made, may not be a sufficient safeguard and it would take a bold optimist to assume such general wisdom.[30]

An effective response to global environmental problems cannot be based on a commitment to science alone but demands new values of worldwide community. Ward and Dubos thus suggest that "it is not wholly irrational to hope that the full realization of planetary interdependence—in biosphere and technosphere alike—may begin to affect man in the depths of his capacity for psychic commitment." Yet in other matters, Ward and Dubos favor decentralization. They see a healthy trend in the grassroots activism characteristic of the environmental movement, noting the great "importance of developing the distinctive genius of each place, each group, and each person—in other words of cultivating individuality." Local allegiances also protect humankind from a centralization that in the past has sometimes yielded efforts to "dragoon other groups into subjection. That kind of `unity' is rejected in our day with unequaled vehemence by all nations, great and small." Ward and Dubos further state that "as a decentralized way of satisfying a million different tastes and needs the market system could hardly be matched." In short, "the world is [today] committed to pluralism and to decentralized decisionmaking."[31]

The ultimate and most menacing form of pollution of the earth's atmosphere is nuclear radiation. In *The Fate of the Earth*, Jonathan Schell argues that the fear of nuclear war may prove to be the catalyst for a new sense of worldwide community, "for nothing underscores our common humanity as strongly as the peril of extinction." Creating a new worldwide community demands fundamental institutional rearrangements; hence, a desperate search must be undertaken to identify "the practical steps by which mankind . . . can reorganize its political life." Schell argues that abolition of the sovereignty of nations must be a starting point because "the connection between sovereignty and war is almost a definitional one—a sovereign state being a state that enjoys the right and the power to go to war." At present, "the peril of extinction is the price that the world pays not for 'safety' or 'survival' but for its insistence on continuing to divide itself up into sovereign nations."[32]

Denationalizing the Public Lands

The progressives saw federal retention of public lands in the West as a particularly important means to promote their goal of establishing a new sense of national unity. The public lands created a common bond among citizens throughout the nation, a shared ownership in a vast property, and a common right of access to the benefits of the lands. Retention of land in public ownership also facilitated the scientific management of American society. Where private property existed, it was difficult to persuade landowners to follow governmental plans. The East was already lost in this regard, but the West could be the showcase for scientific management.

As we well know today, matters turned out otherwise.[33] Federal land management in the West is now under attack from nearly every quarter. Industry complains that federal schemes of natural resource allocation and environmental protection too often lack the certainty required for making sound long-term business investments. Environmentalists complain that federal land managers are usually in league with commodity interests, subsidizing all manner of development at the expense of environmental quality. Few people any longer credit the federal government with sound land management in the national forests, the open rangelands, or even the national parks and wilderness areas. Knitted together, what all these complaints amount to is a widespread attack on the progressive paradigm of scientific management applied to western public lands.

As the progressive gospel fades, no new justification is emerging for retaining the public lands in federal hands. The system today largely survives on inertia. Indeed, the omnipresence of the federal government in the West, symbolized above all by federal landownership, now stands as a significant barrier to the development of stronger state and local communities. And increasingly, some of the bolder thinkers of the libertarian and environmental movements are pointing this out.

Karl Hess, Jr. comes from libertarian stock. Karl Hess, Sr. was for many years a leading writer and participant in libertarian causes. His son moved to the West twenty years ago and has devoted much of his attention to developing a libertarian perspective on the natural resources of the West and the problems of the public lands.

Hess's greatest complaint against the American welfare state is that by centralizing governing power, it has destroyed the possibilities for real community in American life. In *Visions upon the Land*, he asks, "How could people muster the desire and energy to be active and concerned stewards [of the land] when distant bureaucracies assumed their roles and when laws and policies effectively isolated them from meaningful contact with the land and its life?" The current "intrusive laws and distant government" meant that "families, neighborhoods, churches, and voluntary associations . . . were being steadily displaced." The West must find a new capacity for self-government to replace the current "vacuum of power and control." This would mean a reversal of the twentieth-century "centralization of functions that should not be centralized."[34]

Hess is not particularly interested in the free-market prescriptions that occupy many of his fellow libertarians. The freedom he is more concerned with would involve an "ecology of freedom," one that would allow many visions of local community "to compete democratically in the marketplace of ideas and beliefs." Each local community would be free to "envision what its landscapes should look like and would have to have the power to make those landscapes come true." There would be a diversity of community visions, all in competition with one another, and "no single vision could emerge victorious on the merit of force alone." It would be essential that there be "no option on the matter of tolerance" of the right of local groups to govern themselves so as to shape their community according to their own cultural and religious values. All this is part of bringing "democracy to the western range" and creating a world where "visions are free to flourish and citizens are free to pursue them." In short, the most important form of competition for Hess is not the traditional competition among private business firms in the free market; it is, rather, a competition among local communities in the West to create the best places where "people and nature might indeed coexist in harmony."[35]

A good place to start, Hess thinks, is with the public lands. He points out that "more than a century of public-land grazing had proven devastating to arid rangelands and costly to the human and nonhuman life that called those lands home." The West faced "laws and institutions pitting residents against wildlife and bureaucracies against both." As a result, "by almost every indicator, all was not well on the western range." Hence, Hess proposes that "over a twenty-year period—the start and finish to be set by statute—the federal government . . . be required to divest itself of the surface rights to all lands managed by the Forest Service and BLM." The goal would be not privatization of the lands per se but that "public lands would be democratized." Hess proposes a system of distributing shares to the public lands among the American people, a measure that he hopes would result in "the actual transfer of federal lands from managing agencies to an array of citizens, citizen groups, and local communities." It would be a critical step in his grand plan for the revitalization of community on the western range.[36]

Daniel Kemmis is that rare breed who is both a skillful politician—former Democratic party minority leader and speaker of the Montana House of Representatives and former mayor of Missoula, Montana—and a sophisticated intellectual whose writings have recently commanded considerable attention in environmental circles. Kemmis argues in *Community and the Politics of Place* that even an area the size of the original thirteen states was simply "too large an arena for the intensive kind of face-to-face politics" that real community requires. The goal of "civic virtue" was "not going to work in a nation of this size"—and was even less likely to succeed as the United States grew to encompass a continent in the nineteenth century.[37] However, the size of the nation was not a great problem as long as the national government remained a minimal government, as intended by the founders. The basic needs for community would be met at the state and local levels, as reflected in tight constitutional limits placed on the powers of the federal government.

The progressives, however, saw these limits as an artifact, a reflection of an antiquated eighteenth-century political vision of atomistic society. In the twentieth century, the progressives believed, the states and localities should function as components in one grand social system. Therefore, whatever the Constitution said, any genuine sovereignty of the states must be extinguished—a process that required considerable legal gymnastics on the part of law professors and the courts but that was, in fact, gradually accomplished over the course of the century. Stripped of most of their authority and functioning under the heel of federal overseers, state and local governments have seen their ability to establish a strong sense of community greatly eroded. When the national community failed to be sustained in the fashion the progressives had expected, the overall result was an impoverishment of community in all of American life.

Kemmis, however, seeks to redress this situation. His answer is to revitalize state and local community. He writes that Americans must begin to come to terms with the fact that "economically, as well as politically, 'the nation' was not a place but a denial of place." In the economic sphere, radical as the thought may be, revitalization of local community means a growing recognition "that the idea of a national economy may be seriously flawed." States may have to be given a whole new ability to set tariffs, limit in-migration, and otherwise control the flow of people and goods across their borders. Moreover, since "America becoming a nation and America becoming an economy proved . . . to be one and the same story," the unavoidable implication is that curtailing the role of the national economy will mean curtailing the political role of the federal government as well.[38]

As a westerner, Kemmis is well aware that the federal government, especially by virtue of holding almost half the region's land, has direct operational control over much that goes on in the West. In many rural areas, federal officials must grant approval for a wide range of individual land uses, functioning almost as a local zoning board. The requirement to deal with a vast array of federal rules, rigidly administered by federal bureaucracies, and constant congressional meddling means that the West has little ability to control its own fate. Kemmis therefore believes that one great motivation for rethinking the possibilities of community in the West is the very presence of the federal lands.

Indeed, he argues that efforts to establish real communities in the West are "profoundly undermined by these extensive federal holdings." The resolution of land controversies through the mechanism of federal laws and institutions is "always a less satisfying way of inhabiting the place than any of the participants would have chosen." The West must seek to transcend its "colonial heritage"; it must assert a whole new degree of "indigenous control over its own land and resources."[39] Kemmis suggests that the goal of the Sagebrush Rebellion of the late 1970s and early 1980s, the transfer of much of the existing federal lands to the states, was meritorious, even though some of the rebels had narrow and self-serving motives and some of the arguments made at the time were flawed.

In short, if the legitimacy of governmental action is no longer grounded in science, if scientific management is no longer the political religion of the nation, if the nation no longer offers the prospect of true community, then citizens may have to turn elsewhere. State and local governments may have to recover a prominence in American life that they have not held in the United States since the Civil War.

The Role of the Market

The practical prospects for a major decentralization of governing authority in the West may depend on the degree to which people of libertarian inclination and people of environmental inclination join together in a common cause. Yet at present, environmentalists and libertarians mostly travel in different circles. Environmentalists react skeptically to libertarian proposals for the privatization of government functions. The practical results of market forces, many environmentalists think, include the widespread destruction of nature. Surely, many people will conclude, these areas of disagreement will prevent any real coming together of the libertarian and environmental movements.

Yet as libertarian thinkers such as John Baden and Richard Stroup have frequently observed, many of the most environmentally destructive actions have been undertaken by the government.[40] It was not private business but the federal government that built the many dams throughout the West—dams that have proven both economically wasteful and environmentally damaging. Many of the timber sales in Rocky Mountain national forests are money-losing propositions as well as destructive of wilderness and other environmental values. Many wetlands throughout the United States have been filled with the assistance of federal subsidy programs. Indeed, one may well argue that worldwide, governments tend to be the greatest destroyers of nature.

The very principle that plays such a prominent part in libertarian thinking—voluntary agreement as a guiding rule in social relationships—is also surprisingly prominent in much of environmental thinking. The environmental assertion of the right to engage in NIMBY ("not in my backyard") resistance is in essence a declaration for voluntary agreement as a central ordering principle in society. Waste disposal sites, power plants, highways, and many other facilities must be voluntarily accepted. The NIMBY phenomenon is the other side of the coin to the libertarian demand that the power of governmental coercion be curtailed in American life. Environmentalists and libertarians are both seeking to restore rights of the citizenry that were lost to the all-powerful progressive state.

In the future, finding acceptable sites for many industrial and public works facilities is likely to prove possible only with the provision of some form of compensation to the local area. Moreover, it may well turn out that increasingly it is most practical to provide this compensation in the form of a direct monetary payment. Thus, the environmental movement, if perhaps inadvertently, may be paving the way for an injection of market relationships into new parts of American life. Local governments may effectively end up selling, and private firms may end up buying, rights of access.

If libertarians argue for a society grounded in voluntary contractual relationships among holders of legally recognized property rights, environmental activists may be today the leading force in the evolution of a new set of local rights that are the practical equivalent of property rights. The authority granted by a collective private property right (such as a private condominium or community association would hold) and the ability to exclude a use from any given area are the same sort of authority sought by grassroots environmental activists for their communities.[41]

Much as public zoning serves to exclude uses that could also be excluded through the exercise of private property rights, the entire distinction between public and private becomes artificial in small communities.[42] In the United States today, there are private communities, such as Reston, Virginia, and Columbia, Maryland, with populations larger than many local governments and with many of the same service functions as a municipal government. Both have rules for governance that serve to guide an internal political process, and both assess a fee for the use of the common property that is like a local property tax. In short, if a new social pluralism and development of community at the local level is to be achieved, it may not be especially important whether this pluralism is realized in a libertarian framework of a "private" community or an environmental framework of a "public" community.

Some deep ecologists suggest that virtually all trading in goods and services in world markets should be halted, enforcing a new world autarky. Libertarians would undoubtedly object strongly to any attempt to impose such a vision on the world. However, many libertarians would have much less objection to permitting a small local community to erect its own barriers to trade, based on its own local value system. Indeed, it is possible to imagine a world order in which full opportunity exists for every political jurisdiction to participate in trade but the degree of this trading is a matter for local self-determination.

The Separation of Church and State

There is in environmental thought a strong tendency toward seeing nature in religious terms. The writings of John Muir are filled with references to the spiritual inspiration he felt in the wilderness; many current environmentalists follow in this tradition.[43] It is a secularization of a Christian message of long standing that in nature humankind can encounter directly a work of God. As John Calvin wrote more than 500 years ago, for many people "the knowledge of God [is] sown in their minds out of the wonderful workmanship of nature." Indeed, he wrote, it is especially in the presence of nature that humanity can find "burning lamps" that "shine for us ... the glory of its Author" above.[44]

Although many temporary environmentalists would balk at the characterization of environmentalism as a religion, most would surely agree that modern environmentalism is based on a profound sense of morality attached to the question of humans' relationship with nature. Environmental ethics is now a bona fide branch of the formal study of ethics in academic philosophy; nature writing is replete with references to ethics and morality attached to nature; and clearly, beginning with John Muir and the

American transcendentalists, much nature writing and philosophy carries a reverential tone with strong elements of outright religiosity. Environmentalism is a new belief system with roots in both moral philosophy and science, and like other belief systems—religious or not—its adherents work hard to win converts and influence national and world events to support their cause. Members of the environmental movement do, in fact, seek to employ—often quite successfully—the instruments of governmental power to advance their convictions. Whether those convictions are entirely secular or are at least in part religious may be a matter of debate, but there can be no question that environmentalists lobby and proselytize for a moral cause.

Not surprisingly, many libertarians take exception. And indeed, as long as governmental authority remains at the federal level, this source of disagreement will continue to drive a wedge between the libertarian and environmental movements. Libertarians will vigorously oppose steps toward a centralized morality codified at the federal level and grounded in the vision of any one group—progressive, environmental, or otherwise.

If governing responsibilities are significantly decentralized, however, much of this tension will be diminished, if not alleviated altogether. There is likely to be much greater moral agreement within the immediate community served by any one local government. If government acts at this level to promote any one set of moral values, it can do so with much less prospect of infringing on the values of another group. Citizens who strongly object also will find it much easier to move to another community, as compared with leaving a large nation-state.

Libertarian thinkers and deep ecologists face a common issue. If libertarians must consider the fate of a society that by mutual and voluntary agreement rejects liberty, environmentalists must consider the fate of a society that by mutual and voluntary agreement rejects the protection of nature. In Christianity, a similar question had to be faced in earlier centuries: what should be the fate of a society that rejected the proper Christian message? Although Christianity in other times and places, as in Europe in the era of the Crusades, chose war, a tolerance of religious pluralism eventually emerged. For the future peace of the world, a similar pluralistic outlook may be required when questions of pluralism of religions (now including secular as well as traditional) are posed today.

Even in the matter of their own convictions, many environmentalists and libertarians may have more in common than they realize. They can start, for example, with a common rejection of the secular message of the progressive "gospel of efficiency." Moreover, although environmental morality often preaches a greater unity of man and nature, the laws of nature are not always the laws of an idyllic and pastoral world. They are sometimes the laws of the jungle. To "assault" or "rape" nature may not be to violate any condition of existence in nature as Darwin would have understood the matter.

Indeed, rather than advocating the literal act of becoming part of nature, it is more correct to say that environmentalism seeks to inculcate a new morality with respect to the natural world. It is, moreover, a morality that would require human beings to obey higher standards than are found elsewhere in nature. No other creature observes an obligation to protect other species—as the Bible says that Noah was once commanded to do and as the Endangered Species Act of 1973 now seeks to accomplish in the current age. When environmentalists speak of finding moral values and spiritual replenishment in "nature," they are actually speaking of nature not in a literal but in a metaphorical sense. "Nature" in environmental terminology often best translates to "God" in an older religious vocabulary. Nature thus becomes a secular metaphor for a set of values and beliefs that have deep roots in the religious history of Western civilization.

It is, in fact, the task of science to reveal the *actual* laws of nature. In the modern age, science has discovered truths of the natural world to a degree beyond the wildest imaginings of even a century ago. Hence, in expressing opposition to a scientific determination of social arrangements and behavior, deep ecologists and many other environmentalists effectively end up contradicting their own stated views in other respects. To obey the laws of science would be to behave naturally—the very goal of the progressive mentality that is vigorously opposed by deep ecologists and many other environmental thinkers. Environmentalism seeks instead to hold human beings to a standard outside the laws and behavioral rules found in the natural world, as identified by science. Indeed, environmentalism seeks a role for humanity that is more biblical in its origins, a role in which human beings are seen as distinct from other creatures and stand alone—as the Bible explains, alone created in the image of God.

If the arguments of deep ecologists and other environmental thinkers are understood in this way, Buchanan's complaints against progressivism and the environmental criticisms of progressivism have common roots. As Buchanan explains, progressivism reduces humankind to the status of the animal world—it denies any "central difference between my dog and any one of us"—and thus violates a view of humanity distinct from the natural world that is as old as the Judeo-Christian tradition.[45] Even though Buchanan writes in a secular framework, he is in effect saying that progressivism must be rejected because it denies the unique qualities in being human. In making men and women simply another creature subject to the scientific laws of nature, progressivism denies the moral and spiritual dimensions that give human existence a meaning and purpose that transcend the scientific understanding of the natural world. Few environmentalists disagree.

The Next West

The Next West probably will not have seceded from the United States; probably there will still be a United States. Yet the very fact that there is some uncertainty says a great deal in itself. There are powerful new forces at work in the world that mainstream thinkers today have scarcely recognized. The world may have caught a glimpse of the twenty-first century in the breakup of the Soviet Union, an event that caught almost every expert by surprise.

The nation-state is a product of the modern age. The rise of nation-states coincides with the rise of the secular religions of economic progress. In one form or another since Adam Smith, these faiths have shaped the modern world. Marxism was one of these secular religions, grounded, like the others, in the idea that material progress would bring about heaven on earth. The collapse of the Marxist religion occurred prior to the collapse of the Marxist state. Although many economic and other technical reasons have been given for the failure of communism, the fundamental reason may have been simply the loss of religious conviction. Perhaps it is because our social science experts largely exclude religious calculations from their "explanatory models" that their predictive capacities have proven to be so limited.

Faith in another religion of progress, the progressive gospel, is eroding in the United States today. Its fall has not been so rapid or sharp as was the death of Marxism, but few true believers remain. It is difficult today to find people who will zealously defend the notion that science and economic growth will bring heaven on earth. Yet at the beginning of the twentieth century, there was almost a universal conviction—certainly among the secular elite—that solving the economic problems of humankind would also solve its moral and spiritual problems.

Progressivism was the political religion of twentieth-century America, and we are just beginning to come to terms with its demise. As members of a nation of immigrants, most Americans do not have deep ties to one locality going back many centuries, and unlike Europeans, Americans do not have a heritage of an ancient local language. Mobility is so great in American life that most people have little or no sense of place associated with their current location of residence. Hence, unlike, say, Quebec in Canada or Tibet in China, there may not be any region in the United States with a strong interest in an actual secession from the nation, for our feelings for place remain shallow and ill formed.

Nevertheless, powerful centrifugal forces are operating in this country, even if they fall short of movements for secession. They may yield a large-scale decentralization of governing authority, citizen loyalty, and many other matters in the United States. If this should happen, it is likely to take place first in the West. More than any other region of the United States, the West was shaped by progressive principles and thus is likely to feel more strongly any consequences of the crisis of progressive faith. As the most recent part of the country to be settled, the West is still a more open society. Trends of all kinds still often begin in the West and then move eastward. Simply as a matter of physical distance, the West is located farthest from the Washington, D.C., corridors of power, where the last gasps of nationalism will surely be heard.

The West is also particularly attractive to those seekers who reject the progressive gospel and are looking for new religious truths. If new spiritual messages are today being derived from the presence of nature, nowhere in the United States is the opportunity for religious inspiration greater. Religious as well as employment opportunities thus may drive future population levels in the West. Perhaps a "theology of growth," along with the conventional economics of growth, is needed to project the future of the West. The future politics of the West will then also inevitably reflect changing value systems among the new people who are choosing to live in the West, reinforcing the turn against the progressive heritage.

All this said, it should also be acknowledged that the twentieth-century history of progressive dominance has left the West today more tied to federal purse strings than other parts of the country. (By one recent estimate, the net fiscal transfer in 1993 from the federal government to the Rocky Mountain states—total federal spending minus total federal taxes collected in these states—averaged $126 per state resident.[46]) Westerners may have to choose between their "church" and their pocketbook. However, the amounts of money involved are not so great as to preclude the West from following its conscience. As the federal government struggles with its budgetary problems, it has less and less money to spend and is looking to higher grazing, recreation, and other user fees as well as other ways to pass financial burdens to state and local residents. As it does so, maintenance of strong federal ties will offer fewer and fewer financial advantages to the West.

The Next West is likely to be a region in which states and localities take greater responsibility for governance as federal oversight wanes. The West will look less to the "national idea" for community; rather, community will be found within the West, and indeed, in many different ways and many different places, it will grow to reflect a religious pluralism ranging from Mormons to New Agers to deep ecologists and perhaps even deeper ecologists. As the progressive gospel of scientific management wanes, the political philosophy that supports and guides all this may emerge from a sorting out of ideas and beliefs that are found most prominently in the current environmental and libertarian movements. Together, they hold perhaps the brightest, but certainly the most interesting, new hopes for the great American West.

NOTES

1. See Samuel P. Hays, *Conservation and the Gospel of Efficiency: The Progressive Conservation Movement, 1890–1920* (Cambridge, Mass.: Harvard University Press, 1959).

2. See Stephen Skowronek, *Building a New American State: The Expansion of National Administrative Capacities, 1877–1920* (New York: Cambridge University Press, 1982); Robert H. Weibe, *The Search for Order, 1877–1920* (New York: Hill & Wang, 1967); and Richard Hofstadter, *The Age of Reform: From Bryan to F.D.R.* (New York: Vintage Books, 1955).

3. See Dwight Waldo, *The Administrative State: A Study of the Political Theory of American Public Administration* (1948; reprint, New York: Holmes & Meier, 1984).

4. Unsigned editorial, *First Things* 1, no. 2 (April 1990): 8.

5. See Robert H. Nelson, *Reaching for Heaven on Earth: The Theological Meaning of Economics* (Lanham, Md.: Rowman & Littlefield, 1991).

6. The two leading magazines of libertarian opinion, *Reason* and *Liberty*, are published, it might be noted, in California and Washington State, respectively.

7. Harry C. Boyte, *The Backyard Revolution: Understanding the New Citizen Movement* (Philadelphia: Temple University Press, 1980).

8. James M. Buchanan, *The Limits of Liberty: Between Anarchy and Leviathan* (Chicago: University of Chicago Press, 1975).

9. James M. Buchanan, *What Should Economists Do?* (Indianapolis: Liberty Press, 1979), 24, 145.

10. Ibid., 157, 173.

11. Ibid., 281.

12. See Nelson, *Reaching for Heaven on Earth*, 288–296.

13. Buchanan, *What Should Economists Do?*, 280, 90–91, 216, 88.

14. Ibid., 211.

15. Ibid., 226.

16. Ibid., 228–229, 110–111.

17. Bill Devall and George Sessions, *Deep Ecology: Living as if Nature Mattered* (Salt Lake City: Peregrine Smith Books, 1985), 48, 56.

18. Ibid., 56–57, 48.

19. Ibid., 35, 21.

20. Ibid., 43, 145.

21. Ibid., 151, 61, 151, 107.

22. Ibid., 115, 125.

23. Ibid., 169, 20, 18–19.

24. Buchanan, *What Should Economists Do?*, 228.

25. Ernest Callenbach, *Ecotopia* (New York: Bantam Books, 1977), 5.

26. William A. Schambra, "Progresive Liberalism and American 'Community,'" *The Public Interest* (summer 1985): 36.

27. Norman Macrae, *The 2025 Report: A Concise History of the Future, 1975–2025* (New York: Macmillan, 1984), 132, 124.

28. Ibid., 115.

29. Joel Garreau, *The Nine Nations of North America* (New York: Avon Books, 1982), 1, 8.

30. Barbara Ward and René Dubos, *Only One Earth: The Care and Maintenance of a Small Planet* (New York: W. W. Norton, 1972), 195.

31. Ibid., 218, xviii, 189, 19, 189.

32. Jonathan Schell, *The Fate of the Earth* (New York: Avon Books, 1982), 226–227, 219, 187, 210.

33. See Robert H. Nelson, *Public Lands and Private Rights: The Failure of Scientific Management* (Lanham, Md.: Rowman & Littlefield, 1995).

34. Karl Hess, Jr., *Vision upon the Land: Man and Nature on the Western Range* (Washington, D.C.: Island Press, 1992), 245.

35. Ibid., 247, 246, 247, 232, 248.

36. Ibid., 243, 233, 234, 233.

37. Daniel Kemmis, *Community and the Politics of Place* (Norman: University of Oklahoma Press, 1990), 16, 19, 17.

38. Ibid., 102, 99, 85–86.

39. Ibid., 125, 128, 127.

40. John Baden and Richard Stroup, eds., *Bureaucracy versus Enviroment: The Environmental Costs of Bureaucratic Governance* (Ann Arbor: University of Michigan Press, 1981).

41. See Robert H. Nelson, "Private Rights to Government Actions: How Modern Property Rights Evolve," *University of Illinois Law Review* 1986, no. 2 (1986).

42. Robert H. Nelson, *Zoning and Property Rights: An Analysis of the American System of Land Use Regulation* (Cambridge, Mass.: MIT Press, 1977).

43. Roderick Nash, *Wilderness and the American Mind* (New Haven, Conn.: Yale University Press, 1973).

44. John Calvin, "Institutes of the Christian Religion," in Hugh T. Kerr, ed., *Calvin's Institutes: A New Compend* (Louisville, Ky.: Westminster/John Knox Press, 1989), 26–27. See also Robert H. Nelson, "Environmental Calvinism: The Judeo-Christian Roots of Eco-Theology," in Roger Meiners and Bruce Yandle, eds., *Taking the Environment Seriously* (Lanham, Md.: Rowman & Littlefield, 1993).

45. Buchanan, *What Should Economists Do?*, 94.

46. Monica E. Friar and Herman B. Leonard, *The Federal Budget and the States, Fiscal Year 1993*, (Cambridge, Mass.: Office of Senator Daniel Patrick Moynihan and Harvard University, John F. Kennedy School of Government, 28 July, 1994), 34.

CHAPTER ELEVEN

Ideology, Wishful Thinking, and Pragmatic Reform

A Constructive Critique of Free-Market Environmentalism

THOMAS MICHAEL POWER

One enduring remnant of the Reagan revolution, the emphasis on markets and marketlike incentives, will continue to have a significant effect on national environmental policy. The Clinton administration's brand of neoliberal political philosophy endorses many of the "free-market environmental" ideas developed in the Reagan-Bush years. That is made especially clear in the Clinton campaign's *Mandate for Change*, which called for a harnessing of firms' and individuals' "daily self-interest" and the replacement of governmental "command and control" with a more "decentralized market-like" approach in the fight against environmental degradation.[1] Significantly, it was cowritten by a former Environmental Defense Fund staff economist who played a central role in developing the tradable sulfur dioxide permit system that became part of the Clean Air Act. This approach flows directly out of conventional economic theory and the economist's worldview.

In recent years, with antigovernment sentiment seeming to sweep across the nation, the economist's worldview has taken on a new significance in the American West, where federal land and water agencies are under especially bitter attack. A new breed of free-market environmentalist has leaped into public view in recent years, extolling the virtues of the marketplace not merely as a means of creating or expanding national wealth but rather as the best or most efficient way of solving myriad environmental problems. Indeed, some of the West's leading free-market environmentalists have consistently suggested that economic instruments can and should be used as the principal new guides in leading us toward a Next West in which, finally, once and for all, sound economic choices will lead us out of the environmental Dark Ages of command-and-control regulations and politically gerrymandered allocations of federally owned natural resources and into a bright, new era in which a true environmental marketplace will allow citizens to vote for environmental preferences with their dollars. Shorn of the political pressures that force federal land and water agencies to make poor environmental decisions in favor of commodity-interest hegemony, the Next West will be a kind of eco-econ wonderland in which the invisible hand of environmental values will more or less magically cleanse the landscape, increase the value of wilderness and wildlife, and save the "last, best place," the American West.

This chapter will offer a critical examination of free-market environmentalism as it has been presented by some of its leading proponents. It will review efforts by some "conventional" environmentalists to use economic tools in the pursuit of better environmental quality in the West, suggest that some of these tools are indeed helpful and effective if used judiciously and then move on to critique economic tools and the economic mind-set as an environmental panacea. This chapter will make the case that economic tools are appropriate only after hard choices based, essentially, on public values have been made.

Using Economic Tools to Improve Environmental Quality

Many environmentalists are suspicious of both economics and economists, and perhaps they should be, for economics and economists both seem systematically to give the wrong answers to many environmental policy questions: Environmental quality is too costly and not very valuable. Environmental controls hamper productive activity and threaten the foundations of our economy, namely property rights. Zero levels of pollution are irrational; the "optimal" level of pollution is quite high. Health and safety standards and biodiversity protection laws that exclude economic trade-offs are irrational. And so forth.

But many of these same environmentalists have often supported the use of economic tools to control environmental damage. Bottle bills, energy taxes, water markets, elimination of subsidies for commercial users of public lands, and other economic instruments all reflect environmentalists' growing affinity for market tools. Thus, there is ambivalence within the environmental community about the appropriate role of economics and economic instruments in environmental policy.

This ambivalence is not simply the result of confusion on the part of environmentalists. Rather, it represents a healthy respect for the limits of the market and economics paired with an acknowledgment that economic instruments can help promote environmental objectives in certain circumstances. Environmentalists ought to be picking and choosing from among a full range of tools, including both market and nonmarket instruments, as they struggle to protect our increasingly beleaguered natural environment. But we need to become more aware of and articulate about when the market and economics can be used as a productive tool and when altogether different tools are appropriate. This involves forswearing the market and economics as universal ideologies, recognizing the limits and strengths of both, and adopting an explicitly pragmatic approach to solving environmental problems.

A Brief History of Economics

From a historical perspective, environmentalists' suspicions that economics is a less than objective science are warranted. The intellectual mission that Anglo-American economics has been on since before Adam Smith has been to demonstrate the secret social logic of allowing commercial businesses to pursue their profit-maximizing activities unfettered by social controls. That was the function of Smith's image of the "invisible hand" converting, even without the knowledge or agreement of the participants, the selfish, sometimes antisocial behavior of private commercial actors into the public interest. Adam Smith's *Wealth of Nations* began a tradition of economic writing and analysis that had as its primary objective the elimination of social controls on commercial activities. It should not be surprising that the business community enthusiastically supported this intellectual venture, which came to be known as economics.

Economics as a social science has grown beyond these biased and ideological roots, but one can find in its basic structure and policy prescriptions remnants of that origin. That, no doubt, is what makes some environmentalists uneasy when economists offer advice on how better to pursue environmental quality.

The discipline of economics is used by the business community to enhance its private agenda. Business interests contribute heavily to "economic education" organizations that seek to "correct" popular misconceptions about poverty, profits, and environmental damage. A good dose of economics, for instance, is assumed to be useful in counteracting the knee-jerk emotionalism of the clergy when it comes to social issues. Thus, the nation's largest corporations contribute to programs aimed at improving the "economic literacy of the clergy." Similar programs are run for elementary school teachers, judges, and environmental leaders. The board of directors of the Joint Council on Economic Education is a virtual who's who of American business, including many firms with questionable environmental records: Du Pont, ASARCO, ALCOA, AMOCO, Westinghouse, Ashland Inc., and others. Economics is widely recognized by the business community for its convenient built-in bias that helps economists tell some people's stories but not others'.

This does not mean that economics is intellectually bankrupt. It simply means that it has to be used with care and in full recognition of its limitations. That is true of any powerful tool. And economic instruments *are* a powerful environmental tool, a fact clearly recognized by some environmentalists.

Environmentalists as Advocates for the Use of Market Instruments

Environmentalists should be comfortable with a broad range of economic tools aimed at improving or protecting environmental quality. After all, environmental leaders have been the authors and chief advocates of most of them. Consider the following:

1. *Beverage container deposits.* Environmental organizations are the architects of the notion that a price may be placed on empty containers so there is an economic incentive for those containers to be recycled. Deposits are now being considered for other, more dangerous solid wastes such as automobile batteries, automobiles, refrigeration devices, and electronic equipment.

2. *Pricing of irrigation water.* Again, environmentalists are the ones who have insisted that shortages of water in arid regions are often the result of faulty pricing schemes. Environmentalists point to the fact that agri-

cultural users of irrigation water (by far the dominant water users) do not pay prices for water that reflect either the full costs of providing it or its value in alternative uses. They have urged rational economic pricing in order to prevent the need for new water supply projects.

3. *Application of business standards to governmental enterprises.* Many environmental organizations have attacked the subsidies that make various government-sponsored enterprises both viable and environmentally destructive. The fight to prohibit the USDA Forest Service from selling timber below cost is a good example.

4. *Pricing of electrical energy.* In their attempts to reduce demand for new hydroelectric and thermoelectric power plants, environmental organizations have urged that all users of electricity pay prices that reflect the replacement cost of that power. Large industrial customers, who purchase power at levels well below what new sources of supply would cost, are often the target of these proposals for conservation-oriented pricing strategies.

In all these cases—and many more could be cited—environmental groups have urged the use of economic instruments and market incentives to protect the environment, and the affected industries (and usually the government) have strongly opposed such approaches to environmental improvement. This should make clear that economic instruments are not just a concept invented by industry to escape environmental controls. In many situations, there is at least the potential to use those tools effectively to protect environmental quality.

But environmentalists' past use of economic tools and incentives should not be interpreted as a blanket endorsement of market instruments to solve environmental problems. Many environmentalists rightfully remain skeptical about extending this approach to other environmental problems. But their reasons need fuller articulation or this apparent inconsistency will be used to embarrass and weaken the environmental community. Consider, for instance, the hesitancy of some environmentalists to endorse market-based recreation fees on public lands paired with their strong support of the Clinton administration's proposals to impose other market-based fees on commercial users of public lands. There is a potential here for serious embarrassment of environmental organizations. The moral capital of environmentalists is threatened by the special protection they appear to seek for their members' personal interests while enthusiastically endorsing the use of fees that industry decries as punitive. In addition, their hesitancy to fully endorse the use of market instruments is taken as proof of the "watermelon" character of environmentalism: green outside but red inside. Those who wish to characterize environmentalists as authoritarian and antidemocratic will use such arguments with skill.

To escape being misinterpreted in this way, environmentalists must carefully sort through the potentials and limitations of market instruments for protecting and improving environmental quality. There are good reasons for refusing to embrace uncritically the ideology of free-market environmentalism while strongly supporting the use of economic incentives where they can make a significant contribution to environmental quality. We need to work our way carefully through a minefield of ideology and economics to develop a critical but pragmatic position on the use of economic instruments for environmental improvement.

The Cases for and against Recreation Fees

The potential for emergence of an antienvironmental bias from a market-based approach to environmental policy can be seen quite clearly in the question of whether to charge user fees for recreational use of federal lands. The primary argument in favor of such fees is that they are a way to get the public land management agencies to shift their interest away from their attachments to extractive industries.

Currently, land agencies' revenues are closely tied to natural resource extraction: the more timber they harvest, the more mines they permit, the more land they lease for grazing, the larger their budgets. Because recreationists do not pay fees, there is no revenue associated with their interests; thus, the land managers ignore them. The correction for this, some free-market advocates argue, is for recreational users to begin to pay for access to all public lands. The resulting cash flow will attract the interest of the land managers, and in the pursuit of those recreational dollars, land managers will begin to preserve and enhance recreational values. This, we are told, will automatically protect much of the natural landscape because recreational values are much higher than the marginal extractive values that now guide the agencies.

Randal O'Toole of the Oregon-based Thoreau Institute has been one of the most articulate advocates of recreation fees. When combined with the removal of federal subsidies, he argues, recreation fees would go a long way toward eliminating most of the environmental threats to our public lands. O'Toole suggests a concept he calls the "marketization" of our public lands: by following rational pricing practices, much as private owners might, public land managers could avoid the widespread environmental damage we observe in the West. Marketization would right the balance between recreational and extractive uses of the land; thus, environmental harm would be much reduced through the invisible hand of competition. In effect, a new wave of environmental amenity seekers would begin to vote with their dollars for better public land management. Agencies would pay attention because those new dollars would become integral to their budgets.[2]

But Mitch Lansky's *Beyond the Beauty Strip* describes an altogether different result in Maine, where the forested lands are largely in private hands but have been devastated nonetheless. His book bears evidence that the mere use of market devices is simply not a guaranteed prescription for sound land management.[3] Similar environmental disasters on privately owned industrial timberlands in the Pacific Northwest also raise doubts about the environmental magic of private ownership and market forces.

Too strong a bias in favor of markets and the "virtues" of private enterprise tends to mask the outright depredations of private actors on their own lands. It is simply not always the case—as free-market enviros are wont to declare—that private ownership fosters good stewardship. Before we leap to the conclusion that the Forest Service ought to "act like private business," we should carefully investigate stewardship practices on private forestlands.

FINANCIAL INCENTIVES DO MOTIVATE AGENCIES

There is no doubt that when an agency establishes a financial interest in serving a particular clientele, it becomes a strong advocate for that group. Consider the many state fish and wildlife agencies. It is primarily the sale of fishing and hunting licenses that funds fish and wildlife agency operations; hence, those departments have become single-minded advocates for hunting and sport fishing interests. In Montana and Wyoming, fish and wildlife agencies have resisted reintroduction of wolves because they fear wolves will reduce the number of deer available to hunters. In Montana, the Department of Fish, Wildlife, and Parks (DFWP) has opposed listing of the grizzly bear as an endangered species for fear that such listing will eliminate legal hunting of the bear. (Almost unbelievably, until very recently Montana allowed sport hunting of grizzly bears, albeit through a strict quota system that drastically limited the number of bears taken.) In addition, the DFWP has refused to support reintroduction of bighorn sheep in any area where those animals could not be hunted. All over the West, fish and wildlife agencies have developed a vision of their mission that directly reflects their sources of funding.

Those supporting the adoption of substantial recreation fees for public lands hope that the creation of a similar recreation-based cash flow will convince the Forest Service and the Bureau of Land Management of the value of protecting landscapes for recreation.

THE DISTORTING EFFECT OF USER FEES

The example of fish and wildlife agencies should give us some pause. When government agencies rely exclusively on cash flows to guide their policies—as if they were businesses, not agencies that are supposed to reflect the public's interest—some perversity almost always follows. Fish and wildlife agencies have become strong advocates not for all wildlife but just for huntable wildlife. Those agencies often seek to maximize the numbers of favored species regardless of the impact on the natural system as a whole. The situation is analogous to the Forest Service paying attention only to merchantable timber and managing the national forests only for commercially valuable trees or the Bureau of Land Management (BLM) seeing the western landscape only in terms of forage for cattle and sheep.

It is not hard to imagine the potential drawbacks of a successful recreation fee system; simply look at our national parks and the ways in which hordes of visitors threaten the very integrity of those natural areas. If the parks' budgets are tied primarily to the number of visitors they can accommodate and the quantity of services they and their concessionaires can sell, the parks will continue on their seemingly inexorable march toward becoming Disneyesque theme centers.

This threat has been clearly recognized in the ongoing battle over the choice of a new concessionaire for Yosemite National Park and the details of the contract that would govern private business activity in one of our premiere parks. The proposed contract would provide the National Park Service with a share of the revenues proportional to the volume of commercial activity in Yosemite. That, of course, would be a normal business arrangement—a form of marketization, if you will. But it would also give the National Park Service a financial interest in the volume of commercial business conducted within the park. When confronted with a choice between protecting the park "unimpaired for future generations" and maximizing current use and monetary flow, park management may well lean away from protection. The same short-run profit logic that drives private businesses and commodity-oriented public agencies such as the Forest Service may also more strongly influence Yosemite management.

Similarly, the BLM may well be able to make far more money sponsoring off-road vehicle rallies and licensing concessionaires that rent four-wheelers than it could ever make from backpackers or graziers. Currently roadless wildlands might well bring in much more cash if they were opened to motorized tours through snowmobile trails, helicopter lifts into campsites, and Glacier Park Going-to-the-Sun-type roads through all the spectacular mountain country. This isn't fantasy. The congested air traffic over the Grand Canyon and the resulting noise in the canyon have reached crisis proportions, and backcountry skiing in the Wasatch Range in Utah has been almost completely displaced by heli-skiing.

Guiding the management of public lands solely on the basis of cash flows from the interest groups that pay the most is unlikely to lead to anything resembling the preservation of natural ecosystems. It will lead instead to simply a different form of what we see now: monied interests manipulating the landscape for their own purposes. When clear-cuts mar the mountainsides and silt the streams or when mines tear at the earth and destroy entire rivers, the outcome is tragically clear. But it would be no less destructive to have wildlife agencies seeking to eliminate certain types of wildlife, park managers seeking to pave still more of the park, or desert managers organizing off-road vehicle rallies. Marketization would inevitably lead to such abuses; indeed, there is abundant proof that it already has.

Commodity and Use Values versus Environmental Values

There is an important distinction to be made between commodity values and environmental values. When we are focused on relatively common commodities such as timber or forage or minerals, it is perfectly reasonable to expect marketlike or businesslike approaches to work. We already trust the production and use of those commodities primarily to commercial markets. But for most Americans, management of our public lands is not (or should not be) primarily a question of adjusting slightly upward or downward the quantity of two by fours or cattle forage or phosphate rock that makes it to the market. Because the issues at stake in management of public lands go far beyond such narrow commodity issues, it should not be surprising that the economic instruments appropriate to the world of commodities are not so appropriate or effective when what is at stake is not a commodity.

Guiding public land managers by the use of cash flows does not seem to work well simply because many of the objectives for which we want public lands managed cannot have monetary values attached to them. Consider the northern spotted owl or the grizzly bear. Or consider real wilderness. We seek to protect wilderness and the grizzly not as play places or play things for tourists and recreationists but because we wish some part of our natural heritage to be protected from the impacts of human use. Wilderness is supposed to be "untrammeled" by human beings. To protect it, we should, if necessary, be willing to restrict or exclude human use. How, then, are we to attach a monetary value to its use? Market instruments focus on human uses of natural systems and are biased almost exclusively toward use values. But it is important to note that environmental values spill far outside such narrow objectives.

For most Americans, the objectives of public land ownership do not involve primarily human uses of those lands. Instead, the lands are seen as preserves and protected wild landscapes that provide an important backdrop against which we live our lives. Neither human playgrounds nor warehouses of commercial resources are what most Americans now value in public lands. Thus, simply changing which user group pays off the public land managers will not solve the problems threatening those lands.

This critique of user fees should not be interpreted as a rejection of the use of fees generally to rationalize the ways in which our public lands are managed. Fees that cover recreation-related costs such as maintenance of campgrounds, trails, and roads certainly are legitimate. In areas primarily committed to recreation, market-based fees are probably appropriate. We already allow that at ski areas, for instance. It seems unlikely that such fees would exclude low-income folks any more than the cost of camping gear, automobile travel, and the like already do. User fees have a legitimate function in helping fund the management and protection of areas used for recreation. Moreover, correction of perverse incentives within land management agencies should be given top priority. But financial incentives cannot be relied on as the primary guide as to how those natural areas are to be managed and what is to be protected. We cannot simply tell our land managers to protect resources in proportion to how much people are willing to pay for their protection in a free-market auction. To reduce environmental and land management decisions to this type of commercial formula is to abandon the entire purpose of our public lands.

Why We Limit Markets

Markets are not simply neutral technological devices that assist us in more effectively achieving our objectives. They are social institutions, the use of which has profound consequences. All societies purposely limit the reach of the market in order to protect their basic values because they know that markets automatically degrade some things they touch. For instance, we do not allow the buying and selling of votes and judicial decisions; we do not allow the selling of the sexual services of children; we do not allow human beings, even voluntarily, to sell themselves into slavery.

Selling certain things degrades them. Selling praise, selling spiritual favors, selling intimacy, selling the privileges of citizenship, or selling the outcomes of athletic events does not enhance their value; it reduces or destroys their value. Those concerned about protecting environmental values may have this in mind when they question the wisdom of trusting environmental quality to marketlike arrangements.

The Need to Protect Noncommercial Values

The impact of the market goes far beyond the particularly dramatic cases in which markets degrade values. Free-market enthusiasts assume that market-oriented, calculating, self-regarding behavior is all that is needed for a good, responsible society. Such behavior, they assert, should be encouraged, not constrained. But doubters point out how unlikely it is that any decent society can depend so heavily on one type of motivation. Even the commercial market is built around trust and a basic morality that is not narrowly self-regarding. Well-functioning markets do not simply spring into being spontaneously. Rather, they are supported by elaborate public and private social institutions. Our courts, our commercial codes, our contract law, our industrial associations, and our stock, bond, and commodity exchanges are all crucial to our commercial markets working well.

In addition, certain social values incorporating trust and honesty are necessary. Without these social structures, the pursuit of commercial gain degenerates into banditry. This is evident in the drug trade, in frontier societies where social institutions have not yet developed, and in countries, such as Somalia, where institutions have collapsed. By itself, narrow, calculating, self-regarding behavior leads to "bandit capitalism," not to a good society. The extension of marketlike arrangements to more and more aspects of our social life is, indeed, apt to undermine the very social values required for a market economy to function well. Ironically, some people may be less than enthusiastic about such extensions while being quite enthusiastic about the market economy itself.

Motives Matter

There is another disturbing aspect of the use of economic instruments to solve environmental problems. A basic assumption built into the market approach is that motives do not matter; only results do. If bribing polluters out of polluting works, fine. If paying civil servants to obey the law is effective, pay them. Assume the worst of all human beings and arrange incentives to harness the basest human motives. That is the general social logic of free-market environmentalism.

But to most of us, motives do matter. A mistake is not the same as a lie; murder is not the same as self-defense or an accidental killing; prostitution is not the same as love. American jurist Oliver Wendell Holmes once said that even a dog distinguishes between being stumbled over and being kicked. Most of us have at least the sensibilities of that dog. We do care about the motivations of our fellow citizens. It matters to us whether someone seeks to protect the community and its land base because she actually cares; we're apt to be offended if that person "does the right thing" only to protect her pocketbook. We may well have doubts that the earth can be tended well if the only values given expression are those associated with the bottom line. Ethics and conscience matter, and markets can undermine both. That may be why some of us are a bit nervous about uncritically embracing free-market environmentalism. Our concern for the environment has a strong ethical base, and a commercial market mentality hardly seems supportive of that base.

All Preferences Do Not Have Equal Ethical Standing

The basic operating principle behind a market society is that people's preferences, whatever they may be, should be accepted and given importance in proportion to the dollars that back them up. But most of us have strong moral and social values that lead us to be critical of some preferences; indeed, we may seek to oppose them even if they are backed by large sums of money. Money shouldn't be allowed to buy everything. Restrictions on violent behavior or the abuse of children and animals, zoning, and environmental controls all fall into this category. Even when we do not support the use of legal restrictions to constrain the expression of objectionable preferences, most of us would not be comfortable in passively accepting all market outcomes as legitimate. We seek social and cultural means to discourage or constrain certain market outcomes. That is what manners, and public opinion, and community standards are all about. One worrisome thing about allowing the use of public lands to be determined entirely by the highest bid is the implicit legitimization of those outcomes: destructive behavior should not automatically become legitimate and acceptable simply because it is backed by the most money.

This critique of the market and its failures should not be interpreted as an attack on the use of economic instruments to improve environmental quality. Rather, the intent is to make clear the reasons why all societies have constrained the extent of commercial activity. Such an understanding helps us to outline a legitimate realm for the use of economic instruments. It also should help those who are enthusiastic about the use of markets to understand others' hesitancies and assist in the development of instruments that acknowledge those concerns. It is hoped that this discussion will facilitate the adoption of well-thought-out and appropriate economic instruments. Finally, a critical overview allows us to strip away the unexamined ideological component of the package some free-marketeers are trying to sell the environmental community as they pursue their distinctly nonenvironmental agendas. That, too, helps clear the intellectual air.

The Revolutionary Nature of the Environmental Movement

One fundamental fact about environmental protection ensures ongoing conflict between those who currently use and damage environmental resources and those who would protect them. Innovative uses of economic instruments will not make that conflict go away. Environmental protection necessarily involves the transfer of control over valuable resources from one group of people to another. Just one example will suffice: the limited assimilative capacity of our air, water, and land to handle the wastes associated with economic activity. In the past, that capacity could be freely used up by commercial businesses, often at no cost to them, even though such use of the nation's air, water, and land for waste disposal is worth billions of dollars. Over the past several decades, environmentalists have attempted to shift control of these resources away from the commercial sector. The transfer of control over such great wealth cannot take place without considerable conflict. Indeed, revolutions have often been required to accomplish such shifts in wealth, so the ongoing conflict over environmental policy is not surprising. To the extent that economic instruments can reduce the cost of environmental protection, those instruments can make a modest contribution to resolution of the inevitable conflicts. But the fundamental conflict over how the air, water, and land should be used cannot be resolved merely through a change in the instruments used to enforce environmental controls. Only a blindness induced by some form of economics monomania could pretend otherwise.

Isolating the Realm Where Economic Instruments Work

In trying to aim public policy to improve environmental quality, it may help to outline several separable issues:

1. What *level* of each type of environmental degradation is acceptable in *each particular location?*
2. *Who* will be asked to pay the direct costs of reducing the level of degradation to the targeted level?
3. What *policy tools* will be used to reduce pollution to the targeted level and impose the costs in the pattern intended?

Note that the consideration of economic instruments is largely limited to the third question, to be addressed after the first two far more contentious questions have been settled. The discussion of economic instruments should focus on whether they are the best tools available to reach *predetermined* environmental quality levels at a particular site, after a decision has been made about who will directly bear the costs. This is very important. Economic instruments should not be adopted to hide a scaling back of the intended level of environmental quality or to shift the direct costs of environmental controls to different parties. Such a Trojan horse approach would not only impossibly confuse the discussion but also discredit otherwise very valuable and innovative environmental policy tools.

I have referred to the direct costs of pollution control to emphasize the fact that the costs of control will ultimately be borne by the general citizenry in the form of higher prices for various types of products. Some claim that the question of who directly pays does not matter since we all must pay ultimately. That general proposition, however, is false. It matters who directly pays the costs associated with a particular type of economic activity because markets can encourage responsible economic behavior only if the full costs associated with a particular activity are incorporated into prices. Politically shifting costs in an arbitrary manner increases the likelihood that economically irresponsible behavior will be encouraged.

The consideration of economic instruments should take place in a largely win-win context where the objective is primarily to avoid the pure economic waste associated with conventional environmental regulation. That context should be largely distributionally neutral (no major cost shifting between groups or between locations) and should involve previously established pollution control objectives. For example, it may have already been determined that the objective is to reduce sulfur emissions to a level 50 percent below current levels in a particular geographic area and that the direct cost of reduction will be borne by polluters, who will receive special tax benefits for those costs. The question, then, is how best to reach those air quality targets. It is on this much more limited public policy question that economic instruments have something to offer. But note that the really hard and contentious questions have to be settled first.

One of these contentious questions was not at all settled before the inception of the marketable sulfur dioxide permit program created by the Clean Air Act of 1990. That question involved the appropriate geographic distribution of the pollution levels we have decided we can tolerate. When the geographic area over which pollution credits can be traded is very large —nationwide in the case of sulfur dioxide—private trading decisions of polluters can dramatically influence air quality in particular locations. Some areas will see air pollution dramatically improve; others will watch helplessly as serious pollution problems persist indefinitely with the blessing of the law.

This concern has led the State of New York to oppose vigorously any trading of sulfur dioxide permits by its own utilities that might lead to higher levels of pollutants drifting into New York from upwind states. Atlantic coastal utilities have been selling their sulfur dioxide permits to midwestern utilities, which can then avoid reducing their emissions, which are bound ultimately for the Atlantic and New England states. But it was concern over acid rain deposition in those very states that led to the imposition of tighter sulfur dioxide caps in the Clean Air Act. Thus, East Coast states see the tradable permits leading to a perverse result.

In the Midwest, utility customers are also likely to see some perverse results. They will have to pay higher bills in order to finance their utility's purchase of sulfur dioxide permits, but they will not see any reductions in sulfur dioxide emissions from the power plants in their area. Had their utilities been forced to reduce emissions, at least their higher bills would have been offset by the value of cleaner air in their neighborhoods. Now they pay higher bills for "pollution control" but get no pollution control. This, too, is a problem related to the size of the geographic area for pollution permit trading.

The perverse distribution of the resulting pollution has led some environmental organizations to attack the tradable pollution credit mechanism as fundamentally flawed. But that may not really be the case. The real problem is that a fundamental issue was not settled before the trading arrangements were put in place: the levels of environmental quality to be ensured for *all* areas—or the appropriate geographic range for the trading.

The trading arrangement may work better in smaller, more clearly defined airsheds such as the South Coast Air Quality Management District in southern California, where separate tradable permits for three different pollutants will be used to clamp down slowly on the overall levels of each pollutant. But even there, representatives of low-income neighborhoods have objected that they will see no improvement in air quality while more affluent communities will.

For many environmental conflicts, the more divisive questions of how much improvement is appropriate and who should directly bear the costs have not yet been settled. Economic instruments will have little to offer simply because the necessary context in which to consider them has not yet been established. To the extent that economic instruments might dramatically reduce the cost associated with any chosen level of pollution control, discussion of those instruments might help in resolving the other issues. Lowering the cost of reaching a particular level of control may reduce objections both to that level of control and to the imposition of those costs on various parties. So there is *some* interaction between the chosen instruments and the questions of level of control and distribution of cost. But in general, it is useful to consider these questions separately.

The problem of determining the overall level of allowable environmental degradation, along with the equitable distribution of the direct costs of containment, cannot be solved through the market. The political process will continue to be central in the settlement of these more fundamental environmental policy questions.

Ideology versus Instruments

Many of those most strongly committed to the extension of markets to as many aspects of our lives as possible will tend to play down any conflict over who is to bear the direct costs associated with reducing damage to environmental resources. Such free-marketeers tend to believe that equity in the sense of distribution of access to scarce resources or "rights" to a clean and healthful environment is less important than efficient use of resources and protection of existing property rights. But that is hardly a general and widely shared ethical principle. Access to high-quality environments is an important driving force behind the environmental movement. Degradation of environments or absolution of major polluters from any significant financial responsibility for the damage they do is unlikely to be accepted by the citizenry even if it is claimed to be efficient. Fairness, equity, and responsibility are central elements of a democracy. Most citizens are not ready to enshrine efficiency and existing property rights by giving them priority over all other rights. Those who do not share the moral and ideological priorities of the free marketeers may be more critical of the ethical implications of their proposals.

Let's look, for instance, at the concept of legal "takings" and its application to environmental regulations. Under the takings approach, any environmental, health, or safety regulation that reduces the profit opportunities of private citizens would require the government to offer full compensation. It is assumed that individuals so "harmed" had a preregulation property right to pollute or damage the environment in any way they wished and that the public must pay them if that right has been changed or revoked.

To many environmentalists, this is confusing because they see *their* rights to a clean and healthy environment being threatened by the polluters. Yet they are told that the truth is quite the contrary, that the polluters have a preferred constitutional right to poison, damage, or degrade commonly shared environmental resources. Free-marketeers somehow always assign property rights to those doing the polluting rather than to those being damaged by the pollution. Previous behavior is enshrined as a constitutionally protected right that takes precedence over any other concern.

This is not simply a bias but is, rather, a principle within the context of a free-market ideology. Free markets are not seen simply as instruments that allow us to pursue our objectives more efficiently; they are seen as the basic organizing institution of a good society. From this perspective of hard ideology, some free-marketeers see proposals to use market instruments to pursue politically chosen environmental objectives as "collectivism" because the objectives themselves did not emerge from markets. Said one commentator, "This really gets to the heart of the problem with so-called market oriented environmentalism. Too often it sees markets simply as tools for the efficient delivery of environmental goals. . . . But the goals themselves remain collectively determined."[4]

To the most hard-core free-marketeers, markets are a way of life that should replace all other social institutions. This is an interesting philosophical position, even if it is not one that is widely shared. Seeing market extremism buried in proposals disguised as tools to make the pursuit of environmental goals more effective makes a lot of us leery. What exactly is the full package we're being offered? Where do market approaches begin and end?

There is a huge ideological gulf separating the free-marketeers' vision of a good society and the vision of most environmentalists. Environmentalists seek to act collectively to preserve certain qualities associated with the natural and, often, social environments—qualities that are central to the well-being of many people and that usually have the character of public goods. In that sense, environmentalists are fundamentally conservative: they wish things to remain the same or to return to a previous preferred condition. Free-marketeers, on the other hand, are enthusiastic about the constant change a market economy encourages and are extremely suspicious of any collective attempt to change the direction taken by the economy or society. They see purposeful attempts to guide the economy or society as dangerously authoritarian and economically destructive. In other words, we can never know where the economy is going and should simply focus our efforts on productively coping with the opportunities and problems that constantly emerge. We are off on an adventure to an unknown destination; we should learn to enjoy the excitement and change it brings us and trust that the overall result, whatever it is, will be much better than anything that we could have collectively arranged.

Seen in this context, free-marketeers are radical adventurists who explicitly prefer an undirected society that moves rapidly in unexpected directions while generating both problems and opportunities of mind-boggling dimensions. To the free-marketeer, those opportunities more than compensate for the risks and costs associated with the problems. Thus, while environmentalists are the true conservatives, the free-marketeers are radicals willing to risk everything in the name of their faith in the inevitably positive outcome of market forces. Of course, they see environmentalists as arrogant authoritarians who think they know enough to manipulate an infinitely complex social system in the "right" direction.

Extending the Use of Economic Instruments in the Pursuit of Environmental Quality

Despite their misgivings about some of the extremist ideology that often accompanies free-market thinking, environmentalists in the West and elsewhere should continue to pay attention to economic instruments, for there is no denying the facts that incentives matter and marketlike instruments can help protect the environment. Consider the following ideas that have been advanced by environmental organizations.

PURCHASING WATER RIGHTS TO PROTECT IN-STREAM FLOWS

In the West's rural areas, the combined impacts of irrigators often deplete rivers and streams past their capacity to support aquatic life. During years when precipitation and snowmelt are low, these impacts are especially acute.

One reason why this happens is that irrigation water is usually provided at very little cost to farmers and is often used on crops of low value, such as hay. There is little or no incentive to conserve water, since there is little or no penalty for wasting it. Meanwhile, the water being used by irrigators is badly needed to protect the ecological integrity of rivers and streams. Given the explosion of public interest in sport fishing, river recreation, and the wild character of the West's magnificent trout streams, it is probably often the case that irrigation is no longer the most highly valued use of water. But a system of old property rights—western water rights—continues to favor the use of water in low-value agriculture while higher-value recreational and ecological uses remain literally high and dry.

One solution proposed by western environmentalists is to allow fish and wildlife organizations and agencies, water quality agencies, or even private sector environmental groups to purchase water rights from farmers and use them to protect in-stream flows. The water rights would be purchased on the basis of a willing buyer and a willing seller, a straightforward market transaction. What is needed is legal authorization for such transfers in water rights and a regulatory apparatus to protect the purchased in-stream flows. This is a good example of a win-win exchange: under a voluntary system, irrigators could receive compensation for their valuable water rights, river enthusiasts could save rivers, and fish could stay wet and cold.

MONETIZING URBAN TRAFFIC PRIVILEGES

Many of the most serious environmental problems in large metropolitan areas are associated with private use of the automobile. Traffic congestion, air and water pollution, noise, and other problems are all tied to the presence of too many cars. Often, white-collar employee benefits, which include parking privileges adjacent to the workplace, exacerbate the problems.

One proposal is for employers to raise wages to cover the full cash value of parking privileges and then to charge the full cost of providing parking. Those who choose to use mass transit or car pools will thus end up with higher net incomes. No one would be made worse off under this arrangement, but resources might well be saved and environmental costs reduced.

BUYING AND SELLING ENERGY EFFICIENCY IMPROVEMENTS

Supplemental electricity can often be obtained much more cheaply by improving efficiency than by building new generators. By investing in technologies to save electricity, utilities find that they create new "supplies" of energy simply by using less of what's already being generated. Some call this new supply "conservation energy," or energy "created" by conserving.

In many instances, it makes better economic sense for a utility to pay customers to install efficiency measures or switch to alternative fuels than it would for them to take on the enormous and risky investment of building a new power plant. The environmental benefits of creating conservation energy are often enormous, especially when compared with the environmental harm created by bringing new generators on-line.

In their resource planning, utilities are increasingly recognizing the value of conservation energy. In fact, some electric planners are carrying this strategy a step further and offering to improve the energy efficiency of other utilities' customers in return for rights to the electricity freed up by the reduced usage. In the Pacific Northwest, the Bonneville Power Administration is offering to buy the output of such utility programs. Some are suggesting that U.S. utilities pay customers of B.C. Hydro and Power Authority (a British Columbia provincial electric utility) to reduce their electric usage, with the electricity saved to be transferred to the United States.

Once again, these are straightforward commercial transactions with profound environmental consequences.

RAISING GASOLINE PRICES EQUITABLY

Raising the price of gasoline would provide incentives to increase automotive fuel efficiency and decrease the overall amount of driving. Given the high environmental and military costs of developing, protecting, and transporting petroleum, gasoline prices should be high enough to reflect the full social costs. But raising prices also raises objections. People don't want to see higher fuel bills added to their household costs.

One way to get around objections to more expensive gasoline is to incorporate into the price other household costs that are associated with automotive use but are not now collected at the pump. For instance, automobile collision insurance costs are directly tied to miles driven. If these costs were included in the price of gasoline instead of being collected in semiannual insurance premiums, total costs to households would not rise but the price of gasoline would, encouraging more frugal use of it. Moreover, the numbers of drivers covered by insurance would skyrocket. A bill implementing this idea—known as "pay-at-the-pump" insurance—has been introduced in the California legislature.

These examples are purposely speculative to provide a feeling for the range of environmentally productive uses for economic instruments. Once environmentalists' social imaginations are stimulated in this direction, they are likely to generate many more creative uses of markets and incentives to help enhance environmental quality.

Conclusion

Economic instruments for controlling pollution and changing the focus of public land managers can offer more efficient ways to reach environmental quality objectives. At the very least, by reducing the cost of environmental control, they increase the possibility of attaining higher quality standards. Further, many existing regulations do not really limit the amount of any given pollutant that can be emitted in a particular area; in that sense, they do not limit the damage. In contrast, many economic instruments begin by setting a maximum allowable level of environmental degradation and then proceed to attain that level at minimum cost. That, too, is a significant gain. Finally, economic instruments may offer a win-win solution in some environmental conflicts.

But the extension of marketlike arrangements into the realm of environmental protection is neither a cure-all nor without its own serious problems. By itself, a commercial market mentality is not a sufficient ethical base on which a good society can be built. Indeed, the commercial mentality tends to gnaw away at a society's ethical underpinnings. The insider trading, market manipulation, and regulatory corruption scandals of the 1980s should remind us of how faint the ethical dimensions of American business often are. Thus, we must take great care to constantly reinforce the broader ethical foundations on which our society rests. The ideology of free-market environmentalism may do just the opposite, giving us good reason to be critical and cautious as we pragmatically choose economic instruments compatible with long-term environmental integrity and a good society.

Economic instruments can be used only after the most difficult environmental decisions have already been made: what level of degradation will we allow, and who will directly bear the cost? Economic instruments cannot answer these difficult questions and should not be used as a screen to hide the lowering of pollution control targets, the shifting of control costs, or the abandonment of local environmental controls.

Economic instruments should not be confused with deregulation or the pursuit of a more "pure" market society. They are tools to be used only in the context of more sophisticated regulation, not an abandonment of environmental regulation.

The great challenge to environmentalists is to keep their values clear, visible, and in control of the pragmatic choices among environmental policies. There is no need to accept the spurious ideological principles that are often embedded in free-market environmentalism.

NOTES

1. "The Greening of the Market: Making the Polluter Pay." In *Mandate for Change*, W. Marshall and M. Schram, eds. (New York: Berkley Books, 1993).

2. R. O'Toole, "Paying to Play and Preserve: The Case for Recreation Fees on the National Forests," *Forest Watch* 12, no. 11 (June 1992): 18–21.

3. Mitch Lansky, *Beyond the Beauty Strip: Saving What's Left of Our Forests* (Gardiner, Maine: Tilbury House, 1992).

4. L. Scarlett, "Cairncross' Market Collectivism: A Book Review," 1993, *FREE Perspectives* 7(1):9-10, Winter/Spring. [Newsletter of the Foundation for Research on Economics and the Environment, 945 Technology Blvd., Bozeman, MT 59715.]

JOHN A. BADEN is chairman of the Foundation for Research on Economics and the Environment and chairman of the Gallatin Institute, both located in Bozeman, Montana. With Garrett Hardin in 1977, he edited *Managing the Commons,* soon to be republished by Indiana University Press. Baden is a leading voice in the new resource economics; his work has appeared in *Northern Lights,* the *Wall Street Journal,* the *New York Times, Forbes,* and numerous scholarly and popular publications. He and his wife, Ramona Marotz-Baden, operate a family ranch in the Gallatin Valley of Montana.

ROCKY BARKER was for many years senior reporter in charge of special projects for the *Post Register* in Idaho Falls, Idaho. A prolific freelance writer and reporter, he has recently become environmental editor for the *Idaho Statesman* in Boise, and his work has appeared in *High Country News, Buzzworm, Outside,* and many other publications. He is author of *Saving All the Parts: Reconciling Economics and the Endangered Species Act* (Island Press, 1993) and serves as a senior fellow with the Gallatin Institute.

STEPHEN BODIO is well-known for his writing on nature, the outdoors, and sport. His books include *Querencia* (Clark City Press, 1990), *Aloft* (Lyons and Burford, 1990), *A Rage for Falcons,* and *Good Guns.* For a number of years, his essays and articles delighted readers of *Gray's Sporting Journal.*

KARL HESS, JR., holds degrees in economics, history, and ecology. His books include *Visions upon the Land: Man and Nature on the Western Range* (Island Press, 1992) and *Rocky Times in Rocky Mountain National Park* (University Press of Colorado, 1993). In addition, he is editor of a forthcoming Gallatin Institute book titled *Writers on the Range* (University Press of Colorado, 1997). He lives in Las Cruces, New Mexico.

JIM McMAHON was a pioneer in Seattle's recycling business. A former writer-researcher with the Independence Institute in Golden, Colorado, he now directs the Mackinaw River Project for the Illinois chapter of The Nature Conservancy.

ROBERT H. NELSON, an economist, teaches at the University of Maryland's School of Public Affairs. From 1975 to 1993, he was a member of the economics staff of the Office of Policy Analysis in the U.S. Department of the Interior. His books include *The Making of Federal Coal Policy* (Duke University Press, 1983), *Reaching for Heaven on Earth: The Theological Meaning of Economics* (Rowman & Littlefield, 1991), and *Public Lands and Private Rights* (Rowman & Littlefield, 1995).

THOMAS MICHAEL POWER is chairman of the University of Montana's Department of Economics. His new book, *Lost Landscapes and Failed Economies* (Island Press, 1996), explores the myths of the old economy and the emergence of a new economy in the Rocky Mountain region.

MARK SAGOFF is senior research scholar at the University of Maryland's Institute for Philosophy and Public Policy. He is author of *The Economy of the Earth* (Cambridge University Press, 1988), and is a Pew Scholar in conservation and the environment.

DONALD SNOW is executive director of the Northern Lights Research & Education Institute in Missoula, Montana, and associate editor of *Northern Lights* magazine. His books include *Inside the Environmental Movement* and *Voices from the Environmental Movement,* both published by Island Press in 1992. With Deborah Clow, he edited *Northern Lights: A Selection of New Writing from the American West* (Vintage, 1994). He is adjunct professor of environmental studies at the University of Montana and serves as arts and literary director for the Gallatin Institute.

SAMUEL WESTERN, a freelance writer living in Buffalo, Wyoming, is a frequent contributor to the *Economist, High Country News,* and numerous other publications covering the environment and economics in the West.

TOM WOLF is a freelance writer and adjunct professor of Southwest studies at Colorado College in Colorado Springs. He is author of *Colorado's Sangre de Cristo Mountains* (University Press of Colorado, 1995) and numerous magazine, journal, and newspaper articles. He has worked for the Wyoming Outdoor Council and The Nature Conservancy and currently serves as a senior fellow with the Gallatin Institute.

INDEX

Snyder, Gary, 21
Social controls on commercial activi-
ties, 235–36
Social engineering mentality, 210
Social organization of the future, world,
217–18
Social sciences, 214
Soil erosion, 114
Solid Waste Utility in Seattle, 64, 66, 70
South Coast Air Quality Management
District (CA), 247
Soviet Union, former, 228
Space, changing economics of, 116–20
Special interest groups:
advantage over diffuse and disorga-
nized groups, 114
Bureau of Reclamation and water
issues, 123–24
extractive industries promoted by, 119
iron triangle of commodity interests,
124, 184
scientific management perverted by,
104
subsidies, 120
Spence, Gerry, 50
Spirituality, 20
Spotted owls, 31
Sreder-Frechette, K. S., 138
St. John Crèvecoeur, J. Hector, 153
State lands/forests, 27, 42
Stegner, Wallace, 105, 111, 171–72
Stepanian, Armen, 61, 65
Stewardship practices, 126–27, 239
Stream channels, U.S. Forest Service
repairing, 37–38
Stress threshold in ecosystems, 32
Stroup, Richard, 144, 146, 191, 224
Subsidies:
agreement on harm done by, 3
criticisms of subsidies for the West,
190–91
dependence and decentralist vision,
battle between, 187–90

grazing land for animals, 122–23
recycling, 73
special interest groups, 120
victim game, playing the, 173–74
water, 4, 123
welfare state, American, 209–11, 220
for Westerners to subdue nature/sta-
bilize economic life, 112–14, 119
Sulfur emissions, 246–47
Supreme Court, U.S., 53
Surface Mining Control and Reclamation Act of 1977 (SMCRA), 50–52, 56
Sustained-yield management, 27–28, 34,
35, 76

Takings, regulatory, 53, 249
Targhee National Forest (ID), 30
Tax policies on private forestland, 42–43
Taylor, Frederick, 207
Taylor Grazing Act of 1934, 164, 168
Taylor Ranch (CO), 201
Technology:
federal agencies, 142
feudalism, modern, 217
recreation, outdoor, 115–16
resource extraction and development,
112, 117
silvicultural, 27
urbanism, footloose, 183
Texaco vs. *Andrus* (fee exchange program), 54
Thomas, Jack W., 31
Thomson, Rebecca, 54
Thoreau, Henry D., 5, 16
Thoreau Institute (OR), 238
Timber industry:
acres of commercial timberland, 26
antitrust laws, 35
communities dependent on, 188
ecosystem integrity, 32–33
public pressures on, 33–34
Wall Street, 30
see also Forestry